Self-Regulation and Early School Success

Self-regulation has been identified as an important predictor of school readiness and academic achievement in young children. Children who struggle with self-regulation are at risk of experiencing peer rejection and academic difficulties. Teachers report that there is high variability in children's self-regulatory abilities at school entry and that children with an accumulation of risk factors are especially likely to enter school without adequate self-regulation skills. Moreover, early academic skills are often cumulative, so children who fail to acquire early skills are at risk of falling behind their peers academically and facing achievement gaps that widen over time.

Although the relation between self-regulation and school-related outcomes has been clearly documented, our understanding of the pathways through which self-regulation influences early achievement and school success remains unclear. This special issue considers previously neglected areas in the current understanding of self-regulation. The seven articles focus on issues including (a) the complex relations between self-regulation and school readiness, (b) predictors of self-regulation and academic achievement, and (c) advances in measurement of self-regulation and related skills.

Research that continues to investigate the complex relations and mechanisms that influence early self-regulation and related outcomes will inform policy and practice in ways that help all children develop the self-regulation skills they need. The volume will be of interest to researchers in the field of child development or education, and educators and policy makers who are interested in promoting school readiness and academic success.

This book was originally published as a special issue of *Early Education and Development*.

Megan M. McClelland is an Associate Professor in Human Development and Family Sciences at Oregon State University, USA, where she serves as Director of the Healthy Development in Early Childhood Research Core at the Hallie Ford Center for Healthy Children and Families. Her research focuses on school readiness including links between self-regulation and academic achievement from early childhood to adulthood, recent advances in measuring self-regulation, and intervention efforts to improve these skills in young children.

Shauna L. Tominey is a Postdoctoral Associate at Yale University, USA, in the Department of Psychology and at the Yale Child Study Center in the School of Medicine. Her current research is focused on the development of an intervention aimed at promoting preschoolers' social-emotional skills as well the development of programs for children and families targeting the development of social competence and social support as a means of fostering resilience.

Self-Regulation and Early School Success

Edited by
Megan M. McClelland and
Shauna L. Tominey

LONDON AND NEW YORK

First published 2013 by Routledge

2 Park Square, Milton Park, Abingdon, Oxfordshire OX14 4RN
711 Third Avenue, New York, NY 10017

Routledge is an imprint of the Taylor & Francis Group, an informa business

First issued in paperback 2018

Copyright © 2013 Taylor & Francis

This book is a reproduction of *Early Education and Development*, volume 22, issue 03. The Publisher requests to those authors who may be citing this book to state, also, the bibliographical details of the special issue on which the book was based.

All rights reserved. No part of this book may be reprinted or reproduced or utilised in any form or by any electronic, mechanical, or other means, now known or hereafter invented, including photocopying and recording, or in any information storage or retrieval system, without permission in writing from the publishers.

Notice:
Product or corporate names may be trademarks or registered trademarks, and are used only for identification and explanation without intent to infringe.

British Library Cataloguing in Publication Data
A catalogue record for this book is available from the British Library

ISBN13: 978-0-415-82594-8 (hbk)
ISBN13: 978-1-138-37775-2 (pbk)

Typeset in Times New Roman
by Taylor & Francis Books

Publisher's Note
The publisher would like to make readers aware that the chapters in this book may be referred to as articles as they are identical to the articles published in the special issue. The publisher accepts responsibility for any inconsistencies that may have arisen in the course of preparing this volume for print.

Contents

Citation Information vii
Notes on Contributors ix

1. Introduction to the Special Issue on Self-Regulation in Early Childhood
   Megan M. McClelland and Shauna L. Tominey 1

2. The Role of Effortful Control in Mediating the Association Between Maternal Sensitivity and Children's Social and Relational Competence and Problems in First Grade
   Tamar M. Mintz, Bridget K. Hamre, and Bridget E. Hatfield 6

3. Cognitive Flexibility, Approaches to Learning, and Academic School Readiness in Head Start Preschool Children
   Virginia E. Vitiello, Daryl B. Greenfield, Pelin Munis, and J'Lene George 34

4. Children's Effortful Control and Academic Achievement: Mediation Through Social Functioning
   Carlos Valiente, Nancy Eisenberg, Rg Haugen, Tracy L. Spinrad, Claire Hofer, Jeffrey Liew, and Anne Kupfer 57

5. Relations of Children's Effortful Control and Teacher–Child Relationship Quality to School Attitudes in a Low-Income Sample
   Kassondra M. Silva, Tracy L. Spinrad, Nancy Eisenberg, Michael J. Sulik, Carlos Valiente, Snjezana Huerta, Alison Edwards, Natalie D. Eggum, Anne S. Kupfer, Christopher J. Lonigan, Beth M. Phillips, Shauna B. Wilson, Jeanine Clancy-Menchetti, Susan H. Landry, Paul R. Swank, Michael A. Assel, Heather B. Taylor, and School Readiness Consortium 80

6. The Influence of Demographic Risk Factors on Children's Behavioral Regulation in Prekindergarten and Kindergarten
   Shannon B. Wanless, Megan M. McClelland, Shauna L. Tominey, and Alan C. Acock 107

CONTENTS

7. Red Light, Purple Light: Findings From a Randomized Trial Using Circle Time Games to Improve Behavioral Self-Regulation in Preschool
   Shauna L. Tominey and Megan M. McClelland — 135

8. Parent–Teacher Agreement and Reliability on the Devereux Early Childhood Assessment (DECA) in English and Spanish for Ethnically Diverse Children Living in Poverty
   Jennifer Crane, Melissa S. Mincic, and Adam Winsler — 166

Index — 194

Citation Information

The chapters in this book were originally published in *Early Education and Development*, volume 22, issue 3 (May-June 2011). When citing this material, please use the original page numbering for each article, as follows:

Chapter 1
Introduction to the Special Issue on Self-Regulation in Early Childhood
Megan M. McClelland and Shauna L. Tominey
Early Education and Development, volume 22, issue 3 (May-June 2011) pp. 355-359

Chapter 2
The Role of Effortful Control in Mediating the Association Between Maternal Sensitivity and Children's Social and Relational Competence and Problems in First Grade
Tamar M. Mintz, Bridget K. Hamre, and Bridget E. Hatfield
Early Education and Development, volume 22, issue 3 (May-June 2011) pp. 360-387

Chapter 3
Cognitive Flexibility, Approaches to Learning, and Academic School Readiness in Head Start Preschool Children
Virginia E. Vitiello, Daryl B. Greenfield, Pelin Munis, and J'Lene George
Early Education and Development, volume 22, issue 3 (May-June 2011) pp. 388-410

Chapter 4
Children's Effortful Control and Academic Achievement: Mediation Through Social Functioning
Carlos Valiente, Nancy Eisenberg, Rg Haugen, Tracy L. Spinrad, Claire Hofer, Jeffrey Liew, and Anne Kupfer
Early Education and Development, volume 22, issue 3 (May-June 2011) pp. 411-433

Chapter 5
Relations of Children's Effortful Control and Teacher–Child Relationship Quality to School Attitudes in a Low-Income Sample
Kassondra M. Silva, Tracy L. Spinrad, Nancy Eisenberg, Michael J. Sulik, Carlos Valiente, Snjezana Huerta, Alison Edwards, Natalie D. Eggum, Anne S. Kupfer, Christopher J. Lonigan, Beth M. Phillips, Shauna B. Wilson, Jeanine Clancy-Menchetti, Susan H. Landry, Paul R. Swank, Michael A. Assel, Heather B. Taylor, and School Readiness Consortium

Chapter 6
The Influence of Demographic Risk Factors on Children's Behavioral Regulation in Prekindergarten and Kindergarten
Shannon B. Wanless, Megan M. McClelland, Shauna L. Tominey, and Alan C. Acock

Chapter 7
Red Light, Purple Light: Findings From a Randomized Trial Using Circle Time Games to Improve Behavioral Self-Regulation in Preschool
Shauna L. Tominey and Megan M. McClelland

Chapter 8
Parent–Teacher Agreement and Reliability on the Devereux Early Childhood Assessment (DECA) in English and Spanish for Ethnically Diverse Children Living in Poverty
Jennifer Crane, Melissa S. Mincic and Adam Winsler

Notes on Contributors

Alan C. Acock, Human Development & Family Sciences, Oregon State University, USA

Michael A. Assel, Department of Pediatrics, University of Texas Health Science Center at Houston, USA

Jeanine Clancy-Menchetti, Learning Systems Institute, Florida State University, USA

Jennifer Crane, Department of Justice, USA

Alison Edwards, Department of Psychology, Arizona State University, USA

Natalie D. Eggum, School of Social and Family Dynamics, Arizona State University, USA

Nancy Eisenberg, Department of Psychology, Arizona State University, USA

J'Lene George, Department of Psychology, Wenatchee Valley College, USA

Daryl B. Greenfield, Department of Psychology, University of Miami, USA

Bridget K. Hamre, Center for Advanced Study of Teaching & Learning, University of Virginia, USA

Bridget E. Hatfield, Center for Advanced Study of Teaching & Learning, University of Virginia, USA

Rg Haugen, Department of Psychology, Arizona State University, USA

Claire Hofer, Department of Psychology, Arizona State University, USA

Snjezana Huerta, Department of Psychology, Arizona State University, USA

Anne Kupfer, Department of Psychology, Arizona State University, USA

Susan H. Landry, Department of Pediatrics, University of Texas Health Science Center at Houston, USA

NOTES ON CONTRIBUTORS

Jeffrey Liew, Department of Educational Psychology, Texas A&M University, USA

Christopher J. Lonigan, Department of Psychology, Florida State University, USA

Megan M. McClelland, Hallie Ford Center for Healthy Children and Families, Oregon State University, USA

Melissa S. Mincic, Frank Porter Graham Child Development Institute, University of North Carolina, USA

Tamar M. Mintz, Center for Advanced Study of Teaching & Learning, University of Virginia, USA

Pelin Munis, Department of Psychology, University of Miami, USA

Beth M. Phillips, Department of Psychology, Florida State University, USA

School Readiness Consortium

Kassondra M. Silva, School of Social and Family Dynamics, Arizona State University, USA

Tracy L. Spinrad, School of Social & Family Dynamics, Arizona State University, USA

Michael J. Sulik, Department of Psychology, Arizona State University, USA

Paul R. Swank, Department of Pediatrics, University of Texas Health Science Center at Houston, USA

Heather B. Taylor, Department of Pediatrics, University of Texas Health Science Center at Houston, USA

Shauna L. Tominey, Department of Psychology, Yale University, USA

Carlos Valiente, School of Social & Family Dynamics, Arizona State University, USA

Virginia E. Vitiello, Center for Advanced Study of Teaching and Learning, University of Virginia, USA

Shannon B. Wanless, School of Education, University of Pittsburgh, USA

Shauna B. Wilson, Department of Psychology, Florida State University, USA

Adam Winsler, Department of Psychology, George Mason University, USA

Introduction to the Special Issue on Self-Regulation in Early Childhood

Megan M. McClelland and Shauna L. Tominey

In preschool, Ethan was known as "a hitter." If another child took a toy from him, Ethan's impulse was to hit. Ethan would hit his classmates if they bumped into him on the playground or stood too close to him while lining up to use the bathroom. His teacher began stepping in whenever she saw Ethan poised to strike. She tried to help him control his hitting impulse by encouraging him to stop and count to three. One afternoon, Ethan's teacher witnessed the following scene: Another child took a ball from Ethan. Ethan raised his hand and then froze. His teacher could almost hear him counting in his head, "One... two... three..." and she beamed with pride. Then Ethan drew back his leg and kicked.

Like Ethan, we are making great progress in understanding early self-regulation in children, but some of the critical components are yet to be fully understood. Research in the past decade has ignited great interest in the construct of self-regulation, especially as it relates to the education of young children. In particular, with the increased academic focus of many early school environments, self-regulation has been highlighted as a critical component of school readiness and success. Although most children move from preschool to a more structured kindergarten classroom with relative ease, a large number of children without adequate self-regulation experience difficulty once they get to kindergarten (McClelland, Morrison, & Holmes, 2000). This is especially important because recent research has highlighted self-regulation as an important predictor of school readiness and academic achievement (Blair & Razza, 2007; McClelland et al., 2007; Valiente, Lemery-Chalfant, & Castro, 2007). Moreover, studies suggest that children with poor self-regulatory skills are at risk for experiencing peer rejection and academic difficulties (Denham, Brown, & Domitrovich, 2010; Eisenberg, Valiente, & Eggum, 2010). This is problematic because teachers report that there is high variability in children's self-regulatory abilities at kindergarten entry (Rimm-Kaufman, Pianta, & Cox, 2000). Children from low-income families, and those with an accumulation of risk factors, are especially likely to enter school without adequate self-regulation abilities (Mistry, Benner, Biesanz, Clark, & Howes, 2010; Sektnan, McClelland, Acock, & Morrison, 2010). Early academic skills are often cumulative, so children who fail to acquire these skills are at risk of falling behind their peers and facing achievement gaps that widen over time (Entwisle, Alexander, & Olson, 2005).

Although numerous studies have documented the relation between self-regulation and school-related outcomes, our understanding of the pathways through which self-regulation influences these outcomes remains unclear. For instance, the mechanisms through which self-regulation influences school success are not well understood, and few studies have investigated complex pathways between (and through) self-regulation and other outcomes using sophisticated analyses and longitudinal data. Moreover, little research has focused on how these relations operate at various levels (e.g., child, family, classroom, teacher, and school) or examined relations between predictors of these skills (e.g., combinations of demographic risk factors). Research suggests that children with one risk factor are likely to experience many (Dearing, Berry, & Zaslow, 2006). making it important to understand how cumulative risk may impact the development of self-regulation.

Furthermore, considerable debate exists over how best to measure self-regulation in early childhood. Many studies rely on parent or teacher ratings, whereas others focus on direct measures. In addition, few of these measures have been tested using multiple language populations (e.g., English- and Spanish-speaking children). Given the importance of self-regulation for success in school, it is critical that we develop measures that are valid and reliable for use with diverse groups of young children.

In this special issue, we work to fill several gaps in the current understanding of self-regulation. We present seven articles, each of which makes a unique contribution to the self-regulation literature in one the following areas: (a) complex relations between self-regulation and school readiness outcomes, (b) predictors of self-regulation and achievement, and (c) advances in measurement in self-regulation and related skills. The studies included in this special issue utilize a wide range of self-regulation assessments, including teacher and parent reports and direct measures. In addition, several of the articles include large longitudinal samples of children from ethnically diverse and/or low-income populations.

We begin with a collection of articles examining complex (mediating) pathways through which self-regulation influences social and academic outcomes. In the first article, Mintz, Hamre, and Hatfield use data from the National Institute of Child Health and Human Development (NICHD) Study of Early Child Care and Youth Development to examine self-regulation as a mediator between maternal sensitivity (in infancy and toddlerhood) and children's relationships with peers and teachers in early elementary school. They find that early maternal sensitivity is directly related to children's social and relational competence in first grade. Moreover, children's inhibitory control (an aspect of self-regulation) partially mediates the relation between maternal sensitivity and children's social competence. This article highlights the role of child self-regulation as a mechanism variable between parenting and child social competence and has important implications for the inclusion of self-regulation in early childhood and early elementary school curricula.

The next three articles elucidate mediating pathways between self-regulation and school-related outcomes. First, Vitiello, Greenfield, Munis, and George examine indirect relations between cognitive flexibility (a component of self-regulation) and school readiness through three approaches to learning (attention/persistence, competence motivation, and attitude toward learning) in a sample of children from low-income families. These authors demonstrate that children's attention/persistence significantly mediates the relation between cognitive flexibility and school readiness (e.g., knowledge of colors, letters, numbers, sizes, object comparisons, and shapes). Second, Valiente and his coauthors find evidence that social functioning (social competence and externalizing problems) significantly mediates relations between effortful control (one aspect of self-regulation) and academic functioning. Third, Silva and her collaborators examine the quality of relationship with teachers as a mediator between effortful control and school engagement in an ethnically diverse and economically disadvantaged sample. They demonstrate that children's effortful control is positively related to teacher–child relationship quality, which is positively related to children's school attitudes. Taken together, the results from these studies illuminate the mechanisms through which self-regulation is related to children's outcomes. They suggest the importance of attention/persistence as a means through which cognitive flexibility influences school readiness (Vitiello et al., this issue), the value of considering social and emotional processes when focusing on strengthening academic achievement (Valiente et al., this issue), and the significance of examining the quality of the relationships children have with their teachers (Silva et al., this issue) as a way to improve school attitudes. In addition, samples in two of the articles (Silva et al., this issue; Vitiello et al., this issue) focus on children from low-income families who are especially likely to exhibit poor self-regulation. Thus, findings from these studies may be particularly salient to the development of self-regulation interventions in high-risk populations.

Results from the next two articles highlight important predictors of children's self-regulation in early childhood. Using data from a longitudinal study, Wanless, McClelland, Tominey, and Acock examine the impact of demographic factors (family income and language) on behavioral self-regulation and growth in these skills through preschool and kindergarten. They find that children from low-income families begin preschool with significantly lower self-regulation than their peers. Moreover, although low-income English-speaking children are able to catch up to their English-speaking advantaged peers on self-regulation by the end of kindergarten, the children experiencing cumulative risk (e.g., those who are disadvantaged and who are English language learners) remain significantly behind in self-regulation. In the next article, Tominey and McClelland investigate the effectiveness of an intervention using classroom games to improve behavioral self-regulation in preschoolers. They find that treatment group participation significantly predicts gains on a direct measure of self-regulation for children beginning the year with low levels of these skills. In addition, intervention participation predicts gains in letter-word identification in the overall sample. Taken together, these two studies demonstrate the relation between context (family and demographic variables) and intervention efforts of the development of self-regulation in young children.

The last article in this special issue focuses on the measurement of self-regulation and related skills. Crane, Mincic, and Winsler test parent and teacher agreement on the Devereux Early Childhood Assessment (DECA), an assessment of self-regulation and social-emotional skills, in a population of ethnically diverse and economically disadvantaged children. They find that the English and Spanish versions of the DECA reliably measure aspects of self-regulation and social-emotional skills. Moreover, agreement between parents and teachers is highest for children who are average functioning and for parent–teacher pairs who complete the assessment in the same language. These findings suggest that the DECA can be used with diverse samples and underscore the importance of using multiple raters and sources to improve accuracy in measurement.

Taken together, this collection of studies moves us one step closer to understanding the many components and predictors of self-regulation. Research that continues to investigate complex relations and key mechanisms that influence early self-regulation will inform policy and practice in ways that help children, including Ethan, develop the self-regulation skills they need for social and academic success.

REFERENCES

Blair, C., & Razza, R. P. (2007). Relating effortful control, executive function, and false belief understanding to emerging math and literacy ability in kindergarten. *Child Development, 78*, 647–663.

Dearing, E., Berry, D., & Zaslow, M. (2006). Poverty during early childhood. In K. McCartney & D. Phillips (Eds.), *Blackwell handbook of early childhood development* (pp. 399–423). Malden, MA: Blackwell Publishing.

Denham, S. A., Brown, C., & Domitrovich, C. E. (2010). "Plays nice with others": Social–emotional learning and academic success. *Early Education & Development, 21*, 652–680.

Eisenberg, N., Valiente, C., & Eggum, N. D. (2010). Self-regulation and school readiness. *Early Education & Development, 21*, 681–698.

Entwisle, D. R., Alexander, K. L., & Olson, L. S. (2005). First grade and educational attainment by age 22: A new story. *American Journal of Sociology, 110*, 1458–1502.

McClelland, M. M., Cameron, C. E., Connor, C. M., Farris, C. L., Jewkes, A. M., & Morrison, F. J. (2007). Links between behavioral regulation and preschoolers' literacy, vocabulary, and math skills. *Developmental Psychology, 43*, 947–959.

McClelland, M. M., Morrison, F. J., & Holmes, D. L. (2000). Children at-risk for early academic problems: The role of learning-related social skills. *Early Childhood Research Quarterly, 15*, 307–329.

Mistry, R. S., Benner, A. D., Biesanz, J. C., Clark, S. L., & Howes, C. (2010). Family and social risk, and parental investments during the early childhood years as predictors of low-income children's school readiness outcomes. *Early Childhood Research Quarterly, 25*, 432–449. doi:10.1016/j.ecresq.2010.01.002

Rimm-Kaufman, S. E., Pianta, R. C., & Cox, M. J. (2000). Teachers' judgments of problems in the transition to kindergarten. *Early Childhood Research Quarterly, 15*, 147–166.

Sektnan, M., McClelland, M. M., Acock, A., & Morrison, F. J. (2010). Relations between early family risk, children's behavioral regulation, and academic achievement. *Early Childhood Research Quarterly, 25*, 464–479. doi:10.1016/j.ecresq.2010.02.005

Valiente, C., Lemery-Chalfant, K., & Castro, K. S. (2007). Children's effortful control and academic competence. Mediation through school liking. *Merrill-Palmer Quarterly, 53*, 1–25.

The Role of Effortful Control in Mediating the Association Between Maternal Sensitivity and Children's Social and Relational Competence and Problems in First Grade

Tamar M. Mintz, Bridget K. Hamre, and Bridget E. Hatfield

Research Findings: This study examined the extent to which maternal sensitivity in infancy and toddlerhood is associated with children's social and relational competence and problems in the early years of schooling as well as the extent to which this association is mediated by children's effortful control abilities. Data from 1,364 children (705 boys, 659 girls), their mothers, and teachers from the longitudinal National Institute of Child Health and Human Development Study of Early Child Care and Youth Development were used. Maternal sensitivity was assessed by coding semistructured videos of mother–child interactions; effortful control was assessed by maternal report; and children's social competence, problems, and relationships with teachers and peers were assessed by school observations and teacher report. Structural equation models examined the extent to which there was an association between maternal sensitivity and children's social and relational competence and problems as well as the extent to which this association was mediated by children's effortful control skills. Maternal sensitivity had a direct association with children's social and relational competence and problems in 1st grade. Children's inhibitory control partially mediated the association between maternal sensitivity and the quality of children's skills. *Practice or Policy:* The results are discussed in terms of the importance of interventions geared toward improving maternal sensitivity and children's effortful control skills to help children develop better social and relational skills to foster close and supportive relationships with teachers and peers.

Children's abilities to form close and supportive relationships with teachers and peers are predictive of later social and academic success in school (Birch & Ladd, 1997; Hamre & Pianta, 2001; Ladd, 1990; Lerner, Lerner, & Zabski, 1985). Ladd (1990) found that kindergarten children who had more friends and who maintained those friendships throughout the year had better school adjustment and school performance at the end of the school year. Positive teacher–child relationships provide children with school social support that helps them stay identified with and feel positively toward school (La Paro, Pianta, & Stuhlman, 2004; Pianta, 1999; Pianta & Stuhlman, 2004). Yet despite the importance of social relationships for children's development, a survey of kindergarten teachers in United States found that 50% of teachers believed that the majority of the children in their current classrooms lacked competencies in building peer relationships (Rimm-Kaufman, Pianta, & Cox, 2000).

Given the importance of developing social and relational skills for children's school success, it is critical to identify the processes that help children develop these competencies.

Children's earliest social relationships are with their parents, and these relationships are critical to the development of children's emerging social abilities. Early parent–child relationships are associated with later adjustment as children transition to school (Clark & Ladd, 2000). Supportive parenting is associated with popularity among peers (Ladd & LeSieur, 1995), whereas nonsupportive parenting predicts peer rejection and aggression (Carson & Parke, 1996).

In examining the association between early maternal sensitivity and children's social and relational competencies, it is important to identify the developmental mechanisms through which early maternal sensitivity may be associated with later relationships. One likely mediator is *effortful control*, or children's abilities to volitionally control behavior and inhibit undesired responses (Rothbart, 1989). Kochanska, Murray, and Harlan (2000) found that children who received more sensitive and responsive mothering had greater effortful control skills. Research has also shown that children who can regulate their behavior have better social skills than their dysregulated peers (Gresham, 1998) and that effortful control is linked to social competence (Lemery, Essex, & Snider, 2002). The current article examines whether children's effortful control skills mediate the association between maternal sensitivity and children's later social and relational competence and problems.

SOCIAL COMPETENCE AND RELATIONSHIPS IN THE CLASSROOM

An individual's ability to develop social skills is critical for later school success. Forming close, supportive, and nonconflictual relationships with others is a primary task of social competence during the early school years (Birch & Ladd, 1997; National Institute of Child Health and Human Development Early Child Care Research Network [NICHD ECCRN], 2003). Children spend the majority of their days interacting with their teachers and peers during this developmental period (Howes, Hamilton, & Phillipsen, 1998). It logically follows to examine children's emerging social skills by measuring their relational competence and problems in interactions with teachers and peers. In a longitudinal study of children from kindergarten through eighth grade, Hamre and Pianta (2001) found that children who formed high-quality relationships with their teachers in kindergarten displayed better social and academic skills in middle school than their counterparts with poorer teacher relationships. Children's peer relationships are also associated with social success in the classroom. Ladd, Kochenderfer, and Coleman (1996) found that friendships and peer acceptance during the early school years predicted children's school adjustment. Furthermore, effortful control also plays a role in a child's relational and social competence (Eisenberg, Valiente, & Eggum, 2010).

The inability to develop appropriate relational skills is considered a risk factor for problematic school functioning both in the current school year and later years (Asher & Coie, 1990). Children with conflictual relationships with teachers are at risk for later social and behavioral problems in school (Ladd & Burgess, 1999). In a longitudinal study of the behavioral characteristics that place children at risk for maladaptive social functioning, Ladd and Burgess (1999) found that children were most vulnerable if they displayed aggressive behavior, low peer acceptance, and conflictual teacher–child relationships. Children who are unable to form positive and close relationships with peers are more likely to perform poorly in school, feel lonely, and experience psychological or behavioral problems (Ladd & Troop-Gordon, 2003). Not only does the development of relational competencies enable children to succeed in school, but the absence of these skills is associated with children's difficulty with social relationships throughout middle childhood.

Multiple researchers have observed the concordance between children's relationships with their teachers and those with their peers (e.g., Howes, Matheson, & Hamilton, 1994; Howes et al., 1998; Rimm-Kaufman et al., 2002). For example, Howes et al. (1998) found that children's perceptions of their relationships with teachers at age 9 were associated with teachers' ratings of children's relationships with peers. In addition, research indicates that during the preschool years, children's relationships with their teachers are related to their social competence with peers (Howes et al., 1994). Such findings indicate that in early childhood, children's relationships tend to be similar across individuals within a classroom setting.

CHILD AND MATERNAL INFLUENCES ON SOCIAL SKILLS

Research reveals a link between higher levels of maternal sensitivity and the development of subsequent social competence and close relationships. *Maternal sensitivity* was defined by Ainsworth, Biehar, Waters, and Wall (1978) as a mother's availability and responsiveness to a child's needs and her ability to support the child's growing need for autonomy by following the child's signals consistently and appropriately.

Maternal sensitivity, as observed during play tasks in semistructured video interactions, is consistently linked to children's social competence in the NICHD Study of Early Child Care and Youth Development (SECCYD) (NICHD ECCRN, 2002a, 2003). For example, children with mothers who are more sensitive and who engage in responsive interactions have fewer behavioral problems and increased social skills in first grade (NICHD ECCRN, 2003). Other studies also provide support for the relationships between maternal sensitivity and the development of social skills. McElwain and Volling (2004) found that greater maternal sensitivity in infancy was associated with more positive interactions with a friend (selected by the study child) during an observed play session when the children were 4. Furthermore, in a study examining the associations between mother–child and teacher–child relationships on child outcomes in the early years of schooling, Jerome, Hamre, and Pianta (2009) found that lower maternal sensitivity at 54 months predicted greater conflict with teachers in kindergarten to sixth grade. Pianta, Nimetz, and Bennett (1997) found that the overall quality of mother–child interactions predicted children's social adjustment in kindergarten. Thus, maternal sensitivity has been linked to both social competence (e.g., McElwain & Volling, 2004) as well as social and behavioral problems (e.g., Bradley & Corwyn, 2007).

It is important to understand the developmental mechanisms through which maternal sensitivity is linked to the development of social relationships. Effortful control is one possible mechanism, as it is associated both with maternal sensitivity and with social development. *Effortful control*, one component of children's self-regulatory abilities (Caspi & Shiner, 2006), is defined as a level of volitional control that emerges during children's early development (Rothbart, 1989). Rothbart and Bàtes (2006, p. 129) described effortful control as "the efficiency of executive attention, including the ability to inhibit a dominant response and/or to activate a subdominant response, to plan, and to detect errors." Effortful control skills include the ability to voluntarily shift one's attention as well as the capacity to initiate and inhibit behaviors (Caspi & Shiner, 2006; Kieras, Tobin, Graziano, & Rothbart, 2005). Inhibitory control and attentional focusing were both assessed by maternal report in the current study. Examples of inhibitory control in the classroom include raising hands before speaking, taking turns while playing with peers, and waiting in line. Attentional focusing assesses children's abilities to follow a teacher's directions, remain engaged in tasks through completion, and filter out distractions in the classroom setting.

Although effortful control is believed to have a largely constitutional basis, research has demonstrated that it is influenced by environmental experience (Rothbart & Bates, 2006). Recent evidence points specifically to sensitive parenting as a crucial factor in children's development of effortful control skills (Kochanska et al., 2000; Lengua, Honorado, & Bush, 2007; Olson, Bates, Sandy, & Schilling, 2002). Kochanska et al. (2000) found that greater maternal responsiveness at 22 months predicts children's effortful control at both 22 and 33 months. In their longitudinal study of early precursors to children's impulsive and inattentive behavior, Olson and colleagues (2002) demonstrated that lower levels of maternal restrictiveness when children were 6 months were significantly related to children's inhibitory control at 8 years.

There are multiple pathways through which sensitive parenting may promote the development of effortful control. Kopp (1982) described the fact that in early infancy, caregivers provide children with external regulation, but as children develop and parents provide for increasing child autonomy, children's regulation becomes internal. Research found that children of more intrusive mothers performed more poorly on a delay task than children of mothers who supported independence (Silverman & Ragusa, 1990). It is possible that overly involved mothers fail to provide their children with the opportunity to learn to regulate internally. Mothers may also serve as models for their children as to how to manage emotions and behavior, such that more anxious and disapproving mothers model dysregulation and more supportive and warm mothers model how to effectively regulate emotion (Halberstadt, Crisp, & Eaton, 1999). From an attachment perspective, it is also possible that warm and supportive mothering fosters a positive mother–child attachment, which in turn enables children to develop better regulatory skills (Calkins, 2004; Thompson, 2006).

EFFORTFUL CONTROL AND CHILDREN'S SOCIAL COMPETENCE AND RELATIONSHIPS

Research indicates that children who are able to regulate have better social skills than their dysregulated peers (Gresham, 1998) and that effortful control is linked to social competence (Lemery et al., 2002). Children who score lower on measures of effortful control demonstrate more behavior problems than their peers (Eisenberg et al., 2001; Kochanska & Knaack, 2003). Better developed effortful control skills in children are linked to children's prosocial behavior (Rothbart, Ahadi, & Hershey, 1994) and social competence (Calkins, Gill, Johnson, & Smith, 1999). In a study of the transition to school for children with and without intellectual disabilities, McIntyre, Blacher, and Baker (2006) found that inhibitory control (as measured by latency in touching a desired toy) at 36 months was significantly related to teacher-reported problem behavior at 60 months. In terms of broader self-regulation, Eisenhower, Baker, and Blacher (2007) found that children's self-regulatory abilities were significantly correlated with positive teacher–child relationships. Furthermore, observed child self-regulation and mother report of child behavior problems at age 3 accounted for 9.8% of the variance in student–teacher relationships at age 6.

In the school setting, children's effortful control abilities are important in the development of close and supportive relationships with teachers and peers (Gresham, 1998). The transition to school presents new behavioral, academic, and social demands on the child. Thus, the abilities to inhibit one's behavior and shift attention are particularly important skills in predicting school adjustment.

OVERVIEW OF THE PRESENT STUDY

The current study makes several unique contributions to the literature. Numerous studies have elucidated the role of early parenting in children's social development (see Booth-LaForce & Oxford, 2008; Lucas-Thompson & Clarke-Stewart, 2007; NICHD ECCRN, 2003, 2004). However, most of this work broadly examined social competence rather than specifically focusing on the relational aspects of social competence and problems. In addition, few studies have investigated potential mediational pathways that may help to explain the association between parenting and children's social outcomes. The current study extends the literature by examining the potential mediational pathway of child effortful control. In addition, this study extends the literature by focusing specifically on the social skills needed to effectively navigate relationships in the school setting.

There is some evidence that self-regulatory skills may mediate the associations between parenting and social competence in older children (Eisenberg et al., 2001, 2003), but only a few studies have examined this effect with younger children. For example, Spinrad and colleagues (2007) found that toddlers' effortful control mediated the association between maternal support and numerous child outcomes such as externalizing behavior problems, separation distress, and higher social competence. Kochanska and Knaack (2003) found an association between less developed effortful control abilities in toddlerhood and children's externalizing problems at 6 years of age. The current study extends this inquiry by examining whether this mediational association holds true for children's relationships as they begin elementary school. A further strength of the current study is our examination of two components of effortful control (inhibitory control and attentional focusing) to investigate whether these processes have different influences on children's social and relational competence and problems.

The present study utilizes data from the multisite, longitudinal NICHD SECCYD to examine the association between maternal sensitivity in early childhood and children's social and relational functioning in first grade. It also explores the extent to which this association is mediated by children's effortful control—that is, whether sensitive mothers provide their children with tools to learn to control their impulses that in turn contribute to children's social skills and relationships during the early school years.

The study's research questions and hypotheses are as follows. (a) To what extent is exposure to maternal sensitivity in early childhood associated with children's social and relational skill development in first grade? It is hypothesized that higher ratings of maternal sensitivity will be associated with better developed social and relational competence and fewer problems in first grade. (b) To what extent is the association between maternal sensitivity and social and relational competence and problems in the early school years mediated by children's effortful control, such that maternal sensitivity is associated with competencies in children that are related to their development of positive relationships with teachers and peers in first grade? It is hypothesized that children who receive more sensitive mothering will have better developed effortful control skills, which will be associated with better social and relational competencies and fewer social and relational conflicts and problems in first grade.

METHOD

The data used for this study came from the longitudinal NICHD Study of Early Child Care and Youth Development. The study began in 1989 and aimed to investigate the relationships between various child care experiences and child developmental outcomes (NICHD ECCRN, 1993). Data were collected from families, child care settings, and children through multiple methods, including observations, interviews, questionnaires, and individual child assessments.

Participants

Participants were recruited in 1991 from hospitals in or near 10 selected cities (Little Rock, AR; Irvine, CA; Lawrence and Topeka, KS; Boston, MA; Philadelphia, PA; Pittsburgh, PA; Charlottesville, VA; Morganton and Hickory, NC; Seattle, WA; and Madison, WI). Conditional random sampling was conducted to ensure the diversity of participants across sites (please refer to NICHD ECCRN, 2001, for other sample details, including exclusion criteria and sampling procedures). After an initial 1-month interview, data were collected during four phases: Phase I (birth to age 3), Phase II (age 3 through first grade), Phase III (second grade through sixth grade), and Phase IV (7th grade through 10th grade). For the analyses in this study, data from Phases I and II were used. Of the 1,364 study participants, slightly more than half of the children were boys ($n = 705$); 80.4% were Euro-American ($n = 1,097$); and 19.6% were African American ($n = 176$), Asian American ($n = 22$), or other/mixed ethnicity ($n = 69$). In terms of maternal education, 10.2% of mothers had completed fewer than 12 years of schooling ($n = 139$), 21.1% had obtained a high school degree ($n = 287$), 54.2% had a 2- or 4-year college diploma ($n = 739$), and 14.5% had completed at least some graduate work ($n = 198$). When the study children were 1 month of age, 85% of them were living with both their mother and father.

Overview of Data Collection

Mother–child observations occurred in the home when the study child was 6, 15, 24, and 36 months old. Demographic data, including child gender, maternal education, and the family's income-to-needs ratio, were collected when the study child was 1 month of age. Classroom observations took place during first grade. At each data collection time point, mothers participated in interviews and completed questionnaires regarding major life events, family income, and changes in family composition. Teachers completed questionnaires assessing the nature of the child's relationship with themselves and with other children in the classroom.

Measures

Covariates. The covariates used in the current study were child gender, maternal education, and the family's income-to-needs ratio. The income-to-needs ratio was calculated by dividing the total family income by the poverty threshold for the appropriate family size. For the current study, we averaged the income-to-needs ratio from the time the child was 1 month until he or she was 36 months to obtain a more stable estimate of the family's income level over several years.

Maternal sensitivity. Mother–child interactions were conducted when the child was 6, 15, 24, and 36 months old, and trained observers coded the videotapes to assess maternal sensitivity. The 6- and 15-month interactions took place in the child's home, whereas the 24- and 36-month sessions took place in a laboratory. The videotaped interaction at the 6-month visit involved only a free-play session. For the 15-, 24-, and 36-month visit, the mother and child participated in developmentally appropriate play and problem-solving tasks.

A more specific description of the maternal behavior ratings follows. The ratings of maternal behavior looked at (a) sensitivity to non-distress and the extent to which mother–child interaction was characterized by prompt and appropriate responses to the child's social gestures, expressions, and signals and was generally child centered; (b) intrusiveness, or the degree to which the mother imposed her agenda on the child as opposed to interacting in a way that provided a sense of control to the child; (c) positive regard for the child, or the quality and quantity of expressions to the child that connoted the mother's positive feelings toward the child; and (d) respect for autonomy, or the extent to which the mother supported the child's independence and followed his or her lead during the observation period. Overall, this measure assessed how warm, sensitive, attending, supportive, and responsive the mother was to the child's cues.

Composite maternal sensitivity scores were created from the 6-, 15-, and 24-month data from the sums of three 4-point global ratings (mother's sensitivity/responsiveness to non-distress, intrusiveness [reverse scored], and positive regard for the child). At 36 months, the maternal sensitivity composite was the sum of three 7-point ratings (maternal supportive presence, hostility [reverse scored], and respect for the child's autonomy). These sensitivity indicators were standardized and averaged across multiple time points to provide an estimate of the average level of maternal sensitivity across the time period 6 to 36 months. Cronbach's alphas exceeded .7 at every age. Videotapes of the interactions were sent to a location not involved in the data collection. Interrater reliability was attained by assigning

19%–20% of tapes to be watched and coded by two observers, and interrater reliability exceeded .83 at each age for the maternal sensitivity composite scores.

Effortful control. Mothers completed the Child Behavior Questionnaire (CBQ) as a measure of the child's self-regulatory abilities at 54 months. The CBQ was originally designed as a measure of child temperament. However, more recent research (e.g., Kochanska et al., 2000) has conceptualized these same skills as falling under the domain of self-regulation.

The original questionnaire has 196 items that assess 15 dimensions of temperament. For the NICHD SECCYD, only 80 items and eight of the subscales were used. The eight subscales fall under three broad domains of temperament: surgency, negative affectivity, and effortful control. For the current study, we were primarily interested in examining the effortful control domain of self-regulation, as those are the skills most pertinent to children's social development and behavior in the classroom. In the NICHD study, only the Attentional Focusing and Inhibitory Control scales of the CBQ were administered to mothers (the subscales of effortful control not administered were Low Intensity Pleasure and Perceptual Sensitivity). The current study examined whether the two effortful control scales mediated the association between maternal sensitivity and children's relationships with teachers and peers.

The questionnaire consisted of items that described children's reactions to different situations. Items were rated on a 7-point Likert scale ranging from 1 (*extremely untrue*) to 7 (*extremely true*) to capture the child's reactions over the previous 6 months. Cronbach's alphas ranged from .60 to .85 for the eight subscales. The CBQ has been used in many studies and is linked to parents' reports of children's social behavior (Rothbart et al., 1994).

Student–Teacher Relationship Scale (STRS). Teachers completed the STRS (Pianta, 2001).during the spring of first grade to assess the teacher–child relationship. Using this 30-item questionnaire, teachers reported their perceptions of a particular student's relationship with them. Teachers rated how well each statement described their relationship with the study child on a 5-point Likert scale that ranged from 1 (*definitely does not apply*) to 5 (*definitely applies*). The two aspects of the teacher–child relationship that were used for the current study were conflict and closeness. The conflict subscale measures the degree to which the relationship is characterized by antagonistic, disharmonious, or negative interactions. The closeness subscale assesses the extent to which the relationship is characterized by warmth, open communication, and positive interactions. Higher scores on the STRS indicate more positive relationships for the closeness subscale, and lower scores indicate more conflictual relationships.

In terms of the reliability of the STRS, Cronbach's alphas were .86 and .93 for conflict and closeness, respectively. The STRS has been used extensively to measure teacher–child relationships in child care and elementary school (e.g., Birch & Ladd, 1997; Hamre & Pianta, 2001; Jerome et al., 2009). The STRS has been linked to children's and teacher's behaviors in the classroom and associated with observational measures of the quality of teacher–child relationships (e.g., Birch & Ladd, 1997; Howes & Ritchie, 1988).

Classroom Observation System for first grade (COS-1). In the winter to early spring of first grade, classroom observations took place using the COS-1 (NICHD ECCRN, 2002b). All observations took place during the first half of the school day and began with the start of school in the morning. The observation period was approximately 3 hr. Composite scores were developed for children's positive and negative interactions toward the teacher and peers.

Children's positive/neutral interactions with the teacher were a sum of four scores: (a) Child complies with teacher's request (coded when the study child complied with any direct request made by a teacher), (b) child requests (coded when the study child sought help, assistance, or clarification from the teacher), (c) child volunteers (coded when the study child raised his or her hand to answer a question or participate in an activity), and (d) child has social interaction with the teacher (coded when the study child engaged in spontaneous positive or neutral talk with the teacher, not including relaying academic knowledge). Children's negative interactions with the teacher were the sum of three scores: (a) Child does not comply with teacher's request (coded when the study child passively or actively refused to comply with a teacher's direct request), (b) child is negative (coded when the study child demonstrated a variety of negative behavior toward the teacher, including physical or verbal aggression, angry gestures, or making faces), and (c) child is disruptive (coded when the study child demonstrated disruptive and annoying behaviors, including bothering other children, calling out, or acting like the class clown).

Two composites from the COS-1 were used for assessing children's relationships with peers. The first composite measured children's positive relationships with peers and was the sum of three scores: (a) child's cooperative activity with peers (coded when the study child was engaged in an activity in which he or she interacted with peers), (b) child's shared positive affect with peers (coded when the study child giggled, laughed, or smiled with a peer), and (c) child's social interaction with peers (coded when the study child engaged in positive or neutral talk with a peer). Children's negative interactions with peers were a composite of two scores: (a) child's physical aggression with peers (coded when the study child was physically aggressive, for example hitting, tripping, pushing, or pinching) and (b) child's other negative behavior with peers (coded when the study child carried out a negative act toward a peer, including name calling, scolding, taunting, or teasing).

For the COS-1 observation, two 44-min cycles were completed. In each cycle, observers made time-sampled recordings for three 10-min periods of 30-s observe and 30-s record intervals. Thus, there were 30 different minutes in which discrete behaviors were sampled across each of the two observation cycles, for a total of 60 different minutes (i.e., 60 intervals) in which these codes were sampled (NICHD ECCRN, 2003).

Before entering the classrooms, observers were required to pass a videotaped reliability test of six 44-min cycles. To pass the reliability training, observers had to match at least 60% with a master coder on time-sampled codes and match 80% within 1 scale point for the global rating scales. The average agreement for the observers for the gold-standard videotape for the time-sampled codes was .70. For the global teacher and classroom ratings, the average reliability for observers was estimated at .63. Live interrater reliability was assessed by paired visits to classrooms. Correlations between the observers exceeded .60 for 37 of the 44 time-sampled codes, with lower estimates when the behavior was infrequently observed. Correlations between observers for the global teacher and classroom ratings exceeded .70 for 8 of the 11 ratings.

Unstructured peer observation. Unstructured peer observation was used to examine the study child's interactions with peers during recess, the least structured time of the school day. The procedure included 20-min observation cycles during which observers followed a schedule of 30 s observe time and 30 s record time. For the present study, two composite scales were used: (a) negative or aggressive play with peers and (b) shared positive affect with peers. Pearson correlations for the behavioral scales for the unstructured peer observation were moderately to highly correlated.

Social Skills Rating System (SSRS). In addition to the observational measure of children's friendships, teachers completed the SSRS (Gresham & Elliott, 1990) when the child was in first grade. Each item was rated on a 3-point scale from 0 (*never*) to 3 (*very often*). A scale assessing peer competence was created for the NICHD SECCYD by summing nine items from the SSRS and was not part of Gresham and Elliott's (1990) scoring system. The Peer Competence scale was the only scale used for the present study, and it assessed how the target child behaved with peers (e.g., cooperated with peers without prompting, responded appropriately when hit or pushed by other children, made friends easily), with higher scores indicating more positive, skilled interactions with other children. Reliability for the first-grade Peer Competence scale was .85. The validity of the SSRS has been documented in Gresham and Elliott (1990). The Elementary Level form is highly correlated with other teacher report measures, including the Social Behavior Assessment, the Child Behavior Checklist, and the Harter Teacher Rating Scale.

Teacher Report Form (TRF). Teachers also completed the TRF (Achenbach, 1991), a well-validated measure of children's problem behaviors and social competence. Children's behaviors were rated on 3-point scales from 0 (*not true of the child*) to 2 (*very true of the child*), and a computer program was used to determine whether children fell within a clinically significant range. For this study, only the Social Problems scale was used. Extensive reliability and validity information is available for the TRF. Internal consistency of the TRF ranges from .72 to .95, and interrater reliability is .60. Validity studies have demonstrated that children who receive scores in the clinical range are referred more frequently for clinical services and that elevated scores predict a greater severity and duration of difficulties.

Friends or Foes. Teachers completed a survey of the study child's popularity called Friends or Foes that was created for the NICHD SECCYD. The questionnaire examined the study child's ability to make friends and interact with peers. For the present study, only the teacher's rating of the child's peer status was used. Peer status was calculated by summing four items (are there children who like to play with the study child, are there children who do not like to play with the study child [reversed], the study child is well liked by children of the same sex, and the study child is well liked by children of the opposite sex). Internal reliability for ratings of the child's peer status was moderate, with Cronbach's alphas ranging from .81 to .88 over the data collection points.

Attrition and Missing Data

Participants in the current study were followed for 6 years of data collection. Of the original 1,364 children who entered the study, 966 were observed in their first-grade classroom. Mplus 5.1 (Muthén & Muthén, 2007) is a program designed to address latent variable modeling and has properties to estimate the fit of the latent factor structures while accounting for missing data. For the current study, missing data were handled using the default full information maximum likelihood algorithm. Full information maximum likelihood estimation is considered the most efficient and unbiased method of handling missing data and decreases Type I error rates compared to both listwise and pairwise deletion (Enders & Bandalos, 2001).

Analytic Plan

Descriptive statistics, including means and standard deviations, were executed for all covariates, predictors, mediators, and outcome measures. The covariates entered into the model were child gender, maternal education, and the family's income-to-needs ratio. We used structural equation modeling (SEM) to examine both the direct effects of maternal sensitivity on children's social and relational functioning in first grade as well as the extent to which effortful control mediated the association between maternal sensitivity and later relationships. The two domains of effortful control, attentional focusing and behavioral inhibition, were entered separately into the model so that we could examine whether one aspect of effortful control contributed more significantly to children's later relationships. The errors were correlated between inhibitory control and attentional focusing given that the variables were highly correlated ($r = .53$). Correlating the errors of attentional focusing and inhibitory control improved the model fit, and the models presented here include these terms.

We used SEM to combine indices of children's relationships into two latent variables for children's social and relational competence and problems. We collapsed the variables across teachers and peers for two reasons. First, from a theoretical perspective, research suggests that during the early school years when children are developing social and relational skills, it is prudent to assess their skill development more broadly rather than specifically (e.g., by whom the child is interacting with). Second, research indicates that young children tend to have similar types of relationships (e.g., close vs. conflictual) across different contexts and people in early childhood (Howes et al., 1998). In tandem with our theoretical model, preliminary analyses supported combining teacher and student relationships. In preliminary modeling building analyses, positive/neutral teacher interactions demonstrated a nonsignificant influence ($b = -.01$, $p = .68$) on the latent construct of social and relational competence. The likelihood ratio test indicated that dropping the variable did not influence the model fit, and thus this variable was removed from the model to present a more parsimonious model. Therefore, we chose to examine children's social and relational competence and problems across persons in the classroom.

Bootstrapping is a resampling technique used to test for the indirect effects of mediation (MacKinnon, Lockwood, & Williams, 2004). Resampling methods create their own sampling distribution rather than using established distributions of test statistics. These distributions are used to test hypotheses and generate confidence intervals to determine whether indirect mediation has occurred (Williams & MacKinnon, 2008). In bootstrapping, a large number of smaller samples are repeatedly selected from the larger data set to create a sampling distribution. In the current study, 1,000 bootstrap samples were selected to test for indirect effects.

RESULTS

Descriptive statistics for all variables included in the analyses are presented in Table 1; correlations among all independent, mediating, and dependent variables appear in Table 2. To answer the primary research questions, we used SEM to assess the extent to which (a) maternal sensitivity was

TABLE 1
Descriptive Statistics for Independent, Mediator, and Dependent Variables

Variable	M	SD	n	Range
Covariates				
Maternal education (years)	14.23	2.51	1,363	7–21
Income-to-needs ratio	3.27	2.79	1,365	0–18.76
Independent variable				
Maternal sensitivity	−0.02	0.77	1,306	−3.07 to 1.57
Mediator variables (CBQ)				
Effortful control				
Attentional focusing	4.71	0.85	1,023	1.25–6.88
Inhibitory control	4.66	0.78	1,061	2.00–6.70
Outcome variables				
Social and relational competence				
Closeness with teacher (STRS)	33.96	5.04	1,006	12–40
Positive/neutral with peers (COS)	11.90	9.33	966	0–50
Positive play with peers (UPO)	2.88	3.83	966	0–20
Peer status (Friends or Foes)	16.14	3.16	1,000	4–20
Peer competency (SSRS)	15.30	3.62	1,001	4–20
Social and relational problems				
Conflict with teacher (STRS)	10.92	5.17	1,007	7–35
Negative with teacher (COS)	0.033	0.42	966	0–12
Negative with peers (COS)	0.29	0.85	966	0–50
Negative play with peers (UPO)	0.0034	2.86	962	−1.15 to 26.98
Social problems (TRF)	53.94	5.57	1,008	50–83

Note. CBQ = Child Behavior Questionnaire; STRS = Student–Teacher Relationship Scale; COS = Classroom Observation System; UPO = unstructured peer observation; SSRS = Social Skills Rating System; TRF = Teacher Report Form.

TABLE 2
Correlations Among Predictor, Mediator, and Outcome Measures

Variable	1	2	3	4	5	6	7	8	9	10	11	12	13	14	15	16	17
1. Gender	—	.04	.03	.09**	.13**	.16**	.17**	.00	.01	.08*	.06	.15**	-.17**	-.06	-.03	-.12**	-.09**
2. Maternal education		—	.56**	.50**	.28**	.19**	.12**	-.04	.02	.00	.16**	.19**	-.15**	-.06*	-.09**	-.08*	-.15**
3. Income-to-needs ratio			—	.43**	.24**	.22**	.09**	-.04	-.01	-.02	.11**	.12**	-.13**	-.05	-.10**	-.08*	-.12**
4. Maternal sensitivity				—	.32**	.23**	.09**	-.06	.04	.00	.15**	.20**	-.18**	-.08*	-.13**	-.10**	-.19**
5. Attentional focusing					—	.53**	.09**	-.06	.04	-.01	.12**	.19**	-.20**	-.09**	-.10**	-.10**	-.12**
6. Inhibitory control						—	.08*	-.03	.04	.03	.16**	.19**	-.27**	-.08*	-.09**	-.07*	-.19**
7. Closeness with teacher							—	.04	.08*	.09**	.42**	.46**	-.28**	-.03	-.01	.04	-.22**
8. Positive/neutral with teacher								—	-.06	.17**	.00	-.01	.03	-.02	.04	.08*	.03
9. Positive/neutral with peers									—	.15**	.11**	.10**	-.05	-.02	.18**	.03	-.08*
10. Positive play with peers										—	.12**	.12**	-.08**	-.04	-.01	-.07*	-.12**
11. Peer status											—	.66**	-.47**	-.06	-.10**	-.04	-.56**
12. Peer competency												—	-.56**	-.09**	-.10**	-.09**	-.58**
13. Conflict with teacher													—	.03	.14**	.10**	.52**
14. Negative with teacher														—	.06	.06	.03
15. Negative with peers															—	.18**	.08**
16. Negative play with peers																—	.07*
17. Social problems																	—

*$p<.05$. **$p<.01$.

associated with children's social and relational competence and problems, respectively (direct effect), (b) maternal sensitivity was associated with children's effortful control, and (c) children's effortful control was related to their social and relational skills in first grade (indirect effects). The second and third of these questions address mediation, examining the degree to which the association between maternal sensitivity and children's later social skills and relationships is partially mediated by the child's effortful control abilities. SEM provides statistics addressing the overall fit of the hypothesized model compared to the observed data. Because chi-square values are sensitive to sample size and are often found to be statistically significant when the sample size is large, other model fit statistics are frequently used to ascertain the goodness of fit of the model. The root mean square error of approximation (RMSEA) is reported here as an estimate of the fit of the model tested. Steiger (1990) suggested that an RMSEA less than or equal to .05 is considered a close fit, one between .05 and .08 is an adequate fit, one between .08 and .10 is a mediocre fit, and one greater than .10 is not an acceptable fit of the model to the data. Other researchers (e.g., Hu & Bentler, 1999) have recommended that an RMSEA of .06 be used as the cutoff for a good model fit. The overall model indicated good model fit (RMSEA = .046, 90% confidence interval = .03–.05), indicating an improvement of the model fit to the data. In addition, the comparative fit index for these data was .91. Kenny and McCoach (2003) recommended interpreting a comparative fit index between .90 and .95 as an acceptable fit to the data and one above .95 as a good fit, indicating that the current model was an adequate fit.

Direct Effects

Girls were more likely than boys to display higher social and relational competence ($\beta = .12$, $p < .01$). On average, girls scored .12 points higher than boys on the latent construct of social and relational competence. Children whose mothers had more education ($\beta = .14$, $p < .01$) were more likely to be rated higher in social and relational competence. That is, for every 1-year increase in mother's education level, children displayed a .14 increase in social and relational competence. Moreover, even after we accounted for the covariates, there was a positive effect of maternal sensitivity on social and relational competence (see Figure 1). Alternatively, boys were more likely than girls to have higher scores on social and relational problems ($\beta = -.12$, $p < .05$). On average, boys scored .12 points higher than girls on social and relational problems. Children whose mothers who displayed lower sensitivity were more likely to display increased social and relational problems (see Figure 1).

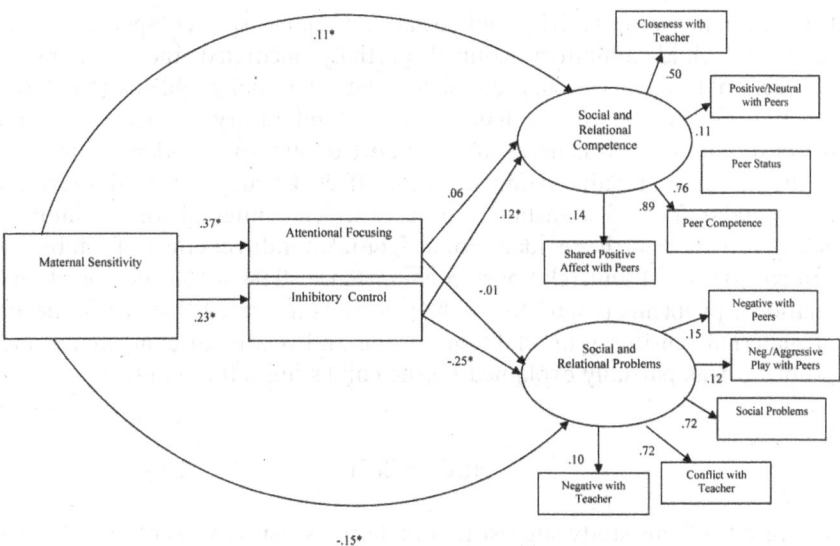

FIGURE 1 Results from a standardized equation model examining the associations between maternal sensitivity, child inhibitory control and attentional focusing, and child social and relational competence and problems in first grade. The model was adjusted for the child gender, maternal education, and income-to-needs ratio. Standardized coefficients are displayed. Neg. = negative. *$p > .05$.

Indirect Effects

In addition to testing the effects of maternal sensitivity on children's social and relational skills, we tested whether this association was partially mediated by children's effortful control skills. Specifically, we tested two components of effortful control: attentional focusing and inhibitory control. We tested these as separate mediators in order to examine the unique contribution of each aspect of the effortful control construct. Results from the SEM model indicated that maternal sensitivity was significantly associated with both attentional focusing ($\beta = .37$, $p < .001$) and inhibitory control ($\beta = .23$, $p < .001$), demonstrating the first necessary step in determining mediation (Baron & Kenny, 1986). What is interesting is that attentional focusing was not significantly associated with either children's social and relational skills or problems in first grade, signifying no further need to examine mediation. However, inhibitory control was significantly associated with both children's social and relational competence ($\beta = .13$, $p < .01$) and problems ($\beta = -.25$, $p < .01$) in first grade. Results indicated a significant indirect effect of inhibitory control ($\beta = .03$, $p > .01$) on the relationship between maternal sensitivity and social and relationship competence. Furthermore, child inhibitory control partially mediated the relationship between maternal sensitivity and social and relational problems ($\beta = -.06$, $p < .01$). Given that the mediating effect of inhibitory control was small for both outcomes, it is necessary to report bootstrap confidence intervals, as they are more reliable estimates of the effect (Cheung, 2007; MacKinnon et al., 2004). The 95% unstandardized confidence interval for the indirect effects provided further evidence of a significant indirect effect of inhibitory control for social and relationship competence (0.04–0.16) and social and relational problems (−0.02 to −0.004). Results indicated that the influence of maternal sensitivity on children's social and relational competence and problems was partially explained by the child's inhibitory control.

DISCUSSION

The results of this study suggest that maternal sensitivity, as observed from infancy through toddlerhood, is significantly associated with children's social and relational competence and problems in first grade. Maternal sensitivity was positively associated with children's social and relational competence and negatively associated with relational problems. These findings are in line with previous longitudinal research suggesting that maternal sensitivity in infancy, toddlerhood, and the preschool years is one of the strongest predictors of children's social development in the early years of school (Pianta & McCoy, 1997; Ramey, Ramey, & Phillips, 1996). The NICHD ECCRN (2003) found that the children of sensitive mothers were rated by their first-grade teachers as having fewer externalizing problems and greater social skills. Although prior research has demonstrated an association between maternal sensitivity and children's later social functioning, this study contributes to the literature by also examining children's relationships within the school setting. Children's relationships with teachers and peers have been linked to both later academic and social–emotional outcomes (Baker, Grant, & Morlock, 2008; Birch & Ladd, 1997; Hamre & Pianta, 2001). Findings from the current study add to this literature by demonstrating that less sensitive parenting is one of the factors that may be associated with the development of social and relational problems during the early school years and, conversely, that greater maternal sensitivity is associated with social and relational skill development.

This study also examined the extent to which associations between early maternal sensitivity and children's relationships in first grade may be explained in part by the development of greater effortful control skills, particularly in the domain of children's inhibitory control. Results demonstrated that inhibitory control partially mediated the association between maternal sensitivity and children's relationships in first grade. This supports the hypothesis that children with more sensitive mothers in early childhood develop regulatory capacities that help them better adjust to the social environment of school. What is interesting is that maternal sensitivity was significantly related to both dimensions of effortful control (attentional focusing and inhibitory control), but only inhibitory control was significantly associated with children's later social competence and relationships. This finding suggests that maternal sensitivity may contribute to the development of children's effortful control skills more broadly. However, consistent with the transactional model of development (Sameroff, 2009), it is also possible that children's behavior influences their parents' reactions. For example, it may be that children with better developed effortful control skills may elicit more sensitive responses from their mothers because it may be easier to be sensitive to such children.

Our results suggest that inhibitory control may be more important to children's relationships in the classroom than attentional focusing. As the demands of school increase, children are required to increasingly inhibit their impulsive responses. They are required to raise their hands before speaking, take turns, and wait in line. In addition to the importance of complying with these requests for academic success, mastery of these skills is required for social success as well. Impulsive children who have difficulty controlling their behavior in the classroom are likely to have difficulty forming close and supportive relationships with their teachers and peers (Ladd, 1999; Spinrad et al., 2006). Attentional focusing assesses children's ability to attend to teachers' directions and remain engaged in classroom tasks. Although this is an important skill for children's academic success, it is likely less related to children's relationships in the classroom. Furthermore, Nathanson, Rimm-Kaufman, and Brock (2009) found that behavioral inhibition was significantly associated with children's kindergarten adjustment, whereas attentional focusing was not. Thus, it appears that the behavioral rather than attentional components of effortful control are more important for children's social and relational success.

Previous research has demonstrated that regulating one's actions is important in the development of social relationships. More impulsive children (i.e., children who have difficulty consciously inhibiting their behavior) have significantly poorer relationships with peers in kindergarten (Gomes & Livesey, 2008) as well as more behavior problems (McClelland, Morrison, & Holmes, 2000). In their study of self-regulation and parenting styles, Nathanson et al. (2009) found that children with poor inhibitory control had more difficulty adjusting to kindergarten than children with better inhibitory control but that attentional focusing was not associated with kindergarten adjustment. Thus, inhibitory control may be the component of effortful control that is most crucial for the development of children's social relationships, particularly in the classroom. Given that in the current study inhibitory control was found to partially mediate both social/relational competence and problems suggests that children's ability to inhibit their impulsive behaviors is important both for the prevention of social problems as well as for the promotion of social and relational competence in the classroom.

Although inhibitory control demonstrates an indirect effect on children's relationships with teachers and peers in first grade, the mediation is only partial. It is likely that in addition to inhibitory control, there are other developmental processes that mediate the association between maternal sensitivity and children's relational capacities. One possible mediator between maternal sensitivity and children's relationships is children's language development. Research indicates that maternal sensitivity contributes to children's cognitive and linguistic development (Landry, Smith, Swank, & Miller-Loncar, 2000). Language development is a critical component of children's social development, as children with stronger language abilities are able to communicate their needs more effectively and have greater social competence (Longoria, Page, Hubbs-Tait, & Kennison, 2009). Because parenting (including maternal sensitivity) contributes to children's linguistic skills, and children's language abilities are linked to social competence during early schooling, testing whether language skills impact the association would be an interesting area for future research.

Study Limitations

Although this study adds to the literature, it does have some limitations. The sample was large and geographically diverse; however, several limits placed on inclusion in the study may limit its generalizability. Families that were not fluent in English, families living in very dangerous areas, families of children with disabilities, mothers younger than age 18, and families with a substance abuse problem were excluded from the study. These exclusion criteria limit the generalizability of the findings to families who fit the criteria represented in the study. There was also limited ethnic and racial diversity within the sample, as 80% of participants were Caucasian. Although 85% of study children were living with both parents at 1 month of age, the current study was not able to examine paternal sensitivity.

Observations for the study were conducted on a single day. This may have limited the robustness and reliability of children's observed behaviors in the classroom. Reliability could have been increased by having observations on multiple days and at different times throughout the day (Downer,

Booren, Lima, Luckner, & Pianta, 2010). It is therefore possible that the association between maternal sensitivity and relational outcomes was underestimated because the single-day observational assessment was not as robust as an assessment over a longer period. In addition it should be noted that Cronbach's alphas for the maternal sensitivity observations were .7, which demonstrates moderate support for internal consistency.

Effortful control was only assessed by maternal report. In future studies, it will be beneficial to assess children's effortful control using direct observation, particularly in the classroom, as that is the most proximal assessment to the outcomes measured. It will be important to assess children's effortful control abilities in the classroom using multiple observation times so that the most valid and reliable estimate is obtained. Furthermore, Cronbach's alphas for the subscales of the CBQ were moderate (ranging from .6 to .85), indicating that items that were grouped together were only moderately associated with one another. However, it should be noted that Rothbart, Ahadi, Hershey, and Fisher (2001) reported similar estimates for internal consistency of the CBQ subscales.

Finally, the study was nonexperimental in design. Although maternal sensitivity was significantly associated with children's later relationships, a causal pathway cannot be concluded. The directionality between maternal sensitivity and effortful control cannot be determined from the findings, and the associations could be merely correlated or have bidirectional associations.

Despite these limitations, the findings from the current study provide support for the importance of sensitive parenting in early childhood for children's development of social and relational competence in first grade. In addition, this study shows support for inhibitory control as a partial mediator between these processes. The results indicate that sensitive parenting has important ramifications for children as they enter school.

Directions for Future Research and Practical Implications

Although this study demonstrates that the association between maternal sensitivity and children's later social and relational competence and problems is partially mediated by the child's inhibitory control abilities, further research is needed to examine these pathways more specifically. Future studies should examine whether maternal sensitivity is more important for children from various backgrounds. The differential susceptibility hypothesis postulates that children who are more sensitive to stimulation and have more difficult temperaments are more sensitive to their rearing experiences than other children (Belsky, Bakermans-Kranenburg, & van IJzendoorn, 2007). Thus, maternal sensitivity may be most important for buffering children who are more biologically predisposed to having difficult temperaments.

Another area for future research is the extent to which children who received less sensitive parenting can improve their social and relational competencies by having a sensitive teacher during their school years. Some researchers suggest that having a supportive and positive relationship with an adult, not necessarily a parent, can help children who are facing multiple risks (Gambone, Klem, & Connell, 2002). It is important to identify the processes that may help children with less sensitive parents to develop relationships with caring adults. This may in turn help such children improve academically, socially, and emotionally.

The current study can help guide intervention research as well. This study points to the association between sensitive parenting in infancy and toddlerhood and later social and relational competence and problems. It therefore appears that the importance of sensitivity extends beyond early childhood and has ramifications for children's relationships as they enter school. Interventions aimed at improving the sensitivity and responsiveness of parents of young children (e.g., Kalinauskiene et al., 2009; Stolk et al., 2008) will likely improve children's relationships beyond early childhood and into the school years.

As this study also demonstrates that inhibitory control is a significant partial mediator between parenting and classroom processes, targeting inhibitory control may be another way to improve children's social and relational skills. Children who are better able to regulate and control their impulsive behavior have less conflict and negative interactions with teachers and peers. Improving children's effortful control, particularly in the domain of inhibitory control, therefore appears to be an important area for intervention to improve children's relationships.

REFERENCES

Achenbach, T. M. (1991). *Manual for the Teacher Report Form and Profile*. Burlington: University of Vermont, Department of Psychiatry.

Ainsworth, M., Biehar, M., Waters, E., & Wall, S. (1978). *Patterns of attachment: A psychological study of the strange situation*. Hillsdale, NJ: Erlbaum.

Asher, S. R., & Coie, J. D. (1990). *Peer rejection in childhood*. New York, NY: Cambridge University Press.

Baker, J. A., Grant, S., & Morlock, L. (2008). The teacher–student relationship as a developmental context for children with internalizing or externalizing behavior problems. *School Psychology Quarterly, 23*, 3–15.

Baron, R. M., & Kenny, D. A. (1986). The moderator–mediator variable distinction in social psychological research: Conceptual, strategic, and statistical considerations. *Journal of Personality & Social Psychology, 51*, 1173–1182.

Belsky, J., Bakermans-Kranenburg, M. J., & van IJzendoorn, M. H. (2007). For better and for worse: Differential susceptibility to environmental influences. *Current Directions in Psychological Science, 16*, 300–304.

Birch, S. H., & Ladd, G. W. (1997). The teacher-child relationship and children's early school adjustment. *Journal of School Psychology, 35*, 61–79.

Booth-LaForce, C., & Oxford, M. L. (2008). Trajectories of social withdrawal from grades 1 to 6: Prediction from early parenting, attachment, and temperament. *Developmental Psychology, 44*, 1298–1313.

Bradley, R. H., & Corwyn, R. F. (2007). Externalizing problems in fifth grade: Relations with productive activity, maternal sensitivity, and harsh parenting from infancy through middle childhood. *Developmental Psychology, 43*, 1390–1401.

Calkins, S. D. (2004). Early attachment processes and the development of emotional self-regulation. In R. F. Baumeister, & K. D. Vohs (Eds.), *Handbook of self-regulation: Research, theory, and applications* (pp. 324–339). New York, NY: Guilford Press.

Calkins, S. D., Gill, K. L., Johnson, M. C., & Smith, C. L. (1999). Emotional reactivity and emotional regulation strategies as predictors of social behavior with peers during toddlerhood. *Social Development, 8*, 310–334.

Carson, J. L., & Parke, R. D. (1996). Reciprocal negative affect in parent child interactions and children's peer competency. *Child Development, 67*, 2217–2226.

Caspi, A., & Shiner, R. L. (2006). Personality development. In W. Damon, & N. Eisenberg (Eds.), *Handbook of child psychology: Vol. 3. Social, emotional, and personality development* (6th ed., pp. 300–365). New York, NY: Wiley.

Cheung, M. W. L. (2007). Comparison of approaches to constructing confidence intervals for mediating effects using structural equation models. *Structural Equation Modeling, 14*, 227–246.

Clark, K. E., & Ladd, G. W. (2000). Connectedness and autonomy support in parent-child relationships. Links to children's socio-emotional orientation and peer relationships. *Developmental Psychology, 36*, 485–498.

Downer, J. T., Booren, L. M., Lima, O. K., Luckner, A. E., & Pianta, R. C. (2010). The Individualized Classroom Assessment Scoring System (inCLASS): Preliminary reliability and validity of a system for observing preschoolers' competence in classroom interactions. *Early Childhood Research Quarterly, 25*, 1–16.

Eisenberg, N., Gershoff, E. T., Fabes, R. A., Shepard, S. A., Cumberland, A. J., Losoya, S. H., ... Murphy, B. C. (2001). Mothers' emotional expressivity and children's behavior problems and social competence: Mediation through children's regulation. *Developmental Psychology, 37*, 475–490.

Eisenberg, N., Valiente, C., & Eggum, N. D. (2010). Self-regulation and school readiness. *Early Education & Development, 21*, 681–698.

Eisenberg, N., Valiente, C., Morris, A. S., Fabes, R. A., Cumberland, A., Reiser, M., ... Lasoya, S. (2003). Longitudinal relations among parental emotional expressivity, children's regulation, and quality of socioemotional functioning. *Developmental Psychology, 39*, 3–19.

Eisenhower, A. S., Baker, B. L., & Blacher, J. (2007). Early student–teacher relationships of children with and without intellectual disability: Contributions of behavioral, social, and self-regulatory competence. *Journal of School Psychology, 45*, 363–383.

Enders, C. K., & Bandalos, D. L. (2001). The relative performance of full information maximum likelihood estimation for missing data in structural equation models. *Structural Equation Modeling, 8*, 430–457.

Gambone, M. A., Klem, A. M., & Connell, J. P. (2002). *Finding out what matters for youth: Testing key links in a community action framework for youth development*. Philadelphia,

PA: Youth Development Strategies, Inc., and Institute for Research and Reform in Education.

Gomes, L., & Livesey, D. (2008). Exploring the link between impulsivity and peer relations in 5- and 6-year-old children. *Child: Care, Health and Development, 34*, 763–770.

Gresham, F. M. (1998). Social skills training with children: Social learning and applied behavioral analytic approaches. In T. S. Watson, & F. M. Gresham (Eds.), *Handbook of child behavior therapy* (pp. 475–497). New York, NY: Plenum Press.

Gresham, F. M., & Elliott, S. N. (1990). *The Social Skills Rating System*. Circle Pines, MN: American Guidance Service.

Halberstadt, A. G., Crisp, V. W., & Eaton, K. L. (1999). Family expressiveness: A retrospective and new directions for research. In P. Philippot, & R. S. Feldman (Eds.), *The social context of nonverbal behavior: Studies in emotion and social interaction* (pp. 109–155). New York, NY: Cambridge University Press.

Hamre, B. K., & Pianta, R. C. (2001). Early teacher-child relationships and the trajectory of children's school outcomes through eighth grade. *Child Development, 72*, 625–638.

Howes, C., Hamilton, C. E., & Phillipsen, L. C. (1998). Stability and continuity of child-caregiver and child-peer relationships. *Child Development, 69*, 418–426.

Howes, C., Matheson, C. C., & Hamilton, C. E. (1994). Maternal, teacher, and child care history correlates of children's relationships with peers. *Child Development, 65*, 264–273.

Howes, C., & Ritchie, S. (1998). Changes in child–teacher relationships in a therapeutic preschool program. *Early Education & Development, 9*, 411–422.

Hu, L., & Bentler, P. M. (1999). Cutoff criteria for fit indexes in covariance structure analysis: Conventional criteria versus new alternatives. *Structural Equation Modeling, 6*, 1–55.

Jerome, E. M., Hamre, B. K., & Pianta, R. C. (2009). Teacher–child relationships from kindergarten to sixth grade: Early childhood predictors of teacher-perceived conflict and closeness. *Social Development, 18*, 915–945.

Kalinauskiene, L., Cekuoliene, D., van IJzendoorn, M. H., Bakermans-Kranenberg, M. J., Juffer, F., & Kusakovskaja, I. (2009). Supporting insensitive mothers: The Vilnius randomized control trial of video-feedback intervention to promote maternal sensitivity and infant attachment security. *Child: Care, Health, and Development, 35*, 613–623.

Kenny, D. A., & McCoach, D. B. (2003). Effect of the number of variables on measures of fit in structural equation modeling. *Structural Equation Modeling, 10*, 333–351.

Kieras, J. E., Tobin, R. M., Graziano, W. G., & Rothbart, M. K. (2005). You can't always get what you want: Effortful control and children's responses to undesirable gifts. *Psychological Science, 16*, 391–396.

Kochanska, G., & Knaack, A. (2003). Effortful control as a personality characteristic of young children: Antecedents, correlates, and consequences. *Journal of Personality, 71*, 1087–1112.

Kochanska, G., Murray, K. T., & Harlan, E. T. (2000). Effortful control in early childhood: Continuity and change, antecedents, and implications for social development. *Developmental Psychology, 36*, 220–232.

Kopp, C. B. (1982). Antecedents of self-regulation: A developmental perspective. *Developmental Psychology, 18*, 199–214.

La Paro, K. M., Pianta, R. C., & Stuhlman, M. (2004). The Classroom Assessment Scoring System: Findings from the prekindergarten year. *The Elementary School Journal, 104*, 409–426.

Ladd, G. W. (1990). Having friends, keeping friends, making friends, and being liked by peers in the classroom: Predictors of children's early school adjustment? *Child Development, 61*, 1081–1100.

Ladd, G. W. (1999). Peer relationships and social competence during early and middle childhood. *Annual Review of Psychology, 50*, 333–359.

Ladd, G. W., & Burgess, K. B. (1999). Charting the relationship trajectories of aggressive, withdrawn, and aggressive/withdrawn children during early grade school. *Child Development, 70*, 910–929.

Ladd, G. W., Kochenderfer, B. J., & Coleman, C. C. (1996). Friendship quality as a predictor of young children's early school adjustment. *Child Development, 67*, 1103–1118.

Ladd, G. W., & LeSieur, K. (1995). Linkages between the family and peer systems: Parents as socializers of children's peer relations. In M. Bornstein (Ed.), *Handbook of parenting* (Vol. 4, pp. 377–409). Hillsdale, NJ: Erlbaum.

Ladd, G. W., & Troop-Gordon, W. (2003). The role of chronic peer difficulties in the development of children's psychological adjustment problems. *Child Development, 74*, 1344–1367.

Landry, S. H., Smith, K. E., Swank, P. R., & Miller-Loncar, C. L. (2000). Early maternal and child influences on children's later independent cognitive and social functioning. *Child Development, 71*, 358–375.

Lemery, K. S., Essex, M. J., & Snider, N. A. (2002). Revealing the relation between temperament and behavior problem symptoms by eliminating measurement confounding: Expert ratings and factor analyses. *Child Development, 73*, 867–882.

Lengua, L. J., Honorado, E., & Bush, N. R. (2007). Contextual risk and parenting as predictors of effortful control and social competence in preschool children. *Journal of Applied Developmental Psychology, 28*, 40–55.

Lerner, J. V., Lerner, R. M., & Zabski, S. (1985). Temperament and elementary school children's academic performance: A test of a "goodness-of-fit" model. *Journal of Child Psychology, 26*, 125–136.

Longoria, A. Q., Page, M. C., Hubbs-Tait, L., & Kennison, S. M. (2009). Relationship between kindergarten children's language ability and social competence. *Early Child Development and Care, 179*, 919–929.

Lucas-Thompson, R., & Clarke-Stewart, K. A. (2007). Forecasting friendship: How marital quality, maternal mood, and attachment security are linked to children's peer relationships. *Journal of Applied Developmental Psychology, 28*, 499–514.

MacKinnon, D. P., Lockwood, C. L., & Williams, J. (2004). Confidence limits for the indirect effect: Distribution of the product and resampling approaches. *Multivariate Behavioral Research, 39*, 99–128.

McClelland, M., Morrison, F. J., & Holmes, D. L. (2000). Children at risk for early academic problems: The role of learning-related social skills. *Early Childhood Research Quarterly, 15*, 307–329.

McElwain, N. L., & Volling, B. (2004). Attachment security and parental sensitivity during infancy: Associations with friendship quality and false belief understanding at age four. *Journal of Social and Personal Relationships, 21*, 639–667.

McIntyre, L. L., Blacher, J., & Baker, B. L. (2006). The transition to school: Adaptation in young children with and without intellectual disability. *Journal of Intellectual Disability Research, 50*, 349–361.

Muthén, L. K., & Muthén, B. O. (2007). *Mplus user's guide.* (5th ed.), Los Angeles, CA.

Nathanson, L., Rimm-Kaufman, S. E., & Brock, L. L. (2009). Kindergarten adjustment difficulty: The contributions of children's effortful control and parental control. *Early Education & Development, 20*, 775–798.

National Institute of Child Health and Human Development Study of Early Child Care. (1993). *The NICHD Study of Early Child Care: A comprehensive longitudinal study of children's lives.* Bethesda, MD: National Institute of Child Health and Human Development.

National Institute of Child Health and Human Development Study of Early Child Care. (2001). Nonmaternal care and family factors in early development: An overview of the NICHD Study of Early Child Care. *Journal of Applied Developmental Psychology, 22*, 457–492.

National Institute of Child Health and Human Development Early Child Care Research Network. (2002a). Early child care and children's development prior to school entry. *American Educational Research Journal, 39*, 133–164.

National Institute of Child Health and Human Development Early Child Care Research Network. (2002b). The relation of global first grade classroom environment to structural classroom features, teacher, and student behaviors. *Elementary School Journal, 102*, 367–387.

National Institute of Child Health and Human Development Early Child Care Research Network. (2003). Social functioning in first grade: Associations with earlier home and child care predictors and with current classroom experience. *Child Development, 74*, 1639–1662.

National Institute of Child Health and Human Development Early Child Care Research Network. (2004). Fathers' and mothers' parenting behavior and beliefs as predictors of children's social adjustment in the transition to school. *Journal of Family Psychology, 18*, 628–638.

Olson, S. L., Bates, J. E., Sandy, J. M., & Schilling, E. M. (2002). Early developmental precursors of impulsive and inattentive behavior: From infancy to middle childhood. *Journal of Child Psychology and Psychiatry, 43*, 435–447.

Pianta, R. C. (1999). *Enhancing relationships between children and teachers*. Washington, DC: American Psychological Association.

Pianta, R. C. (2001). *Student-Teacher Relationship Scale*. Lutz, FL: Psychological Assessment Resources.

Pianta, R. C., & McCoy, S. (1997). The first day of school: The predictive validity of early school screening. *Journal of Applied Developmental Psychology, 18*, 1–22.

Pianta, R. C., Nimetz, S. L., & Bennett, E. (1997). Mother-child relationships, teacher-child relationships and adjustment in preschool and kindergarten. *Early Childhood Research Quarterly, 12*, 263–280.

Pianta, R. C., & Stuhlman, M. W. (2004). Teacher-child relationships and children's success in the first years of school. *School Psychology Review, 33*, 444–458.

Ramey, S. L., Ramey, C. T., & Phillips, M. M. (1996). *Head Start children's entry into public school: An interim report on the National Head Start-Public School Early Childhood Transition Demonstration Study*. Washington, DC: U.S. Department of Health and Human Services.

Rimm-Kaufman, S. E., Early, D. M., Cox, M. J., Saluja, G., Pianta, R. C., Bradley, R. H., & Payne, C. (2002). Early behavioral attributes and teachers' sensitivity as predictors of competent behavior in the kindergarten classroom. *Journal of Applied Developmental Psychology, 23*, 451–470.

Rimm-Kaufman, S. E., Pianta, R. C., & Cox, M. J. (2000). Teachers' judgments of problems in the transition to kindergarten. *Early Childhood Research Quarterly, 15*, 147–166.

Rothbart, M. K. (1989). Temperament and development. In G. A. Kohnstamm, J. E. Bates, & M. K. Rothbart (Eds.), *Temperament in childhood* (pp. 187–247). New York, NY: Wiley.

Rothbart, M. K., Ahadi, S. A., & Hershey, K. L. (1994). Temperament and social behavior in childhood. *Merrill Palmer Quarterly, 40*, 21–39.

Rothbart, M. K., Ahadi, S. A., Hershey, K. L., & Fisher, P. (2001). Investigations of temperament at three to seven years: The Children's Behavior Questionnaire. *Child Development, 72*, 1394–1408.

Rothbart, M., & Bates, J. (2006). Temperament. In N. Eisenberg, W. Damon, & L. M. Richard (Eds.), *Handbook of child psychology: Vol. 3, Social, emotional, and personality development* (6th ed., pp. 99–166). Hoboken, NJ: John Wiley & Sons, Inc.

Sameroff, A. (2009). *The transactional model of development: How children and contexts shape each other*. Washington, DC: American Psychological Association.

Silverman, I. W., & Ragusa, D. M. (1990). Child and maternal correlates of impulse control in 24-month-old children. *Genetic, Social, and General Psychology Monographs, 116,* 435–473.

Spinrad, T. L., Eisenberg, N., Cumberland, A., Fabes, R. A., Valiente, C., Shepard, S. A., ... Guthrie, I. K. (2006). Relation of emotion-related regulation to children's social competence: A longitudinal study. *Emotion, 6,* 498–510.

Spinrad, T. L., Eisenberg, N., Gaertner, B., Popp, T., Smith, C. L., Kupfer, A., ... Hofer, C. (2007). Relations of maternal socialization and toddlers' effortful control to children's adjustment and social competence. *Developmental Psychology, 43,* 1170–1186.

Steiger, J. H. (1990). Structural model evaluation and modification: An interval estimation approach. *Multivariate Behavioral Research, 25,* 173–180.

Stolk, M. N., Mesman, J., van Zeijl, J., Alink, L. R. A., Bakermans-Kranenburg, M. J., van IJzendoorn, M. J., ... Koot, H. M. (2008). Early parenting intervention aimed at maternal sensitivity and discipline: A process evaluation. *Journal of Community Psychology, 36,* 780–797.

Thompson, R. A. (2006). The development of the person: Social understanding, relationships, conscience, self. In N. Eisenberg, & W. Damon (Eds.), *Handbook of child psychology: Vol. 3. Social, emotional, and personality development* (6th ed., pp. 24–98). New York, NY: Wiley.

Williams, J., & MacKinnon, D. P. (2008). Resampling and distribution of the product methods for testing indirect effects in complex models. *Structural Equation Modeling, 15,* 23–51.

Cognitive Flexibility, Approaches to Learning, and Academic School Readiness in Head Start Preschool Children

Virginia E. Vitiello

Daryl B. Greenfield and Pelin Munis

J'Lene George

Research Findings: The purpose of this study was to examine whether approaches to learning significantly mediated relations between cognitive flexibility (a component of executive functions) and school readiness in Head Start preschoolers. A total of 191 children from 22 Head Start classrooms were directly assessed on cognitive flexibility and school readiness. In addition, teachers rated children's approaches to learning in 3 domains (competence motivation, attention/persistence, and attitude toward learning) using the Preschool Learning Behaviors Scale (P. A. McDermott, L. F. Green, J. M. Francis, & D. H. Stott, 2000). Results of multilevel mediation analyses revealed that 1 component of approaches to learning—attention/persistence—significantly mediated the relation between cognitive flexibility and school readiness. These results suggest that part of the effect of cognitive flexibility on school readiness may be related to cognitive flexibility supporting children's approaches to learning. *Practice or Policy:* This information may be useful to researchers and practitioners attempting to improve school readiness by improving children's cognitive flexibility. The findings suggest, at a very preliminary level, that improvements to children's cognitive flexibility may lead to improved approaches to learning as well as academic school readiness. This information is important to consider as preschool programs increasingly target children's executive functions.

In recent years, researchers have sought to understand how self-regulatory skills like executive functions are related to individual differences in young children's achievement. *Executive functions* are cognitive skills, including working memory, inhibition, and cognitive flexibility, that are involved in performing goal-directed actions (Blair & Peters, 2003). Studies suggest that executive functions are involved in a broad range of cognitive and behavioral processes critical to daily functioning; deficits in these skills have been implicated in developmental disabilities, learning disabilities, and behavior problems (Brophy, Taylor, & Hughes, 2002; Pennington & Ozonoff, 1996; Welsh, 2002). It is increasingly clear that executive functions are fundamental to children's academic achievement as well (Bull & Scerif, 2001; St. Clair-Thompson & Gathercole, 2006). However, the mechanisms driving the relationship between executive functions and achievement are not fully understood. One possible explanation is that strong executive functions support the performance of adaptive behaviors that contribute to learning, commonly referred to as children's *approaches to learning*. The current study examined this possibility by testing relations between cognitive flexibility (one component of executive functions), approaches to learning, and academic school readiness in preschool children at risk for school failure because of poverty. Children who have stronger cognitive flexibility may be better able to select and activate positive approaches to learning in response to learning situations compared to children with poorer cognitive flexibility, leading to better academic school readiness.

Preschool children raised in contexts of poverty are at high risk for academic difficulty and school failure (Reynolds & Temple, 2008). For these children, supporting the development of academic school readiness skills, including knowledge of colors, numbers, letters, and basic vocabulary, is particularly important: Although children in poverty tend to enter school already behind their more affluent peers, children who enter school with stronger early academic skills make greater achievement gains in elementary school (Duncan et al., 2007; Ramey & Ramey, 2004). Furthermore, income levels and family experiences are associated with preschool and early school-age children's executive skills, such that lower income children and those exposed to less positive early home environments have lower executive skills (National Institute of Child Health and Human Development Early Child Care Research Network, 2003, 2005). Some preschool programs are increasingly attempting to improve low-income children's school readiness by explicitly targeting executive functions, including cognitive flexibility (e.g., Diamond, Barnett, Thomas, & Munro, 2007). Understanding the pathways of influence from executive functions like cognitive flexibility to academic school readiness in at-risk preschoolers is an important goal because a better understanding of these relations could lead to more effective, targeted intervention strategies.

COGNITIVE FLEXIBILITY

Cognitive flexibility, also called *switching*, is a particularly complex executive skill involving the ability to shift between two or more competing response alternatives (Davidson, Amso, Anderson, & Diamond, 2006); for example, when a preschooler cleans up blocks and beads by sorting them into different bins or a second grader does a worksheet that alternates between addition and subtraction problems. Extensive research has been conducted on cognitive flexibility in preschool children, focusing especially on its role in cognition and information processing. This research suggests that cognitive flexibility involves multiple skills, including activating new response sets, inhibiting previously activated response sets, and maintaining response rules in working memory (Chevalier & Blaye, 2008; Davidson et al., 2006). In addition, several studies have linked cognitive flexibility to academic school readiness and achievement in young children. In a predominantly middle-class sample, cognitive flexibility measured at 4 to 5 years of age was positively correlated with literacy and math scores over the first 3 years of elementary school (Bull, Espy, & Wiebe, 2008). In a study of Head Start preschool children, cognitive flexibility positively predicted gains in language and literacy (Bierman, Nix, Greenberg, Blair, & Domitrovich, 2008). In another study that followed Head Start children from preschool into kindergarten, researchers found that cognitive flexibility measured in kindergarten was marginally related to kindergarten achievement (although cognitive flexibility measured in Head Start was not related to achievement gains from Head Start into kindergarten; Blair & Razza, 2007).

Thus, prior research provides some support for the notion that cognitive flexibility is involved in actively processing information and that higher cognitive flexibility is associated with better academic school readiness for preschoolers. It is not clear, though, whether the relation between cognitive flexibility and academic school readiness is entirely due to the role that cognitive flexibility plays in information processing or whether part of the relation may be due to its role in selecting and activating appropriate responses to learning situations. Although relatively little research has been conducted linking cognitive flexibility to preschool children's observable behaviors, such as their approaches to learning, both theory and prior research suggest such a relation.

APPROACHES TO LEARNING

Adaptive learning behaviors, frequently referred to as *approaches to learning*, include motivation, persistence, frustration tolerance, initiative, and a positive disposition toward learning (Kagan, Moore, & Bredekamp, 1995). Research has shown that preschool and early elementary school children with positive approaches to learning have higher school readiness and achievement outcomes than children with poor approaches to learning (Fantuzzo, Perry, & McDermott, 2004; McClelland, Morrison, & Holmes, 2000; McWayne, Fantuzzo, & McDermott, 2004). These children are better able to attend to and actively participate in learning activities, show interest in new and difficult tasks, and demonstrate persistence in the face of challenge. Of interest in the current study were three components of approaches to learning: competence motivation, attention/persistence, and attitude toward learning. *Competence motivation* refers to a child's tendency to choose challenging tasks, work independently at tasks, and show positive affect in relation to tasks (Morgan, MacTurk, & Hrncir, 1995). *Attention/persistence* refers to a child's ability to focus on tasks, resist distractions, and persist appropriately (McWayne et al., 2004). *Attitude toward learning* encompasses a child's ability to tolerate frustration, cooperate, and accept help when needed (McWayne et al., 2004). These constructs encompass overt behavioral and affective responses to learning situations that serve to bring children into greater contact with learning opportunities in the classroom.

THEORETICAL RATIONALE

The theoretical rationale for examining links between cognitive flexibility and approaches to learning is based on a cognitive application of control theory (Johnson, Chang, & Lord, 2006; Lord & Levy, 1994). According to this theory, the performance of goal-directed actions depends on feedback between multiple hierarchically organized processes. At the highest levels these processes are geared toward attaining abstract, long-term goals and can include social interactions or complex behaviors, such as organizing friends for a game of tag or eliciting a teacher's help in writing a letter to a friend. Lower level processes, including biological perception and cognitive skills, are focused on subconscious, short-term goals such as signal detection or response selection. Feedback between these levels results in coordinated, complex, goal-directed behavior. This feedback can come from the top down or bottom up—for example, a new goal can lead to the activation of cognitive processes, or new perceptual information can lead to the formation of new goals (Johnson et al., 2006).

According to this theory, executive functions, including cognitive flexibility, are part of a cognitive system involved in activating appropriate responses and suppressing inappropriate responses toward meeting goals (Johnson et al., 2006). Thus, the current study proposed that cognitive flexibility can be recruited to support the attainment of higher level, abstract learning goals by selecting and activating appropriate responses to learning opportunities. To put this in concrete terms, in the preschool context, an abstract, long-term goal (set in part by adults) is to learn basic concepts such as letters, numbers, and colors. To reach the goal of learning effectively, children have to demonstrate positive approaches to learning; in other words, they must display motivation, attention, persistence, and a positive attitude toward learning, behaviors that bring children into greater contact with learning opportunities (Schaefer & McDermott, 1999). Initiating and maintaining these positive approaches to learning may depend in part on children's ability to select and activate relevant behaviors, attitudes, and motivation. In effect, prior research has shown that progress toward the abstract goal (learning) is supported by positive approaches to learning (McWayne et al., 2004). The current study proposed that positive approaches to learning may in turn be supported by strong cognitive flexibility.

SUPPORT FOR LINKS BETWEEN COGNITIVE FLEXIBILITY AND APPROACHES TO LEARNING

Evidence is accumulating that suggests a link between cognitive flexibility and observable child behaviors. The majority of this research has focused on social competence and behavior problems rather than approaches to learning. For example, in a study of children followed from first to third grade, first-grade cognitive flexibility was found to be positively related to third-grade social competence (Nigg, Quamma, Greenberg, & Kusché, 1999). In first-grade students, higher scores on cognitive flexibility were associated with decreased internalizing and externalizing behavior problems from first to second grade (Riggs, Blair, & Greenberg, 2003). These studies support the notion that cognitive flexibility is associated with important social and behavioral skills: Children with stronger cognitive flexibility may be better able to activate appropriate responses to peers and social interactions within the classroom.

Initial research also suggests that cognitive flexibility is related to children's approaches to learning. Low cognitive flexibility has been linked to teacher reports of impulsivity, hyperactivity, and inattention in children from ages 6 to 16 (Riccio et al., 1994), indicating that cognitive flexibility may be related to attention within the classroom context.

Very little is known about relations between cognitive flexibility and other components of approaches to learning such as children's motivation and attitudes toward learning. The extant research suggests that cognitive processes, including cognitive flexibility, are related to motivation in preschool children (Chang & Burns, 2005). However, these studies have tended to focus on the role that motivation plays in supporting cognitive flexibility (Pessoa, 2009). An alternative possibility is that cognitive flexibility supports children's ability to be motivated and enthusiastic by selecting and activating these tendencies in response to learning activities. Evidence suggests that general executive functions are involved in the regulation of emotions like anger, disappointment, and frustration, factors that in turn can affect early learning (Carlson & Wang, 2007; Hoeksma, Oosterlaan, & Schipper, 2004; Howse, Calkins, Anastopoulos, Keane, & Shelton, 2003), although these studies did not specifically examine cognitive flexibility. Research has also suggested that cognitive flexibility is involved in activating and regulating attitudes in adults (Poldrack, Wagner, Stanley, Phelps, & Banaji, 2008). Overall, however, very little is known about relations between cognitive flexibility, motivation, and attitudes in preschool children, representing a significant gap in knowledge. It may be that cognitive flexibility is involved in selecting and activating positive responses to learning opportunities, such as motivation to learn and a positive attitude toward learning. The current study addressed this knowledge gap preliminarily by examining these relations.

THE CURRENT STUDY

In summary, although evidence suggests that approaches to learning and cognitive flexibility are both potentially important contributors to academic achievement (Bierman et al., 2008; McWayne et al., 2004), the relations among them are not well understood. Based on control theory and evidence from the existing literature, we hypothesized that approaches to learning would mediate relations between cognitive flexibility (a component of executive functions) and school readiness among at-risk preschoolers enrolled in the public Head Start preschool program. In testing this hypothesis, we aimed to establish that (a) cognitive flexibility is related to school readiness, (b) cognitive flexibility is related to approaches to learning, and (c) the indirect pathway from cognitive flexibility to school readiness through approaches to learning is significant. Preschool children enrolled in Head Start were directly assessed on measures of cognitive flexibility and school readiness. Teachers rated children's approaches to learning using the Preschool Learning Behaviors Scale (PLBS), which produced a total score for approaches to learning and subscale scores for competence motivation, attention/persistence, and attitude toward learning (McDermott, Green, Francis, & Stott, 2000). To better understand the complex relations between cognitive flexibility and approaches to learning, we tested the mediation first using the total score for approaches to learning and then using the subscale scores. To account for the nested nature of the data (children within classrooms), we tested mediation models using a multilevel modeling framework (Krull & MacKinnon, 2001).

METHOD

Participants

Participants in the study were 196 children from 23 classrooms within two urban Head Start centers in southern Florida. Both centers served predominantly African American populations, and instruction was in English. Teachers from these classrooms distributed consent forms to all parents in their classrooms ($N = 414$). Additional consent forms were sent out to non-responding parents 2 weeks after the first forms were distributed. A total of 47% of parents consented to their children's participation in the study, and 1% of parents declined. The remaining parents did not return consent forms.

Of the initial sample of 196 children, 4 children were missing data on one or more measures and one classroom had only 1 participating child, which meant that classroom effects could not be estimated for that classroom in a multilevel framework. Excluding these children resulted in a final sample of 22 classrooms and 191 children. Ages ranged from 36 to 60 months ($M = 48$ months, $SD = 7$). Participating children were predominantly African American (92%) and Hispanic (7%). Finally, 49% were female.

Procedures

This project was approved by the university institutional review board. Data collection took place in the spring. Child demographic data were collected from parents and center records. Direct assessments were conducted at the participating Head Start centers. To the extent possible, assessments were conducted in quiet locations free of distractions. The cognitive flexibility task was administered in a session that lasted 15 to 20 min per child. Approximately 2 weeks later the school readiness assessment was administered, requiring 15 to 30 min per child. Children were given stickers at the end of each testing session. Concurrently with the collection of the direct assessments, teachers were asked to complete rating scales of approaches to learning for each participating child.

Measures

Cognitive flexibility. Cognitive flexibility was assessed using a 33-item oddity switching task in which children were shown arrays of three pictures and asked to point to the picture that was different from the others (Greenfield, 1992). On each item the criterion for determining which picture was different changed, requiring children to switch response strategies when responding to each item. For example, for one item children were shown one arrow pointing up and two arrows pointing down and had to choose the odd picture out based on spatial orientation. For the subsequent item, children were shown a violin, a trumpet, and a pickup truck and had to choose based on superordinate category. This task primarily assesses cognitive flexibility but also taps into problem solving and inhibition to some degree; some overlap when testing executive functions in young children is common (Hughes & Graham, 2002). Correct responses were scored as 1 and incorrect responses were scored as 0, with a possible range of 0 to 33.

In a low-income kindergarten sample, performance on the cognitive flexibility task was positively correlated with achievement and teacher-reported approaches to learning (George & Greenfield, 2005). In the same sample of low-income children, performance on the task was moderately stable from Head Start into kindergarten ($r = .36$, $p < .001$) and was significantly correlated with concurrently administered executive tasks measuring inhibition ($r = .16$, $p = .043$) and sequencing ($r = .17$, $p = .028$) in Head Start (Greenfield, 2000). Cronbach's alpha for the current study was .75, indicating adequate internal consistency.

Approaches to learning. Approaches to learning was assessed using the PLBS (McDermott et al., 2000). The PLBS is a 29-item measure developed for use with low-income preschool children that asks teachers to rate children's approaches to learning on a 3-point scale (most often applies, sometimes applies, and doesn't apply). Teachers rate behaviors in three areas: competence motivation (e.g., "shows a lively interest in the activities"), attention/persistence (e.g., "tries but concentration soon fades"), and attitude toward learning (e.g., "gets aggressive or hostile when frustrated"). Raw scores for each subscale were converted into area conversion t scores ($M = 50$, $SD = 10$) based on the national standardization sample (McDermott et al., 2000). Cronbach's alphas for the three subscales on the standardization sample were .85 (competence motivation), .83 (attention/persistence), and .75 (attitude toward learning; McDermott et al., 2000). For the current sample, alphas were .87, .81, and .74, respectively.

The PLBS was standardized on a nationally representative sample of preschool children ages 3 to 5.5 (McDermott, Leigh, & Perry, 2002). Scores showed small to moderate correlations with measures of children's verbal and nonverbal ability ($rs = .15-.34$, $p < .05$) and moderate to large correlations with teacher reports of social skills ($rs = .33-.76$, $p < .001$) and internalizing and externalizing behavior problems ($rs = -.32$ to $-.69$, $p < .05$). Test–retest reliability was assessed for a subsample of Head Start children and was found to be high (.80–.94 for the subscales and total score).

Academic school readiness. Academic school readiness was directly assessed using the Bracken Basic Concepts Scale–Revised School Readiness Composite (BBCS-R; Bracken, 1998). The BBCS-R consists of six subtests assessing knowledge of colors, letters, numbers, sizes, object comparisons, and shapes. The subtest scores are summed to provide a raw score, which is then converted to a scaled score based on the child's chronological age. Scaled scores have a mean of 10 and a standard deviation of 3. Internal consistency estimates based on the standardization sample were .93, .96, and .97, for 3-, 4-, and 5-year-olds, respectively, and test–retest reliability was .88, indicating high stability (Bracken, 1998).

The BBCS-R was nationally normed on a sample of children ages 2 years, 6 months, to 8 years selected to reflect census estimates for age, gender, geographical location, ethnicity, and parent education (Bracken, 1998). Scores in kindergartners have been shown to predict kindergarten children's retention and teacher reports of learning problems as well as direct assessments of prereading skills in first grade (Panter & Bracken, 2009). BBCS-R scores at 4 years were also positively associated with assessments of low-income children's language use and vocabulary at 2.5 years (Loeb, Fuller, Kagan, & Carrol, 2004).

Analytic Approach

The data were analyzed in several steps. Descriptive analyses were conducted first, including descriptive statistics and correlations among variables. Analyses were also conducted to assess the effects of age and gender on all variables to identify potentially important covariates. The effects of ethnicity were not tested because of the homogeneity of the sample, which was predominantly African American.

Next, a series of multilevel models were conducted to test for mediation. For all analyses, Level 1 represented variability between children nested within classrooms, and Level 2 represented variability between classrooms. Mediation was tested following Krull and MacKinnon's (2001) guidelines for testing mediation when all variables are at Level 1. This approach is similar to the procedures outlined by Baron and Kenny (1986) and involves establishing that (Step 1) the predictor (cognitive flexibility) significantly predicts the outcome (school readiness), (Step 2) the predictor significantly predicts the mediators (approaches to learning total score, competence motivation, attention/persistence, and attitude toward learning), and (Step 3) the mediators significantly predict the outcome variable after the predictor is controlled. If the effect of the predictor on the outcome is reduced after the mediator is controlled, then there is evidence of mediation. In the current study, the significance of the mediation was tested using the Sobel test (Baron & Kenny, 1986; Krull & MacKinnon, 2001). All variables were centered on the group mean in keeping with recommendations for models in which Level 1 predictors are of interest (Enders & Tofighi, 2007). Prior to centering, gender was scored as 0 for boys and 1 for girls.

RESULTS

Descriptive Analyses

All of the study variables were found to be normally distributed. Means and standard deviations for cognitive flexibility, approaches to learning, and school readiness are presented in Table 1. According to published norms for the BBCS-R (Bracken, 1998), 78% of current participants could be categorized as having "average" or "advanced" school readiness scores, whereas 20% of the participants could be categorized as "delayed" and 1% ($n = 2$) as "very delayed." Thus, the majority of children in this high-risk sample were functioning at or above the level expected for their age group.

TABLE 1
Means (SD) for Cognitive Flexibility, Approaches to Learning, and School Readiness Scores

Variable	Full Sample ($N=191$)	Girls ($n=93$)	Boys ($n=98$)
Cognitive flexibility[a]	15.62 (5.33)	15.60 (5.23)	15.63 (5.47)
Approaches to learning total score[b]	47.34 (12.04)	49.83 (11.0)	45.02 (12.55)
Attention/persistence[b]	47.30 (10.46)	49.22** (9.58)	45.49 (10.78)
Competence motivation[b]	47.35 (11.14)	49.30** (10.35)	45.51 (11.59)
Attitude toward learning[b]	50.23 (10.39)	52.04** (9.35)	48.51 (11.06)
School readiness[c]	8.88 (2.80)	9.58** (2.38)	8.22 (2.99)

[a]Scores ranged from 6 to 31.
[b]Standard scores have a mean of 50 and a standard deviation of 10.
[c]Scores ranged from 3 to 16.
**$p < .01$.

Age. Pearson correlations were computed to assess relationships between age, cognitive flexibility, and approaches to learning (see Table 2). Significant positive relationships ranging from .31 to .41 were found between age and cognitive flexibility, competence motivation, attention/persistence, and attitude toward learning ($p < .01$). As expected, the correlation between age and school readiness was not significant, as the BBCS-R controls for age in its standardized scores.

Gender. An independent samples t test was conducted to assess gender differences on cognitive flexibility, approaches to learning, and school readiness. Levene's test for equality of variances was significant for attitude toward learning and school readiness ($ps = .03$ and .02, respectively): There was greater variability in scores for boys than for girls. Significant gender differences were found for competence motivation, attention/persistence, attitude toward learning, and school readiness. On average, girls scored nearly 4 standard points (about two fifths of a standard deviation) higher

TABLE 2
Correlations Between Study Variables

Variable	1	2	3	4	5	6
1. Age	—	.41**	.31**	.31**	.33**	.06
2. Cognitive flexibility		—	.29**	.30**	.29**	.19**
3. Competence motivation			—	.80**	.76**	.22**
4. Attention/persistence				—	.73**	.30**
5. Attitude toward learning					—	.13
6. School readiness						—

**$p < .01$.

than boys on competence motivation, attention/persistence, and attitude toward learning: $t(189) = -2.38$, $t(189) = -2.52$, and $t(189) = -2.38$, respectively; all $ps < .01$. For school readiness, girls scored 1.36 standard points (nearly half of a standard deviation) higher on average than boys, $t(189) = -3.45$, $p < .01$. There were no gender differences on the cognitive flexibility task, $t(189) = 0.04$, ns. Means and standard deviations for all variables by gender are presented in Table 1.

Correlations among study variables. Pearson correlations among cognitive flexibility, approaches to learning, and school readiness are presented in Table 2. There were low positive correlations ranging from .19 to .29 between cognitive flexibility, school readiness, and the approaches to learning variables (all $ps < .01$). Lastly, there were significant positive correlations ranging from .73 to .80 between the approaches to learning variables (all $ps < .01$).

Multilevel Mediation Analyses

Approaches to learning (total score) as the mediator. The first set of analyses tested the approaches to learning total score as the mediator between cognitive flexibility and academic school readiness. First we used a multilevel model to test the relation between cognitive flexibility and academic school readiness, controlling for age and gender (see Table 3). The fully unconditional model indicated that 9.9% of the variance was due to differences between classrooms. Next, age and gender were entered into the model as predictors at Level 1; together, these control variables accounted for 5.2% of the between-child variance in school readiness. Finally, cognitive flexibility was entered into the model. The equations for the final model predicting school readiness were as follows:

Level 1: $Y_{ij} = \beta_{0j} + \beta_{1j}(age) + \beta_{2j}(gender) + \beta_{3j}(cognitive\ flexibility) + \gamma_{ij}$
Level 2: $\beta_{0j} = \gamma_{00} + u_{0j}$
$\beta_{1j} = \gamma_{10}$
$\beta_{2j} = \gamma_{20}$
$\beta_{3j} = \gamma_{30}$

Cognitive flexibility was significantly and positively associated with school readiness scores at Level 1 and explained an additional 7.6% of the variance within classrooms (see Table 3, Step 1).

Next, the relation between cognitive flexibility and the approaches to learning total score was tested (see Table 3, Step 2). We found that 46% of the variance in approaches to learning scores was due to differences between classrooms; 9.1% of the child-level variance was accounted for by

TABLE 3
Analyses Testing Approaches to Learning (Total Score) as a Mediator

Parameter	Step 1: Flexibility Predicting School Readiness		Step 2: Flexibility Predicting Approaches to Learning (Total Score)		Step 3: Flexibility and Approaches to Learning Predicting School Readiness	
	Estimate	SE	Estimate	SE	Estimate	SE
Fixed effects						
Intercept (γ_{00})	8.85***	0.30	45.49***	1.87	8.87***	0.29
Age (γ_{10})	−0.04	0.03	0.18	0.11	−0.05	0.03
Gender (γ_{20})	1.45***	0.37	3.72***	1.21	1.21**	0.38
Flexibility (γ_{30})	0.14***	0.04	0.40**	0.13	0.11***	0.04
Approaches to learning (γ_{40})					0.07**	0.02
Random effects						
Level 1 (r_{ij})	6.09***	0.66	63.56***	6.93	5.85***	0.64
Level 2 (u_{0j})	1.02*	0.65	66.37**	24.36	0.97*	0.62

*$p < .05$. **$p < .01$. ***$p \leq .001$.

age and gender. Cognitive flexibility was significantly and positively associated with approaches to learning and accounted for an additional 4.3% of the child-level variance.

Finally, approaches to learning was tested as a predictor of academic school readiness with age, gender, and cognitive flexibility controlled (see Table 3, Step 3). Both approaches to learning and cognitive flexibility were independently associated with academic school readiness; approaches to learning accounted for 2.8% of the variance in the outcome. A Sobel test indicated that approaches to learning significantly mediated the relation between cognitive flexibility and academic school readiness ($z = 2.09$, $p = .037$).

Individual components of approaches to learning: competence motivation, attention/persistence, and attitude toward learning. Three sets of models were then run to test each of the approaches to learning variables separately as mediators. Models first tested relations between cognitive flexibility and each component of approaches to learning. The equations for these models were as follows:

Level 1: $Y_{ij} = \beta_{0j} + \beta_{1j}(age) + \beta_{2j}(gender) + \beta_{3j}(cognitive\ flexibility) + \gamma_{ij}$
Level 2: $\beta_{0j} = \gamma_{00} + u_{0j}$
$\beta_{1j} = \gamma_{10}$
$\beta_{2j} = \gamma_{20}$
$\beta_{3j} = \gamma_{30}$

For competence motivation (see Table 4, Step 2), the results of the unconditional model showed that 39.0% of the variance was attributable to differences between classrooms. Age and gender accounted for 6% of the child-level variance. Cognitive flexibility explained a small but significant amount of the variance beyond age and gender (3.7%).

For attention/persistence (see Table 5, Step 2), 32.9% of the variance was due to differences between classrooms. Age and gender accounted for 9.7% of the child-level variance. Cognitive flexibility accounted for an additional 5.5% of the variance in attention/persistence.

For attitude toward learning, 50.7% of the variance was attributable to differences between classrooms. Age and gender accounted for 7.6% of the variance at Level 1. Cognitive flexibility accounted for 1.9% of the variance.

Finally, multilevel models tested whether the approaches to learning variables significantly mediated the relations between cognitive flexibility and academic school readiness with age and gender controlled. An example of the equations for this final model using competence motivation is as follows:

Level 1: $Y_{ij} = \beta_{0j} + \beta_{1j}(age) + \beta_{2j}(gender) + \beta_{3j}(cognitive\ flexibility)$
$+ \gamma_{ij}(competence\ motivation) + \gamma_{ij}$

Level 2: $\beta_{0j} = \gamma_{00} + u_{0j}$
$\beta_{1j} = \gamma_{10}$
$\beta_{2j} = \gamma_{20}$
$\beta_{3j} = \gamma_{30}$
$\beta_{4j} = \gamma_{40}$

TABLE 4
Analyses Testing Competence Motivation as a Mediator

Parameter	Step 2: Flexibility Predicting Competence Motivation		Step 3: Flexibility and Competence Motivation Predicting School Readiness	
	Estimate	SE	Estimate	SE
Fixed effects				
Intercept (γ_{00})	45.91***	1.65	8.87***	0.29
Age (γ_{10})	0.13	0.11	−0.04	0.03
Gender (γ_{20})	3.13**	1.23	1.29**	0.38
Flexibility (γ_{30})	0.37**	0.13	0.12***	0.04
Competence motivation (γ_{40})			0.05*	0.02
Random effects				
Level 1 (r_{ij})	65.42***	7.08	5.95***	0.65
Level 2 (u_{0j})	45.91**	19.00	0.95*	0.61

*$p < .05$. **$p < .01$. ***$p \leq .001$.

TABLE 5
Analyses Testing Attention/Persistence as a Mediator

Parameter	Step 2: Flexibility Predicting Attention/Persistence		Step 3: Flexibility and Attention/Persistence Predicting School Readiness	
	Estimate	SE	Estimate	SE
Fixed effects				
Intercept (γ_{00})	46.12***	1.52	8.87***	0.29
Age (γ_{10})	0.19†	0.10	−0.05	0.03
Gender (γ_{20})	3.55**	1.18	1.15**	0.37
Flexibility (γ_{30})	0.45***	0.13	0.10***	0.04
Attention/persistence (γ_{40})			0.09***	0.02
Random effects				
Level 1 (r_{ij})	60.93***	6.65	5.68***	0.62
Level 2 (u_{0j})	40.64*	11.24	1.01*	0.64

†$p < .10$. *$p < .05$. **$p < .01$. ***$p \leq .001$.

For competence motivation, the final model explained 15.0% of the child-level variability (see Table 4, Step 3). Both cognitive flexibility and competence motivation were positively associated with academic school readiness. A Sobel test of the mediation approached significance ($z = 1.73$, $p = .083$).

For attention/persistence, the final model accounted for 18.4% of the child-level variability (see Table 5, Step 3). Cognitive flexibility and attention/persistence were both positively associated with academic school readiness. A Sobel test of the mediation was significant ($z = 2.51$, $p = .012$).

For attitude toward learning, the final model accounted for 14.3% of the child-level variability. Cognitive flexibility ($b = .15$, $SE = .04$, $p < .001$) but not attitude toward learning ($b = .04$, $SE = .02$, $p < .10$) was significantly associated with academic school readiness. A Sobel test of the mediation was not significant ($z = 1.34$, $p = .181$).

DISCUSSION

According to control theory, multiple levels of increasingly complex processes interact to produce complex, goal-directed behaviors (Johnson et al., 2006). The results of this study provide preliminary support for the use of control theory to understand how cognitive flexibility may be associated with better school readiness outcomes among at-risk preschoolers. The results suggest that cognitive flexibility, a lower order cognitive process, was related to children's ability to attend and persist appropriately within the classroom. Attention/persistence, in turn, was associated with children's school readiness. These findings provide initial evidence in support of the study's main hypothesis that approaches to learning mediate the relation between cognitive flexibility and school readiness.

The first set of models tested in this study examined whether approaches to learning as a whole mediated the relation between cognitive flexibility and school readiness. The first analysis supported the hypothesis that cognitive flexibility was positively associated with school readiness in this low-income preschool sample, providing additional evidence that cognitive flexibility may contribute to academic outcomes in children as young as 3 to 5 years old, in keeping with previous research (Bierman, Torres, Domitrovich, Welsh, & Gest, 2009; Blair & Razza, 2007). However, it is important to note that flexibility accounted for a relatively small proportion of the variance in scores after age and gender were controlled. This is consistent with previous research that tends to show small but significant effects of executive functions on learning, especially when components of executive functions are examined individually (Bull & Scerif, 2001; Hooper, Swartz, Wakely, de Kruif, & Montgomery, 2002). Given that cognitive flexibility and school readiness were both measured in the spring of a single school year, this study also adds to existing research demonstrating that cognitive flexibility is significantly associated with concurrently measured achievement (Blair & Razza, 2007). Longer term longitudinal designs may find a larger impact across time; indeed, some existing evidence suggests that early measures of executive functions continue to predict achievement over several years (Gathercole, Brown, & Pickering, 2003).

Analyses also suggested that cognitive flexibility was positively associated with the approaches to learning total score and that the indirect effect from cognitive flexibility to approaches to learning to school readiness was significant. At a preliminary level, this supports the hypothesis that strong cognitive flexibility may be involved in selecting and activating positive, appropriate approaches to learning and that children with lower levels of cognitive flexibility may have difficulty selecting and activating these positive approaches.

To further explore relations between the constructs, in the second step in this study we aimed to determine whether associations with school readiness were mediated by each individual component of approaches to learning. Cognitive flexibility was significantly and positively associated with competence motivation, but the indirect effect through competence motivation was not significant. It has previously been suggested that motivation may increase children's ability to control cognition and behavior (Chang & Burns, 2005); for example, a child who is interested in dinosaurs may be better able than a less interested peer to complete a difficult dinosaur activity. The current study indicates very preliminarily that the reverse may also be true: A child with strong cognitive flexibility may be better able than a child with poor cognitive flexibility to select and activate motivated responses to learning situations. However, the relation between cognitive flexibility and motivation did not account for a significant portion of the total relation between cognitive flexibility and school readiness. It is possible that a longitudinal study measuring these constructs over time would have given the mediation process more time to work and uncovered a significant mediation effect. Further studies in this area, especially longitudinal studies, are needed to explore these relations.

Children's attention/persistence was positively associated with cognitive flexibility and significantly mediated the relation between cognitive flexibility and school readiness. This finding serves as an initial step in better understanding relations between cognitive flexibility and behavioral indicators of attention and persistence in preschoolers. It is important here to carefully distinguish between cognitive flexibility and attention/persistence: Although the constructs are conceptually related, cognitive flexibility is part of the executive control system that regulates attention and monitors progress toward goals; attention itself is a limited-capacity resource that is directed by the executive control system in accordance with task demands (Corbetta & Shulman, 2002; Posner, Sheese, Odludas, & Tang, 2006), and persistence involves maintaining attention and working at a difficult or long task for an extended period of time. Although prior studies have shown that cognitive flexibility is related to attention maintenance during actual task performance (e.g., Posner et al., 2006), the current study provides evidence to suggest associations between cognitive flexibility and a more dispositional, overt, behavioral aspect of attention: teachers' reports of children's ability to maintain attention and appropriately persist at classroom activities. This finding further suggests that attention and persistence may explain part of the relation between cognitive flexibility and school readiness, potentially suggesting that increasing children's cognitive flexibility may have positive effects on both attention/persistence and school readiness through this pathway. This potential pathway of influence needs to be examined in further research.

Another finding that emerged from this study is that cognitive flexibility was significantly associated with children's attitudes toward learning. The attitude toward learning variable incorporated frustration tolerance and learning-related interactions with teachers and peers (McDermott et al., 2000). Previous studies have found relationships between executive functions and similar constructs, such as emotion regulation (Carlson & Wang, 2007; Leerkes, Paradise, O'Brien, Calkins, & Lange, 2008; Wolfe & Bell,

2007). Although the relation between the two variables was relatively small in this study, it warrants further study.

For all three components of approaches to learning, cognitive flexibility explained relatively small amounts of variance. This may be due in part to method variance, as cognitive flexibility was directly assessed and approaches to learning were rated by teachers. However, it also suggests that there may be other important contributors to children's approaches to learning that were not included in the current model. Other components of executive functions, including inhibition and working memory, may be related to approaches to learning; this possibility should be examined in future studies. Studies have also suggested that approaches to learning are affected by children's behavior problems and peer relationships (Coolahan, Fantuzzo, Mendez, & McDermott, 2000; Dominguez & Greenfield, 2009). In addition, aspects of parenting and the classroom environment may affect children's approaches to learning, including parents' educational involvement and teachers' level of emotional support (Fantuzzo, McWayne, Perry, & Childs, 2004; Hamre & Pianta, 2001). Future studies should attempt to better understand influences on children's approaches to learning by including these important factors.

Another implication of these findings is that a large part of the effect of flexibility on school readiness was not mediated by children's approaches to learning. What, then, may account for the effect? Other factors, such as relationships with peers and teachers, may act as mediators. Research has linked general executive functions to social relationships with peers (Nigg et al., 1999), and social competence has in turn been linked to achievement outcomes (Caprara, Barbaranelli, Pastorelli, Bandura, & Zimbardo, 2000); likewise, teacher–child relationships are associated with achievement (O'Connor & McCartney, 2007) and may rely to some degree on children's executive functions and cognitive flexibility specifically. Lastly, a large part of the relation may be attributable to information processing: Research with adults has shown that cognitive flexibility is involved in transferring new information into long-term storage (Chein & Schneider, 2005). Further research is needed to identify additional mediators of this relation and to explore the role of cognitive flexibility in young children's information processing.

It is interesting that although age was correlated with the approaches to learning variables, it was not a significant predictor in any of the models. This suggests that a child being older than his or her peers in the classroom is not associated with stronger approaches to learning. It may be that supports within the classroom environment help children engage in learning irrespective of their age. Gender, in contrast, was a consistent predictor of outcomes and suggested that girls had higher approaches to learning and school readiness scores compared to boys. This is consistent with prior studies showing that girls receive higher ratings on approaches to learning than boys and perform better on early academic measures (e.g., Fantuzzo, Perry, et al., 2004).

This study has several limitations. The most significant limitation is that all measures were collected within a short time frame, giving a cross-sectional snapshot of children's skills rather than picture of development over time. Although we used this design to shed light on a potential mediation model, true mediation models require data to be collected at three distinct time points in order for researchers to be able to infer a degree of causal ordering. Therefore, the current study must be viewed as offering preliminary evidence for a potential mediation rather than definitive evidence of causal relations. Alternative models may also be possible; for example, competence motivation, attitude toward learning, and attention/persistence may be associated with children's ability to demonstrate cognitive flexibility. Within a correlational research framework, some of the strongest evidence for causal relations comes from collecting data on all constructs of interest across three or more waves and testing lagged associations; future studies using this type of design would shed greater light on potential causal relations among these constructs.

Also, we measured a single component of executive functions, limiting our ability to generalize findings to executive functions more broadly defined. A comprehensive assessment may have revealed larger effects and provided a more nuanced picture of the relations under study. Moreover, the measure of cognitive flexibility used in the current study was not a pure measure—it also relied to some degree on children's ability to problem-solve and inhibit incorrect responses. Although this drawback is common to measures of executive functions in young children (Hughes & Graham, 2002), it still limits the interpretation of the findings. Future studies may be better able to isolate this important construct by creating latent factors using multiple measures of cognitive flexibility.

Another limitation is the low rate of parental consent for the study. This may have been due to teachers' buy-in to the project—teachers were asked to distribute consent forms to parents, and consent rates varied substantially across classrooms (ranging from 1 to 20 children). Because child characteristics rather than teacher characteristics were of interest, and because classroom effects were controlled through multilevel modeling, this is not likely to have significantly biased results. However, efforts to increase future response rates should include either increasing teacher buy-in or recruiting parents directly.

A final but important limitation is the lack of definitive conceptual differentiation between cognitive flexibility and approaches to learning. Theory and evidence suggest that the two constructs are distinct but importantly related (e.g., Bierman et al., 2008; Johnson et al., 2006), but research examining the nature of the relation is lacking. The current article proposes one possible explanation for relations between the constructs, but further research, including research on better ways of measuring both constructs, is needed.

Despite these limitations, the current study adds to the understanding of relations between cognitive flexibility, approaches to learning, and school readiness. With further corroboration from subsequent studies, early educators may want to specifically target the cognitive flexibility of at-risk children in order to support the development of positive approaches to learning and school readiness. Using games or activities that challenge children's ability to be flexible, such as, perhaps, a matching game in which a visual cue determines which matching strategy to use or a sorting activity in which children are asked to sort toys in different ways, may support cognitive flexibility and lead to greater attention and persistence in the classroom. However, more research into the causal nature of these relations is needed before specific recommendations can be made.

The results of this study suggest that control theory may be an appropriate framework for understanding the relations between executive functions and school readiness (Johnson et al., 2006). Both cognitive flexibility and approaches to learning are important contributors to school readiness in Head Start children, and both may be important skill sets to target in at-risk preschool children. This study indicates that cognitive flexibility is a significant predictor of some aspects of children's approaches to learning. Furthermore, it provides evidence that attention/persistence mediates the relationship between cognitive flexibility and school readiness. These findings will be important to consider as preschool programs move toward intervening directly to improve children's executive functions and approaches to learning.

REFERENCES

Baron, R. M., & Kenny, D. A. (1986). The moderator-mediator variable distinction in social psychological research: Conceptual, strategic and statistical considerations. *Journal of Personality and Social Psychology, 51*, 1173–1182.

Bierman, K. L., Nix, R. L., Greenberg, M. T., Blair, C., & Domitrovich, C. E. (2008). Executive functions and school readiness intervention: Impact, moderation, and mediation in the Head Start REDI program. *Development and Psychopathology, 20*, 821–843.

Bierman, K. L., Torres, M. M., Domitrovich, C. E., Welsh, J. A., & Gest, S. D. (2009). Behavioral and cognitive readiness for school: Cross-domain associations for children attending Head Start. *Social Development, 18*, 305–323.

Blair, C., & Peters, R. (2003). Physiological and neurocognitive correlates of adaptive behavior in preschool among children in Head Start. *Developmental Neuropsychology*, *24*, 479–497.

Blair, C., & Razza, R. P. (2007). Relating effortful control, executive function, and false belief understanding to emerging math and literacy ability in kindergarten. *Child Development*, *78*, 647–663.

Bracken, B. (1998). *The Bracken Basic Concepts Scale—Revised*. San Antonio, TX: The Psychological Corporation.

Brophy, M., Taylor, E., & Hughes, C. (2002). To go or not to go: Inhibitory control in "hard to manage" children. *Infant and Child Development*, *11*, 125–140.

Bull, R., Espy, K. A., & Wiebe, S. A. (2008). Short-term memory, working memory, and executive functioning in preschoolers: Longitudinal predictors of mathematical achievement at age 7 years. *Developmental Neuropsychology*, *33*, 205–228.

Bull, R., & Scerif, G. (2001). Executive functioning as a predictor of children's mathematics ability: Inhibition, switching, and working memory. *Developmental Neuropsychology*, *19*, 273–293.

Caprara, G. V., Barbaranelli, C., Pastorelli, C., Bandura, A., & Zimbardo, P. G. (2000). Prosocial foundations of children's academic achievement. *Psychological Science*, *11*, 302–306.

Carlson, S. M., & Wang, T. S. (2007). Inhibitory control and emotion regulation in preschool children. *Cognitive Development*, *22*, 489–510.

Chang, F., & Burns, B. M. (2005). Attention in preschoolers: Associations with effortful control and motivation. *Child Development*, *76*, 247–263.

Chein, J. M., & Schneider, W. (2005). Neuroimaging studies of practice-related change: fMRI and meta-analytic evidence of a domain-general control network for learning. *Cognitive Brain Research*, *25*, 607–623.

Chevalier, N., & Blaye, A. (2008). Cognitive flexibility in preschoolers: The role of representation, motivation, and maintenance. *Developmental Science*, *11*, 339–353.

Coolahan, K., Fantuzzo, J., Mendez, J., & McDermott, P. (2000). Preschool peer interactions and readiness to learn: Relationships between classroom peer play and learning behaviors and conduct. *Journal of Educational Psychology*, *92*, 458–465.

Corbetta, M., & Shulman, G. L. (2002). Control of goal-directed and stimulus-driven attention in the brain. *Nature Reviews Neuroscience*, *3*, 201–216.

Davidson, M. C., Amso, D., Anderson, L. C., & Diamond, A. (2006). Development of cognitive control and executive functions from 4 to 13 years: Evidence from manipulations of memory, inhibition, and task switching. *Neuropsychologia*, *44*, 2037–2078.

Diamond, A., Barnett, W. S., Thomas, J., & Munro, S. (2007, November 30). Preschool program improves cognitive control. *Science*, *318*, 1387–1388.

Dominguez, X., & Greenfield, D. (2009). Learning behaviors mediating the effects of behavior problems on academic school readiness. *NHSA Dialog*, *12*, 1–17.

Duncan, G. J., Dowsett, C. J., Claessens, A., Magnuson, K., Huston, A. C., Klebanov, P., ... Japel, C. (2007). School readiness and later achievement. *Developmental Psychology*, *43*, 1428–1446.

Enders, C. K., & Tofighi, D. (2007). Centering predictor variables in cross-sectional multilevel models: A new look at an old issue. *Psychological Methods*, *12*, 121–138.

Fantuzzo, J., McWayne, C., Perry, M. A., & Childs, S. (2004). Multiple dimensions of family involvement and their relations to behavioral and learning competencies for urban, low-income children. *School Psychology Review*, *33*, 467–480.

Fantuzzo, J., Perry, M. A., & McDermott, P. (2004). Preschool approaches to learning and their relationship to other relevant classroom competencies for low-income children. *School Psychology Quarterly*, *19*(3), 212–230.

Gathercole, S. E., Brown, L., & Pickering, S. J. (2003). Working memory assessments at school entry as longitudinal predictors of national curriculum attainment levels. *Educational and Child Psychology, 20*(3), 109–122.

George, J., & Greenfield, D. B. (2005). Examination of a structured problem-solving flexibility task for assessing approaches to learning in young children: Relation to teacher ratings and children's achievement. *Applied Developmental Psychology, 26*, 69–84.

Greenfield, D. B. (1992). *Manual for the oddity flexibility task*. Miami, FL: University of Miami.

Greenfield, D. B. (2000). [Transition demonstration project]. Unpublished raw data.

Hamre, B. K., & Pianta, R. C. (2001). Early teacher-child relationships and the trajectory of children's school outcomes through eighth grade. *Child Development, 72*, 625–638.

Hoeksma, J. B., Oosterlaan, J., & Schipper, E. M. (2004). Emotion regulation and the dynamics of feelings: A conceptual and methodological framework. *Child Development, 75*, 354–360.

Hooper, S. R., Swartz, C. W., Wakely, M. B., de Kruif, R. E. L., & Montgomery, J. W. (2002). Executive functions in elementary school children with and without problems in written expression. *Journal of Learning Disabilities, 35*(1), 57–68.

Howse, R. B., Calkins, S. D., Anastopoulos, A. D., Keane, S. P., & Shelton, T. L. (2003). Regulatory contributors to children's kindergarten achievement. *Early Education & Development, 14*, 101–119.

Hughes, C., & Graham, A. (2002). Measuring executive functions in childhood: Problems and solutions? *Child and Adolescent Mental Health, 7*(3), 131–142.

Johnson, R. E., Chang, C.-H., & Lord, R. G. (2006). Moving from cognition to behavior: What the research says. *Psychological Bulletin, 132*, 381–415.

Kagan, S. L., Moore, E., & Bredekamp, S. (1995). *Reconsidering children's early development and learning: Toward common views and vocabulary*. Washington, DC: National Education Goals Panel.

Krull, J. L., & MacKinnon, D. P. (2001). Multilevel modeling of individual and group level mediated effects. *Multivariate Behavioral Research, 36*(2), 249–277.

Leerkes, E. M., Paradise, M., O'Brien, M., Calkins, S. D., & Lange, G. (2008). Emotion and cognition processes in preschool children. *Merrill-Palmer Quarterly, 54*(1), 102–124.

Loeb, S., Fuller, B., Kagan, S. L., & Carrol, B. (2004). Child care in poor communities: Early learning effects of type, quality, and stability. *Child Development, 75*, 47–65.

Lord, R. G., & Levy, P. E. (1994). Moving from cognition to action: A control theory perspective. *Applied Psychology: An International Review, 43*, 335–398.

McClelland, M. M., Morrison, F. J., & Holmes, D. L. (2000). Children at risk for early academic problems: The role of learning-related social skills. *Early Childhood Research Quarterly, 15*(3), 307–329.

McDermott, P. A., Green, L. F., Francis, J. M., & Stott, D. H. (2000). *Preschool learning behaviors scale*. Philadelphia, PA: Edumetric and Clinical Science.

McDermott, P. A., Leigh, N. M., & Perry, M. A. (2002). Development and validation of the Preschool Learning Behaviors Scale. *Psychology in the Schools, 39*, 353–365.

McWayne, C. M., Fantuzzo, J. W., & McDermott, P. A. (2004). Preschool competency in context: An investigation of the unique contribution of child competencies to early academic success. *Developmental Psychology, 40*, 633–645.

Morgan, G. A., MacTurk, R. H., & Hrncir, E. J. (1995). Mastery motivation: Overview, definitions, and conceptual issues. In R. H. MacTurk, & G. A. Morgan (Eds.), *Mastery motivation: Origins, conceptualizations, and applications*, (pp. 1–18). Norwood, NJ: Ablex.

National Institute of Child Health, & Human Development Early Child Care Research Network. (2003). Do children's attention processes mediate the link between family predictors and school readiness? *Developmental Psychology, 39*, 581–593.

National Institute of Child Health, & Human Development Early Child Care Research Network. (2005). Predicting individual differences in attention, memory, and planning in first graders from experiences at home, child care, and school. *Developmental Psychology, 41*, 99–114.

Nigg, J. T., Quamma, J. P., Greenberg, M. T., & Kusché, C. A. (1999). A two-year longitudinal study of neuropsychological and cognitive performance in relation to behavioral problems and competencies in elementary school children. *Journal of Abnormal Child Psychology, 27*, 51–63.

O'Connor, E., & McCartney, K. (2007). Examining teacher-child relationships and achievement as part of an ecological model of development. *American Education Research Journal, 44*, 340–369.

Panter, J. E., & Bracken, B. A. (2009). Validity of the Bracken School Readiness Assessment for predicting first grade readiness. *Psychology in the Schools, 46*, 397–409.

Pennington, B. F., & Ozonoff, S. (1996). Executive functions and developmental psychopathology. *Journal of Child Psychology and Psychiatry, 37*(1), 51–87.

Pessoa, L. (2009). How do emotion and motivation direct executive functions? *Trends in Cognitive Sciences, 13*, 160–166.

Poldrack, R. A., Wagner, A. D., Stanley, D., Phelps, E., & Banaji, M. (2008). The neural basis of implicit attitudes. *Current Directions in Psychological Science, 17*, 164–170.

Posner, M. I., Sheese, B. E., Odludas, Y., & Tang, Y. (2006). Analyzing and shaping human attentional networks. *Neural Networks, 19*, 1422–1429.

Ramey, C. T., & Ramey, S. L. (2004). Early learning and school readiness: Can early intervention make a difference? *Merrill-Palmer Quarterly, 50*, 471–491.

Reynolds, A. J., & Temple, J. A. (2008). Cost-effective early childhood development programs from preschool to third grade. *Annual Review of Clinical Psychology, 4*, 109–139.

Riccio, C. A., Hall, J., Morgan, A., Hynd, G. W., Gonzalez, J. J., & Marshall, R. M. (1994). Executive functions and the Wisconsin Card Sorting Test: Relationship with behavioral ratings and cognitive ability. *Developmental Neuropsychology, 10*, 215–229.

Riggs, N. R., Blair, C. B., & Greenberg, M. T. (2003). Concurrent and 2-year longitudinal relations between executive function and the behavior of 1st and 2nd grade children. *Child Neuropsychology, 9*(4), 267–276.

Schaefer, B. A., & McDermott, P. A. (1999). Learning behavior and intelligence as explanations for children's scholastic achievement. *Journal of School Psychology, 37*, 299–313.

St. Clair-Thompson, H. L., & Gathercole, S. E. (2006). Executive functions and achievements in school: Shifting, updating, inhibition, and working memory. *Quarterly Journal of Experimental Psychology, 59*, 745–759.

Welsh, M. C. (2002). Developmental and clinical variations in executive functions. In D. L. Molfese, & V. J. Molfese (Eds.), *Developmental variations in learning* (pp. 139–185). Mahwah, NJ: Erlbaum.

Wolfe, C. D., & Bell, M. A. (2007). The integration of cognition and emotion during infancy and early childhood: Regulatory processes associated with the development of working memory. *Brain and Cognition, 65*(1), 3–13.

Children's Effortful Control and Academic Achievement: Mediation Through Social Functioning

Carlos Valiente

Nancy Eisenberg and Rg Haugen

Tracy L. Spinrad

Claire Hofer

Jeffrey Liew

Anne Kupfer

Research Findings: The purpose of this study was to test the premise that children's effortful control (EC) is prospectively related to their academic achievement and to specify mechanisms through which EC is related to academic success. We used data from 214 children (M age at Time 1 [T1] = 73 months) to test whether social functioning (e.g., social competence and externalizing problems) mediated the relations between EC and academic achievement. Children's adult-reported and observed EC were assessed at T1. Parents' and teachers' reports of social functioning were obtained 2 years later (T2), whereas teachers' and children's reports of academic achievement were obtained 4 years after T2 (T3). Children's T2 social functioning fully mediated the relation between T1 EC and T3 academic achievement in a structural equation model. *Practice or Policy:* Findings highlight the importance of considering social and emotional processes when attempting to improve academic achievement and have implications for curriculum developers and professionals working in preschool programs and elementary schools.

It is clear that children's academic achievement plays a central role in their opportunities for continued learning, academic progress, mental and physical health, and future employment (Bureau of Labor Statistics, 2004; Caspi, Elder, & Bem, 1987; Ensminger & Slusarcick, 1992; U.S. Department of Education, 2004). In an effort to understand why some school children fail to achieve at the desired levels, and why many kindergarten teachers note that a high percentage of their students have difficulty following directions, working in a group, or interacting with peers (Rimm-Kaufman, Pianta, & Cox, 2000), investigators from several disciplines have focused on the role of regulatory abilities/effortful control (EC) in children's academic achievement (Blair & Razza, 2007; McClelland et al., 2007; Valiente, Lemery-Chalfant, & Swanson, 2010). An often separate body of literature supports the premise that relationships with peers and the experience of problem behaviors also have implications for learning and achievement (Ladd, Herald, & Kochel, 2006; Welsh, Parke, Widaman, & O'Neil, 2001). The purpose of the present study was to bring together findings from these literatures in an effort to more fully explain why EC is predictive of academic achievement. We hypothesized that the relation between children's EC and their academic achievement is mediated by their social functioning. We tested this hypothesis in a 6-year prospective study.

EC is a group of temperamentally based skills viewed as the basis of self-regulation. Rothbart and Bates (2006) defined *EC* as "the efficiency of executive attention—including the ability to inhibit a dominant response and/or to activate a subdominant response, to plan, and to detect errors" (p. 126). EC develops rapidly in the preschool years and continues to improve in the early school years (Carlson, 2005; Rothbart & Bates, 2006). EC can be measured in a variety of ways, but adults' reports of children's attentional control (the abilities to effortfully focus and shift attention) and inhibitory control (the capacity to effortfully suppress inappropriate approach responses under instructions or in novel or uncertain situations) are perhaps most often used. EC can also be assessed behaviorally, and these tasks often measure persistence, attentional regulation, or the delay of gratification (Kochanska, Murray, & Harlan, 2000; Spinrad,

Eisenberg, & Gaertner, 2007). High levels of EC are adaptive in many contexts and may be especially useful in a classroom setting where children are required to modulate emotional reactivity and behaviors that would otherwise disrupt classroom activities.

Posner and his colleagues' work on the alerting, orienting, and executive attention networks is useful for clarifying the significance and meaning of EC (Posner & Rothbart, 2007; Rothbart, Sheese, & Posner, 2007). The alerting network maintains sensitivity toward incoming information, and the orienting network involves aligning attention with incoming messages (e.g., moving one's eyes toward stimuli). The focus of our investigation is on the more advanced executive attention network, which functions to monitor and resolve conflicts with other neural networks. The process of resolving conflicts involves the activation or suppression of other neural networks and is hypothesized to play a central role in regulatory efforts (Cole, Armstrong, & Pemberton, 2010; Posner & Rothbart, 2007). Regulatory abilities are particularly important given the contextual demands of early elementary classrooms, in which sitting still, attending to instructional materials, and ignoring distracting stimuli are crucial for performing well.

EC AND ACHIEVEMENT

In a seminal review, Raver (2002) made a compelling case for considering students' emotional development in models of school success, noting that self-regulation may impact academic achievement through a number of mechanisms. Raver and others have argued that students' EC provides academic advantages by helping children to focus on their assignments and avoid moving from task to task without completing required assignments (Duncan et al., 2007; Zimmerman, 1998). Motivational mechanisms are also likely to support the association between EC and achievement. Students high in EC are likely to be good at initiating, sustaining, and regulating their motivation for goal-directed learning, and there is clear evidence that motivation for learning is positively related to achievement (Meece, Anderman, & Anderman, 2006; Zimmerman, 1998). Finally, interpersonal mechanisms may mediate the relation between components of EC and achievement. Blair and Diamond (2008) noted that when children have poor self-regulation, school becomes difficult and unpleasant because compliance is challenging, attention control is difficult, and often relationships with teachers are characterized by annoyance and frustration. A large and robust body of literature demonstrates that EC is predictive of high-quality social relationships with both peers and teachers, and these relationships may promote students' academic success (Hamre & Pianta,

2001; Rothbart & Bates, 2006; Valiente, Lemery-Chalfant, Swanson, & Reiser, 2008).

Since the publication of Raver's (2002) report, a number of investigators have demonstrated that EC and related constructs predict many components of achievement. For example, in a series of studies, McClelland and colleagues (McClelland et al., 2007; Ponitz, McClelland, Matthews, & Morrison, 2009) demonstrated that observational measures of behavioral regulation are concurrently and prospectively related to scores in mathematics, literacy, and vocabulary. Moreover, attentional regulation has been related to standardized measures of achievement (Duncan et al., 2007; National Institute of Child Health and Human Development [NICHD] Early Child Care Research Network, 2003). A number of investigators also have reported concurrent and prospective relations between adults' reports of EC and children's academic success, both for students in the United States (Blair & Razza, 2007; Valiente, Lemery-Chalfant, & Castro, 2007; Valiente et al., 2008) and for those in China (Zhou, Main, & Wang, in press). It is noteworthy that many of the studies conducted in the United States included a significant percentage of minority children (mainly Hispanic children), and the relations between EC and achievement were quite similar for Caucasian and Hispanic children (McClelland et al., 2007; Valiente et al., 2008).

These findings provide relatively clear and consistent evidence that some of the central components of EC are related to achievement concurrently and over 1 to 2 years. What is not clear is whether these relations exist over longer periods of time and why these relations exist. A central goal of this article was to test whether the interpersonal mechanisms discussed previously—specifically social competence and externalizing problems—mediate the relations between EC and academic achievement. Statistical support for such mediation would require that EC predict the measures of social functioning and social functioning predict achievement when EC is controlled (MacKinnon, Lockwood, Hoffman, West, & Sheets, 2002). There were good reasons to believe that these requirements would be met.

Indeed, there are a number of reasons to expect EC to contribute to children's social functioning. EC could be expected to impact the way children process information and modulate emotion, which is likely to contribute to social competence and the control of externalizing behavior (Dodge, Coie, & Lynam, 2006). In fact, the capacity to divert attention from nonconstructive thoughts to more positive perspectives is associated with low levels of anger, anxiety, and depression (Derryberry & Reed, 2002; Rothbart & Bates, 2006; Silk, Steinberg, & Morris, 2003). Moreover, planning behavior, which is part of EC, is often positively related to high levels of social functioning (Eronen, Nurmi, & Salmela-Aro, 1997).

Results from many studies support the hypothesis that EC is predictive of social functioning. Inhibitory control has been related to internalized compliance, low selfish/antisocial solutions to hypothesized dilemmas, and low externalizing problems (Kochanska & Knaack, 2003; Kochanska, Murray, & Coy, 1997; Martel et al., 2007). Similarly, children's effortful attention focusing and shifting have often been negatively related to externalizing problems, concurrently and prospectively, for children in the United States, China, Indonesia, and Europe (Eisenberg, Pidada, & Liew, 2001; Eisenberg et al., 2009; Muris, Meesters, & Blijlevens, 2007; Muris, Meesters, & Rompelberg, 2007; Zhou, Lengua, & Wang, 2009). Conversely, a number of investigators have reported positive relations between children's EC and their social competence (Eisenberg, Gershoff, et al., 2001; Rothbart & Bates, 2006; Spinrad et al., 2006; Valiente et al., 2008).

SOCIAL FUNCTIONING AND ACHIEVEMENT

As noted previously, children's social competence is hypothesized to predict academic achievement, and Eisenberg, Sadovsky, and Spinrad (2005) hypothesized that social competence might mediate the relations between EC and achievement. Students who are accepted by their peers and who develop and maintain friendships are likely to benefit from being included in classroom activities that provide high-quality opportunities for learning and exposure to educational materials (Wentzel, Baker, & Russell, 2009). There is also evidence that the number of mutual friends a child has and being accepted by peers are important precursors to achievement (Ladd, Birch, & Buhs, 1999). Students who are not accepted by their peers are often less motivated to participate in classroom activities and are at risk for withdrawing from learning opportunities (Wentzel et al., 2009). In a 2-year longitudinal study, Welsh et al. (2001) demonstrated that social competence was positively related to achievement. In one of the few studies to test for the presence of mediation, Valiente et al. (2008) found that teacher- and parent-reported social competence partially mediated the relations between EC and achievement. These findings are informative, but the data were concurrent, and data from longitudinal studies in which the predictor, mediator, and outcome are all measured at different assessments are needed in order to better test the relevant associations.

The co-occurrence of externalizing problems and low levels of academic achievement has been a research focus for some time (Hinshaw, 1992). Externalizing behaviors are quite likely to interfere with appropriately engaging in classroom activities, and children prone to aggressive behavior may spend less time than less aggressive peers on tasks and may miss learning opportunities while being disciplined for their misbehavior (Arnold, 1997; Coie & Dodge, 1988; Hoglund, 2007). More aggressive children may also experience academic challenges because they have more difficulty than less aggressive peers forming and maintaining close relationships with their teachers (Jerome, Hamre, & Pianta, 2009). Despite relatively clear reasons to expect externalizing problems to predict achievement, findings are mixed, with some investigators finding no consistent direct relations between the constructs (Duncan et al., 2008) and others finding that relations are primarily mediated by the teacher–child relationship (Stipek & Miles, 2008). In contrast, in perhaps the longest longitudinal study to date addressing this issue, children who were consistently high in aggression from age 2 years, 9 months, were more likely than their peers to experience academic challenges when in third grade (NICHD Early Child Care Research Network, 2004).

Despite theoretical reasons to expect externalizing problems to be a mediator of the relation between EC and academic accomplishment, there are few relevant empirical data. The only direct test of mediation of which we are aware involved a kindergarten sample, and in this study externalizing problems did not predict standardized measures of math or literacy when the indices of EC were in the model (Graziano, Reavis, Keane, & Calkins, 2007). However, these authors examined concurrent associations in kindergarten and simultaneously considered the student–teacher relationship (which was a significant predictor and might overlap in prediction with externalizing problems). Perhaps, as noted by Rimm-Kaufman and Pianta (2000), the hypothesized mechanisms need more time to evolve in order to impact students' math and literacy skills and, thus, mediational processes might emerge over time. It is also possible that externalizing problems are more disruptive in the later elementary school years, as such behaviors would be more noticeable and atypical than those occurring in kindergarten (NICHD Early Child Care Research Network, 2004).

THE PRESENT STUDY

During the past decade, the number of investigators reporting relations between EC and academic achievement has grown markedly. It now seems relatively clear that EC is concurrently positively related to academic achievement; there is much less support for prospective relations between these constructs or evidence of the pathways through which EC might influence students' learning and achievement. The first aim of this study was to test whether children's reported and observed EC were prospectively related to their academic achievement across a 6-year time period. Our second aim was to test whether children's social functioning acted as a statistical mediator of the relations between EC and achievement. We expected positive relations between EC and achievement and expected that social functioning would mediate these relations. We used data from a multi-reporter, multi-method longitudinal study to test our predictions. To examine whether the hypothesized model was robust across several key demographic variables, we explored the potential moderating role of children's sex, socioeconomic status (SES), and age. The associations between sex and achievement are complex, with some findings showing that girls outperform boys and others demonstrating the reverse relation or no relation (Frome & Eccles, 1998; Jordan, Kaplan, Oláh, & Locuniak, 2006; Simpkins, Davis-Kean, & Eccles, 2006; Valiente et al., 2008). Family SES, and especially income, is also a robust predictor of achievement. Families that earn higher incomes may provide more educational opportunities and materials to their children, and these children are also likely to experience lower levels of the chaos and educational disruptions that are associated with low income (Davis-Kean, 2005). Therefore, we included sex and SES as covariates in the equations when we tested the major hypotheses. Because children ranged in age from 4 to 8 at Time 1 (T1), and because age is sometimes positively related to the constructs under consideration, we also included age as a covariate.

METHOD

Participants

Families in this study were involved in a 6-year longitudinal study (Eisenberg, Cumberland, Spinrad, Fabes, Shepard, Reiser, et al., 2001). Parents were recruited to participate at one of four schools or through ads placed in schools, newspapers, and flyers. A key goal of the larger study was to examine relations between parenting, temperament, and problem behaviors in a sample of children experiencing a range of problem behaviors. Therefore, prior to being included in the study, parents completed the Child Behavior Checklist (Achenbach, 1991b). All children who received a T score above 59 (which is on the borderline of the clinical cutoff) on either the externalizing or internalizing subscale were asked to participate in the study. A matching procedure based on parents' education and occupation, children's age, and race was used to match children whose T scores were below 60 on both internalizing and externalizing to those who scored above 59 on one or both types of problems (not all eligible children were invited to continue with the study). Thus, the sample included children with one or both types of problem behaviors (at a borderline level or higher) as well as children with scores below the borderline cutoff for both types of problem behaviors. Using this procedure resulted in a continuum of children's scores on both types of problem behaviors from low to relatively high. A total of 214 children were recruited, and data were collected from children, their parents, and teachers. Based on parent report of problem behaviors and the criterion of a T score of 60 or above as the cutoff for problem behaviors, 79 children were nondisordered, 31 were high in internalizing problems, 47 were high in externalizing problems, and 57 were high in both internalizing and externalizing problems. These children were not higher in externalizing problems than those in another study conducted in the same school district using all families who volunteered (i.e., with no selection process; Zhou, Hofer, Eisenberg, Reiser, Spinrad, Fabes, 2007).

At T1, 214 children (96 girls and 118 boys) between the ages of 55 and 97 months ($M = 73$) participated. A total of 193 children (88 girls and 105 boys) participated at Time 2 (T2), which was 2 years after T1, and 159 children (71 girls and 88 boys) participated at Time 3 (T3), which was 4 years after T2 (note that T3 in this study has been labeled T4 in other articles because there was an assessment between T2 and T3 in this study). The majority of families were working and middle class (T1 mean income = \$41,000, $SD = \$25,000$; 15% of the families earned less than \$15,000 per year). Mean family income was between \$40,000 and \$60,000 at T2 and T3. At each assessment, approximately 70% of parents had completed some college education. The majority of participants were Caucasian: 77% at T1, 80% at T2, and 78% at T3. Hispanics composed 12% of the sample at T1, 12% at T2, and 11% at T3. At each assessment less than 5% of the sample was Native American, African American, or Asian. Families were paid \$25 at T1 and \$30 thereafter.

We conducted a series of tests to explore whether there were differences on reported or observed EC, social competence, externalizing problem behaviors, mothers' education, fathers' education, income, sex, or race between those who continued at either T2 or T3 and those who did not complete measures after T1. Children who had data only at T1 ($n = 15$) were rated by teachers as having lower levels of EC and social competence, and parents reported lower incomes than those with data after T1, $ts(193, 192, 192) = -2.13, -2.12$, and -2.17, respectively, $ps < .05$. Children who attritted after T1 were also more likely than would be expected by chance to be minorities, $\chi^2(5) = 19.59, p < .001, N = 213$. We also compared those with data at each assessment ($N = 155$) to those who missed an entire assessment ($n = 59$) on reported or observed EC, social competence, externalizing problem behaviors, mothers' education, fathers' education, income, sex, and race.

Children who missed an assessment persisted less on the puzzle task, had fathers with lower levels of education, and had families that earned lower incomes than those with complete data, $ts(210, 204, 192) = -2.65, -2.97$, and -1.97, $ps < .01, .01$, and $.05$, respectively.

Procedure

One parent (usually the mother) and the child came to a university laboratory to complete a series of questionnaires and tasks. At each assessment, during the middle and end of the school years, we mailed questionnaires to children's teachers.

SES. At T1, parents provided an estimate of their combined family income as well as the number of years of education both parents had completed. As shown in Table 1, income and education were all significantly and moderately interrelated.

EC. At T1, parents and teachers completed the attention shifting (e.g., "Can easily shift from one activity to another"; 9 items), attention focusing (e.g., "When drawing or coloring in a book, shows strong concentration"; 9 items for parents and 8 items for teachers), and inhibitory control (e.g., "Can lower his/her voice when asked to do so"; 13 items) subscales of the Children's Behavior Questionnaire (Rothbart, Ahadi, Hersey, & Fisher, 2001). Alphas for attention shifting, attention focusing, and inhibitory control subscales were .80, .74, and .84 for parents and .86, .85, and .88 for teachers, respectively. Parents' reports of attention shifting were related to attention focusing and inhibitory control, $rs(207, 204) = .37$ and $.74$, $ps < .01$, respectively; and attention focusing was positively related to inhibitory control, $r(204) = .61, p < .01$. An identical pattern emerged for teachers' reports of these variables, $rs(193, 187, 187) = .61, .76$, and $.78$, respectively, $ps < .01$. As a result, we averaged these scales within reporter to form parent- and teacher-report scores for EC.

At T1, we also obtained an observed measure of EC during a laboratory visit. Children were seated in front of a puzzle that had a clear Plexiglas back and a cloth-covered front. Children inserted their hands through the cloth (which prevented the children from seeing the puzzle), and observers in a different room could see whether they were cheating by lifting the cloth. The experimenter set the timer for 4 min and told the children that they would receive a prize if they completed the puzzle within the allotted time. They were also told not to look at the puzzle. The experimenter then left the room. We used the amount of time children persisted (e.g., worked

TABLE 1
Descriptive Statistics and Zero-Order Correlations for Study Variables

Variable	1	2	3	4	5	6	7	8	9	10	11	12
1. Income	—											
2. Mothers' education	.44**	—										
3. Fathers' education	.39**	.53**	—									
4. T1 EC: Parent report	.07	.03	.14*	—								
5. T1 EC: Teacher report	.17*	.15*	.25**	.49**	—							
6. T1 EC: Puzzle	.12†	.05	.07	.28**	.24**	—						
7. T2 Social competence: Parent report	.11†	−.01	.18*	.56**	.42**	.23**	—					
8. T2 Social competence: Teacher report	.14*	.04	.13†	.33**	.48**	.24**	.47**	—				
9. T2 EXT: Parent report	−.10	−.07	−.11†	−.51**	−.40**	−.09†	−.44**	−.23**	—			
10. T2 EXT: Teacher report	−.18*	−.08	−.23**	−.30**	−.42**	−.20*	−.31**	−.69**	.24**	—		
11. T3 AA: Child report	.25*	.18*	.47**	.22*	.33*	.21*	.25*	.25*	−.08	−.20*	—	
12. T3 AA: Teacher report	.29**	.30**	.42**	.22*	.41*	.21*	.31*	.27**	−.16*	−.15*	.66**	—
M	40.96	14.12	14.04	4.41	4.87	0.55	3.20	3.09	12.79	9.57	6.14	5.49
SD	25.31	2.49	3.05	0.74	1.02	0.30	0.55	0.73	7.79	11.46	2.31	2.19

Note. T1 = Time 1; EC = effortful control; T2 = Time 2; EXT = externalizing problem behaviors; AA = academic achievement.
†$p < .10$. *$p < .05$. **$p < .01$.

on the puzzle without cheating) divided by the total time spent completing the puzzle as an observed index of EC (interrater reliability: $r[197] = .97$).

Social competence. At T2, parents and teachers rated children's social competence on a modified version of Harter's (1982) Perceived Competence Scale for Children (Eisenberg et al., 1995; Eisenberg, Gershoff, et al., 2001). Socially appropriate behavior (e.g., "This child is usually well behaved"; $\alpha = .76$ for parents and .87 for teachers) was the average of four items. Popularity (e.g., "This child has a lot of friends"; $\alpha = .76$ for parents and .91 for teachers) was the average of three items. Consistent with prior research (Eisenberg, Gershoff, et al., 2001; Valiente et al., 2008), parents' reports of socially appropriate behavior and popularity were substantially correlated, $r(184) = .43$, $p < .001$; as were teachers' reports, $r(180) = .59$, $p < .001$. Thus, the scales were averaged within reporter to form separate measures of parent- and teacher-reported social competence.

Externalizing problem behaviors. Mothers used the Child Behavior Checklist and teachers used the Teacher Report Form (Achenbach, 1991a, 1991b) at T2 to rate children's externalizing problem behaviors. Items were coded on a scale of 0 (*not true*) to 2 (*very true*) per standard procedures. Alphas for externalizing problems were .89 for mothers (30 items) and .96 for teachers (29 items).

Academic achievement. Children's T3 academic achievement was reported on by teachers and children ($1 = C-$ or below, $2 = C$, $3 = C+$, $4 = B-$, $5 = B$, $6 = B+$, $7 = A-$, $8 = A$, $9 = A+$). This method of assessment is similar to Pierce, Hamm, and Vandell's (1999) "mock report card" for assessing academic competence, and we adapted it to reflect the plus/minus grading system used in many of the local schools. The validity of this index is supported by correlations of .80 and higher between students' self-reported grades and scores on report cards (Graham, Updegraff, Tomascik, & McHale, 1997).

RESULTS

We computed two *t* tests at T1 to explore the relations between children's sex and parent- and teacher-reported EC. At T2, because multiple measures were available per reporter (e.g., social competence and externalizing problems), we computed a multivariate analysis of variance to examine these relations, and at T3 we computed *t* tests for teacher- and then child-reported achievement. At T1, girls were higher on parent- and teacher-rated EC and observed EC than boys, $ts(207, 193, 210) = 3.26, 3.35$, and 3.20, respectively, $ps < .002$. There was a significant multivariate analysis of variance involving T2 teacher- but not T2 parent-reported data, multivariate $Fs(2, 177$ and $2, 180) = 5.05$ and 1.79, $p < .007$ and ns, respectively. Teachers rated girls higher on social competence and lower on externalizing problems than boys, $Fs(1, 178) = 7.57$ and 9.28, $ps < .01$, respectively. Children and teachers reported higher levels of T3 academic achievement for girls than boys, $ts(121$ and $134) = 2.43$ and 4.15, $ps < .02$ and $.001$, respectively. In addition, age was positively related only to parent-reported and observed EC, $rs(207$ and $210) = .16$ and $.13$, respectively, $ps < .05$. Variables did not exceed the cutoffs for skewness, kurtosis, and outliers identified by West, Finch, and Curran (1995). There were no multivariate outliers (Cook, 1977).

Table 1 contains descriptive statistics and the zero-order relations between the main study variables. We were interested in assessing whether the variables expected to load on latent constructs were correlated and whether the pattern of correlations supported the hypothesized process of mediation. The across-reporter relations within construct were always significant and moderate in magnitude (e.g., parents' reports of EC were significantly positively related to teachers' reports of EC), suggesting that latent variables could be created in the structural equation modeling context. In support of our predictions regarding mediation, both reported and observed EC were positively related to the measures of social competence, negatively related to externalizing problems, and positively related to the measures of academic achievement. In addition, social competence (positively) and externalizing problems (negatively) were prospectively related to academic achievement. Therefore, the zero-order correlations were consistent with the requirements for mediation.

We used MPlus (Version 5.2; Muthén & Muthén, 1998–2005) and full information maximum likelihood estimation to account for missing data when testing our hypothesis using structural equation modeling. We estimated the within-reporter covariances among the error terms of the indicators (e.g., the error term for parent-reported EC was allowed to correlate with the error term for parent-reported social competence) to reduce bias associated with using the same reporters for latent variables (Kenny & Kashy, 1992; Thomson & Williams, 1984). To simplify the presentation, we do not present these parameters in Figure 1.

It is noteworthy that the measures of social competence were consistently negatively related to externalizing problems. Therefore, and because both measures were related to achievement, we created a latent variable that was indicated by the measures of both social competence and externalizing problems. The model displayed in Figure 1 fit the data well, $\chi^2(59) = 76.27$, $p < .09$, $N = 214$; comparative fit index $= 97$; root mean square error

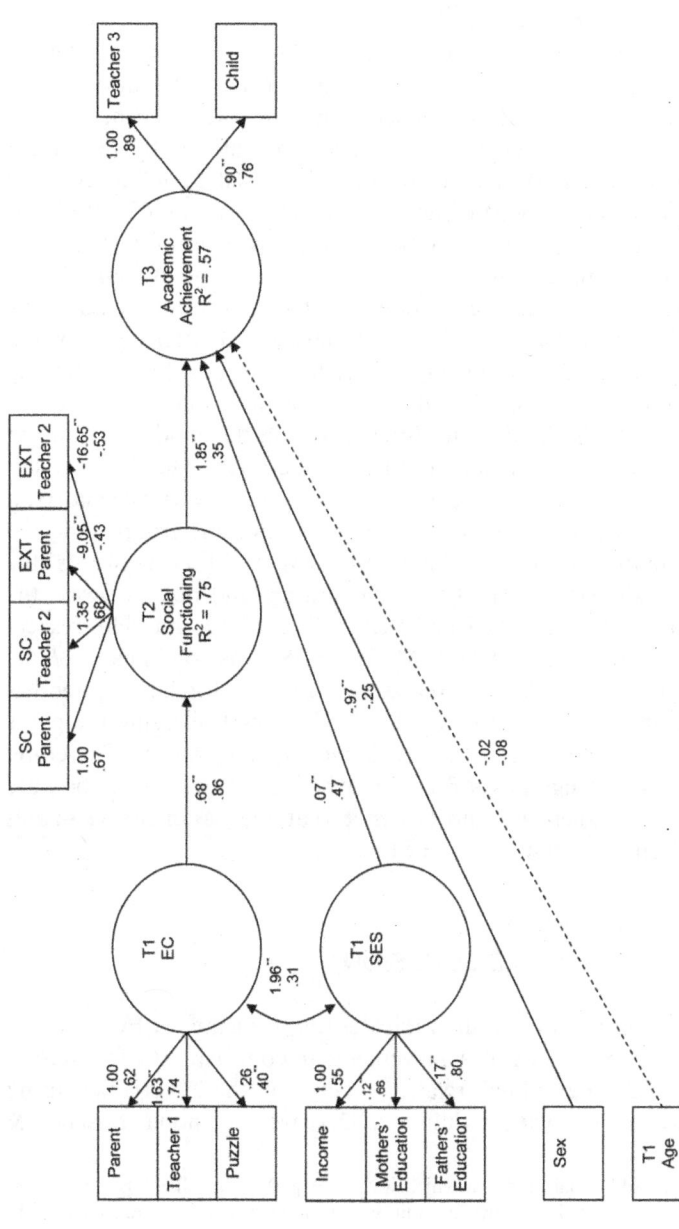

FIGURE 1 Estimated model. The mediated model with unstandardized estimates (standardized estimates are in parentheses). Estimated, but not included in the figure, covariances between age and SES, age and EC, and sex (1 = female, 2 = male) and SES were not significant. There was a significant covariance between sex and EC (unstandardized coefficient = −.08**, standardized coefficient = −.35). Solid lines represent significant paths. SC = social competence; EXT = externalizing problems; T1 = Time 1; T2 = Time 2; T3 = Time 3; EC = effortful control; SES = socioeconomic status. *p < .05. **p < .01.

of approximation = .04. Consistent with our hypotheses, EC was positively related to social functioning, and social functioning in turn was positively related to achievement, even when SES, age, and sex were used as covariates (i.e., as predictors of academic achievement).[1] To formally test mediation and to avoid problems associated with the nonnormal distribution of the indirect effect (e.g., the product of the coefficient from the independent variable to the mediator and the coefficient from the mediator to the dependent variable are generally nonnormally distributed), we used a confidence interval method recommended by MacKinnon and colleagues (2002). Both the upper and lower confidence limits are based on the product of two random variables from tables produced by Meeker, Cornwell, and Aroian (1981). Mediation is significant when the confidence intervals do not include zero. The confidence intervals based on the unstandardized coefficients shown in Figure 1 were 0.37 and 2.29, supporting the prediction that social functioning mediated the relation between EC and academic achievement.

We did not expect the findings to differ based on the child's sex, but we computed a Box's M as a first step in testing moderation. The Box's M statistic tests whether there are differences in the variance/covariance matrix; if Box's M is significant, one is justified in estimating multiple group models to examine the potential source of moderation (Winer, 1971). However, the nonsignificant Box's Ms indicated that sex and age did not moderate the pattern of findings, $Fs(91, 18,967$ and $91, 13,975) = 1.19$ and .830, respectively, *ns*. In contrast, the Box's M for SES was significant, $F(66, 20,290) = 1.64$, $p < .001$. In follow-up analyses using multiple group models in which we compared chi-square based on freeing and releasing the paths displayed in Figure 1, we did not find evidence of moderation. Therefore, although Box's M was significant for SES (which is not surprising because it is a sensitive test), there was no evidence that the parameter estimates varied for children low versus high in SES.

DISCUSSION

A rapidly growing body of literature indicates that measures of EC are often concurrently related to academic achievement. In contrast, very few studies have explored the longitudinal relations between these variables using research designs that span more than 1 or 2 years (cf. Shoda, Mischel, &

---

[1] We estimated an additional model in which we added paths from SES, age, and sex to social functioning. None was significant. In addition, when we estimated a model similar to the one in Figure 1 but with the social functioning measures assessed at T3, the significance of the paths was the same as shown in Figure 1.

Peake, 1990). In addition, only recently have investigators begun to specify the pathways and mechanisms through which EC influences academic achievement. The primary purpose of the present inquiry was to describe the longitudinal relations among EC, social functioning, and academic achievement. Based on theoretical (Eisenberg et al., 2005; Valiente & Eisenberg, 2008) and empirical (Ponitz et al., 2008, 2009; Valiente et al., 2007, 2008) findings, we predicted that EC would be positively related to academic achievement; we further expected quality of social functioning to mediate these relations. The results support our predictions.

Children who were rated by adults as having high levels of EC and who persisted on a mildly frustrating task when in early elementary school (i.e., kindergarten to third grade) achieved academically at relatively high levels when in middle school or high school (i.e., 6 years after T1). Our confidence in the findings is strengthened because the relations were found both within and across reporter when both reported and observed data for EC were used. The pattern of findings suggests that there is a robust relation between EC and academic achievement and supports the notion that attentional and inhibitory control are important contributors to school success (Blair, 2002; Ponitz et al., 2009). The data presented here complement findings of positive concurrent relations of behavioral regulation, working memory, inhibitory control, and attention with literacy and math skills when children are both in preschool and in the early elementary years (Bronson, Tivnan, & Seppanen, 1995; Howse, Calkins, Anastopoulos, Keane, & Shelton, 2003; NICHD Early Child Care Research Network, 2003). Our findings also extend the limited number of prospective studies that span more than 1 to 2 years and are consistent with findings that preschoolers' regulatory abilities predict their SAT scores (Shoda et al., 1990).

Blair (2002) has argued that EC, and particularly attentional regulation, is relevant for academic performance because when students' attentional abilities are limited and focused on several tasks, students often experience difficulties integrating new material. The work of Posner and colleagues (Posner & Rothbart, 2007; Rothbart et al., 2007) on the executive attention system is consistent with Blair's predictions and highlights the importance of considering the contextual demands placed on young children's ability to frequently monitor and evaluate incoming stimuli. These explanations have roots in the cognitive literature (Ruff & Rothbart, 1996) and are supported by findings that children who have difficulty with attention often have poor reading and language skills (McGee, Partridge, Williams, & Silva, 1991; Tamis-LeMonda & Bornstein, 1989), perhaps because difficulties in focusing on tasks or moving from task to task as needed interfere with both learning and completing tasks.

In support of Eisenberg et al.'s (2005) model and our predictions, there is evidence that the relation between EC and academic achievement is mediated by students' social functioning. The longitudinal associations between EC and quality of social functioning replicate a robust body of literature (see Rothbart & Bates, 2006, for a review). Children's EC is believed to affect their social functioning by contributing to how emotion is modulated and how information is processed. When children are able to rein in their behavior and adhere to social standards, they are likely to avoid engaging in aversive or aggressive behaviors in social interactions and are more likely to act in socially appropriate ways.

The findings in this study support the hypothesis that part of the reason why children high in EC perform well in school is that they are relatively competent in terms of their social behavior. These data are consistent with cross-sectional findings that students' social competence partially mediates the associations between EC and grades (Valiente et al., 2008) and strengthen evidence that students' peer interactions are longitudinally related to their academic success (Welsh et al., 2001; Wentzel et al., 2009). When children are low in EC and, as a consequence, are disruptive and engage in aggressive activities, they are likely to receive less substantial support from their peers, which in turn is likely to negatively impact their academic performance. This is especially noteworthy given that many models of instruction require students to engage in social interactions in small-group settings; students who experience difficulty in the peer domain are relatively unlikely to benefit from peer collaboration or cooperative learning groups.

The associations between social functioning and achievement contradict Duncan et al.'s (2007) finding that externalizing problems and social skills are not related to later academic achievement. The lack of correspondence between findings may stem from differences in when externalizing problems and social skills were assessed. Duncan et al. (2007) measured these constructs prior to school entry, and we obtained these data during the early elementary years. Perhaps disruptive behavior is more problematic for learning and achievement during this developmental period, in part because such behavior would be less normative than during the preschool period.

Strengths and Limitations

This investigation has several methodological strengths. First, data were obtained from multiple informants (children, their parents, and teachers), and we also gathered data using questionnaires and observations. Moreover, the teachers who served as reporters differed at all three assessments.

Therefore, it is unlikely that the pattern of findings was inflated because of shared reporter or method variance. Second, in addition to documenting prospective associations between EC and achievement, we identified mechanisms that may underlie these relations. Third, we controlled for a number of potential covariates, and we examined whether SES, children's sex, or age moderated the hypothesized model. The lack of moderation suggests that this pattern can be generalized to children varying in SES, sex, and age. It is noteworthy that age was not a significant moderator. Students ranged in age from 55 to 97 months at T1 and 127 to 169 months age T3 (during which time they were in fifth to ninth grade), suggesting that similar processes operate across a range of development. Nevertheless, future work that more directly tests whether the hypothesized relations are similar for younger and older children is needed. Despite these strengths, there are key areas that could be improved in future research. First, the inclusion of indices of IQ in subsequent models would be valuable. It is possible that the magnitude of the relations between EC (or social functioning) and achievement would be reduced when IQ is in the model, but based on the extant literature it is very likely that relations would continue to be significant (Blair & Razza, 2007; Gottfried, 1990; Masten et al., 2005). Second, the findings reported here are for a primarily Caucasian sample; based on other work with more diverse samples (Valiente et al., 2008; Zhou et al., in press), we believe the processes will replicate cross-ethnically and cross-racially, but additional evidence is necessary before we are able to generalize the findings to other groups. Third, in future inquiries it would be quite valuable to consider reciprocal models. Hinshaw (1992) and others have argued that there are likely bidirectional relationships between externalizing problems and academic achievement. A better appreciation for how social functioning and academic achievement influence each other as children progress through early elementary school would provide a richer understanding of how to intervene and prevent further deterioration in the social and academic domains. Finally, there were some differences between families who completed data at all assessments (more than 75% of the families) and those who missed one or more assessments. Although we relied on the most current methods for imputing missing data, it would clearly be more advantageous to have obtained complete data. Finally, we could not control for grade point average at an earlier age to assess prediction of change in children's grade point average by EC and social functioning, which would have provided a stronger test of potential causal relations.

Notwithstanding these limitations, the pattern of findings presented here has educational implications. Our model highlights the value of considering students' social and emotional functioning in models of school success. There is mounting evidence that attentional abilities and inhibitory control can be improved via training experiences and interventions and that growth in these domains positively impacts academic success (Bierman, Nix, Greenberg, Blair, & Domitrovich, 2008; Diamond, Barnett, Thomas, & Munro, 2007; Domitrovich, Cortes, & Greenberg, 2007). Based on the current findings, we believe a focused effort to improve EC is advantageous because growth in this area is likely to produce both social advantages (e.g., high levels of social competence and low levels of problem behaviors) *and* academic advantages. Many activities that can be used to improve self-regulation are relatively inexpensive or free and can be administered in the classroom. Given the many demands placed on teachers, it is likely that administrators need to provide clear messages supporting the modest amount of time needed to promote students' EC in order for teachers to engage in such activities.

REFERENCES

Achenbach, T. M. (1991a). *Integrative guide for the 1991 CBCL/4-18, YSR, and TRF profiles.* Burlington: University of Vermont, Department of Psychiatry.

Achenbach, T. M. (1991b). *Manual for the Child Behavior Checklist/4-18 and 1991 profile.* Burlington: University of Vermont, Department of Psychology.

Arnold, D. H. (1997). Co-occurrence of externalizing behavior problems and emergent academic difficulties in young high-risk boys: A preliminary evaluation of patterns and mechanisms. *Journal of Applied Developmental Psychology, 18*, 317–330.

Bierman, K. L., Nix, R. L., Greenberg, M. T., Blair, C., & Domitrovich, C. E. (2008). Executive functions and school readiness intervention: Impact, moderation, and mediation in the Head Start REDI program. *Development and Psychopathology, 20*, 821–843.

Blair, C. (2002). School readiness: Integrating cognition and emotion in a neurobiological conceptualization of children's functioning at school entry. *American Psychologist, 57*, 111–127.

Blair, C., & Diamond, A. (2008). Biological processes in prevention and intervention: The promotion of self-regulation as a means of preventing school failure. *Development and Psychopathology, 20*, 899–911.

Blair, C., & Razza, R. P. (2007). Relating effortful control, executive function, and false belief understanding to emerging math and literacy ability in kindergarten. *Child Development, 78*, 647–663.

Bronson, M. B., Tivnan, T., & Seppanen, P. S. (1995). Relations between teacher and classroom activity variables and the classroom behaviors of prekindergarten children in Chapter 1 funded programs. *Journal of Applied Developmental Psychology, 16*, 253–282.

Bureau of Labor Statistics. (2004). [Tabulations: 2004]. Retrieved from ftp://ftp.bls.gov/pub/special.requests/lf/aat7.txt

Carlson, S. M. (2005). Developmentally sensitive measures of executive function in preschool children. *Developmental Neuropsychology, 28*, 595–616.

Caspi, A., Elder, G. H., & Bem, D. J. (1987). Moving against the world: Life-course patterns of explosive children. *Developmental Psychology, 23*, 308–313.

Coie, J. D., & Dodge, K. A. (1988). Multiple sources of data on social behavior and social status in the school: A cross-age comparison. *Child Development, 59*, 815–829.

Cole, P. M., Armstrong, L. M., & Pemberton, C. K. (2010). The role of language in the development of emotion regulation. In S. D. Calkins & M. A. Bell (Eds.), *Child development at the intersection of emotion and cognition: Human brain development* (pp. 59–77). Washington, DC: American Psychological Association.

Cook, R. D. (1977). Detection of influential observation in linear regression. *Technometrics, 19*, 15–19.

Davis-Kean, P. E. (2005). The influence of parent education and family income on child achievement: The indirect role of parental expectations and the home environment. *Journal of Family Psychology, 19*, 294–304.

Derryberry, D., & Reed, M. A. (2002). Anxiety-related attentional biases and their regulation by attentional control. *Journal of Abnormal Psychology, 111*, 225–236.

Diamond, A., Barnett, W. S., Thomas, J., & Munro, S. (2007, November 30). Preschool program improves cognitive control. *Science, 318*, 1387–1388.

Dodge, K. A., Coie, J. D., & Lynam, D. (2006). Aggression and antisocial behavior in youth. In W. Damon (Series Ed.) & N. Eisenberg (Vol. Ed.), *Handbook of child psychology: Vol. 3. Social, emotional, personality development* (6th ed., pp. 719–788). Hoboken, NJ: Wiley.

Domitrovich, C. E., Cortes, R. C., & Greenberg, M. T. (2007). Improving young children's social and emotional competence: A randomized trial of the preschool "PATHS" curriculum. *Journal of Primary Prevention, 28*, 67–91.

Duncan, G. J., Dowsett, C. J., Claessens, A., Magnuson, K., Huston, A. C., Klebanov, P., ... Japel, C. (2007). School readiness and later achievement. *Developmental Psychology, 43*, 1428–1446.

Duncan, G. J., Dowsett, C. J., Claessens, A., Magnuson, K., Huston, A. C., Klebanov, P., ... Japel, C. (2008). "School readiness and later achievement": Correction to Duncan et al. (2007). *Developmental Psychology, 44*, 232.

Eisenberg, N., Cumberland, A. J., Spinrad, T. L., Fabes, R. A., Shepard, S. A., Reiser, M. et al. (2001). The relations of regulation and emotionality to children's externalizing and internalizing problem behavior. *Child Development, 72*, 1112–1134.

Eisenberg, N., Fabes, R. A., Murphy, B., Maszk, P., Smith, M., & Karbon, M. (1995). The role of emotionality and regulation in children's social functioning: A longitudinal study. *Child Development, 66*, 1360–1384.

Eisenberg, N., Gershoff, E. T., Fabes, R. A., Shepard, S. A., Cumberland, A. J., Losoya, S. H., ... Murphy, B. C. (2001). Mother's emotional expressivity and children's behavior problems and social competence: Mediation through children's regulation. *Developmental Psychology, 37*, 475–490.

Eisenberg, N., Pidada, S., & Liew, J. (2001). The relations of regulation and negative emotionality to Indonesian children's social functioning. *Child Development, 72*, 1747–1763.

Eisenberg, N., Sadovsky, A., & Spinrad, T. (2005). Associations among emotion-related regulation, language skills, emotion knowledge, and academic outcomes. *New Directions in Child and Adolescent Development, 109*, 109–118.

Eisenberg, N., Valiente, C., Spinrad, T. L., Cumberland, A., Liew, J., Reiser, M., ... Lasoya, S. H. (2009). Longitudinal relations of children's effortful control, impulsivity, and negative emotionality to their externalizing, internalizing, and co-occurring behavior problems. *Developmental Psychology, 45*, 988–1008.

Ensminger, M. E., & Slusarcick, A. L. (1992). Paths to high school graduation or dropout: A longitudinal study of a first-grade cohort. *Sociology of Education, 65*, 95–113.

Eronen, S., Nurmi, J.-E., & Salmela-Aro, K. (1997). Planning-oriented, avoidant, and impulsive social reaction styles: A person-oriented approach. *Journal of Research in Personality, 31*, 34–57.

Frome, P. M., & Eccles, J. S. (1998). Parents' influence on children's achievement-related perceptions. *Journal of Personality and Social Psychology, 74*, 435–452.

Gottfried, A. E. (1990). Academic intrinsic motivation in young elementary school children. *Journal of Educational Psychology, 82*, 525–538.

Graham, J. E., Updegraff, K. A., Tomascik, C. A., & McHale, S. M. (1997). Someone who cares: Evaluation of school advisor programs in two community settings. *Applied Developmental Science, 1*, 28–42.

Graziano, P. A., Reavis, R. D., Keane, S. P., & Calkins, S. D. (2007). The role of emotion regulation in children's early academic success. *Journal of School Psychology, 45*, 3–19.

Hamre, B. K., & Pianta, R. C. (2001). Early teacher-child relationships and the trajectory of children's school outcomes through eighth grade. *Child Development, 72*, 625–638.

Harter, S. (1982). The Perceived Competence Scale for Children. *Child Development, 53*, 87–97.

Hinshaw, S. P. (1992). Externalizing behavior problems and academic underachievement in childhood and adolescence: Causal relationships and underlying mechanisms. *Psychological Bulletin, 111*, 127–155.

Hoglund, W. L. G. (2007). School functioning in early adolescence: Gender-linked responses to peer victimization. *Journal of Educational Psychology, 99*, 683–699.

Howse, R. B., Calkins, S. D., Anastopoulos, A. D., Keane, S. P., & Shelton, T. L. (2003). Regulatory contributors to children's kindergarten achievement. *Early Education & Development, 14*, 101–119.

Jerome, E. M., Hamre, B. K., & Pianta, R. C. (2009). Teacher-child relationships from kindergarten to sixth grade: Early childhood predictors of teacher-perceived conflict and closeness. *Social Development, 18*, 915–945.

Jordan, N. C., Kaplan, D., Oláh, L. N., & Locuniak, M. N. (2006). Number sense growth in kindergarten: A longitudinal investigation of children at risk for mathematics difficulties. *Child Development, 77*, 153–175.

Kenny, D. A., & Kashy, D. A. (1992). Analysis of the multitrait-multimethod matrix by confirmatory factor analysis. *Psychological Bulletin, 112*, 165–172.

Kochanska, G., & Knaack, A. (2003). Effortful control as a personality characteristic of young children: Antecedents, correlates, and consequences. *Journal of Personality, 71*, 1087–1112.

Kochanska, G., Murray, K., & Coy, K. C. (1997). Inhibitory control as a contributor to conscience in childhood: From toddler to early school age. *Child Development, 68*, 263–277.

Kochanska, G., Murray, K., & Harlan, E. T. (2000). Effortful control in early childhood: Continuity and change, antecedents, and implications for social development. *Developmental Psychology, 36*, 220–232.

Ladd, G. W., Birch, S. H., & Buhs, E. S. (1999). Children's social and scholastic lives in kindergarten: Related spheres of influence? *Child Development, 70*, 1373–1400.

Ladd, G. W., Herald, S. L., & Kochel, K. P. (2006). School readiness: Are there social prerequisites? *Early Education & Development, 17*, 115–150.

MacKinnon, D. P., Lockwood, C. M., Hoffman, J. M., West, S. G., & Sheets, V. (2002). A comparison of methods to test mediation and other intervening variable effects. *Psychological Methods, 7*, 83–104.

Martel, M. M., Nigg, J. T., Wong, M. M., Fitzgerald, H. E., Jester, J. M., Puttler, L. I., ... Zucker, R. A. (2007). Childhood and adolescent resiliency, regulation, and executive functioning in relation to adolescent problems and competence in a high-risk sample. *Development and Psychopathology, 19*, 541–563.

Masten, A. S., Roisman, G. I., Long, J. D., Burt, K. B., Obradović, J., Riley, J. R., ... Tellegen, A. (2005). Developmental cascades: Linking academic achievement and externalizing and internalizing symptoms over 20 years. *Developmental Psychology, 41*, 733–746.

McClelland, M. M., Cameron, C. E., Connor, C. M., Farris, C. L., Jewkes, A. M., & Morrison, F. J. (2007). Links between behavioral regulation and preschoolers' literacy, vocabulary, and math skills. *Developmental Psychology, 43*, 947–959.

McGee, R., Partridge, F., Williams, S., & Silva, P. A. (1991). A twelve-year follow-up of preschool hyperactive children. *Journal of the American Academy of Child & Adolescent Psychiatry, 30*, 224–232.

Meece, J. L., Anderman, E. M., & Anderman, L. H. (2006). Classroom goal structure, student motivation, and academic achievement. *Annual Review of Psychology, 57*, 487–503.

Meeker, W. Q., Cornwell, L. W., & Aroian, L. A. (1981). *Selected tables in mathematical statistics: Vol. VII. The product of two normally distributed random variables*. Providence, RI: American Mathematical Society.

Muris, P., Meesters, C., & Blijlevens, P. (2007). Self-reported reactive and regulative temperament in early adolescence: Relations to internalizing and externalizing problem behavior and "big three" personality factors. *Journal of Adolescence, 30*, 1035–1049.

Muris, P., Meesters, C., & Rompelberg, L. (2007). Attention control in middle childhood: Relations to psychopathological symptoms and threat perception distortions. *Behaviour Research and Therapy, 45*, 997–1010.

Muthén, L. K., & Muthén, B. O. (1998–2005). *Mplus user's guide* (3rd ed.). Los Angeles, CA: Author.

National Institute of Child Health and Human Development Early Child Care Research Network. (2003). Do children's attention processes mediate the link between family predictors and school readiness? *Developmental Psychology, 39*, 581–593.

National Institute of Child Health and Human Development Early Child Care Research Network. (2004). Trajectories of physical aggression from toddlerhood to middle childhood. *Monographs of the Society for Research in Child Development, 69*, 1–129.

Pierce, K. M., Hamm, J. V., & Vandell, D. L. (1999). Experiences in after-school programs and children's adjustment in first-grade classrooms. *Child Development, 70*, 756–767.

Ponitz, C. C., McClelland, M. M., Jewkes, A. M., Connor, C. M., Farris, C. L., & Morrison, F. J. (2008). Touch your toes! Developing a direct measure of behavioral regulation in early childhood. *Early Childhood Research Quarterly, 23*, 141–158.

Ponitz, C. C., McClelland, M. M., Matthews, J. S., & Morrison, F. J. (2009). A structured observation of behavioral self-regulation and its contribution to kindergarten outcomes. *Developmental Psychology, 45*, 605–619.

Posner, M. I., & Rothbart, M. K. (2007). Research on attention networks as a model for the integration of psychological science. *Annual Review of Psychology, 58*, 1–23.

Raver, C. C. (2002). Emotions matter: Making the case for the role of young children's emotional development for early school readiness. *Social Policy Report, 16*(3), 3–18.

Rimm-Kaufman, S. E., & Pianta, R. C. (2000). An ecological perspective on the transition to kindergarten: A theoretical framework to guide empirical research. *Journal of Applied Developmental Psychology, 21*, 491–511.

Rimm-Kaufman, S. E., Pianta, R. C., & Cox, M. J. (2000). Teachers' judgments of problems in the transition to kindergarten. *Early Childhood Research Quarterly, 15*, 147–166.

Rothbart, M. K., Ahadi, S. A., Hersey, K. L., & Fisher, P. (2001). Investigations of temperament at three to seven years: The Children's Behavior Questionnaire. *Child Development, 72*, 1394–1408.

Rothbart, M. K., & Bates, J. E. (2006). Temperament. In W. Damon (Series Ed.) & N. Eisenberg (Vol. Ed.), *Handbook of child psychology: Vol. 3. Social, emotional, personality development* (6th ed., pp. 99–166). Hoboken, NJ: Wiley.

Rothbart, M. K., Sheese, B. E., & Posner, M. I. (2007). Executive attention and effortful control: Linking temperament, brain networks, and genes. *Child Development Perspectives, 1*, 2–7.

Ruff, H. A., & Rothbart, M. K. (1996). *Attention in early development: Themes and variations.* London, England: Oxford University Press.

Shoda, Y., Mischel, W., & Peake, P. K. (1990). Predicting adolescent cognitive and self-regulatory competencies from preschool delay of gratification: Identifying diagnostic conditions. *Developmental Psychology, 26,* 978–986.

Silk, J. S., Steinberg, L., & Morris, A. S. (2003). Adolescents' emotion regulation in daily life: Links to depressive symptoms and problem behavior. *Child Development, 74,* 1869–1880.

Simpkins, S. D., Davis-Kean, P. E., & Eccles, J. S. (2006). Math and science motivation: A longitudinal examination of the links between choices and beliefs. *Developmental Psychology, 42,* 70–83.

Spinrad, T. L., Eisenberg, N., Cumberland, A., Fabes, R. A., Valiente, C., Shepard, S. A., ... Guthrie, I. K. (2006). Relation of emotion-related regulation to children's social competence: A longitudinal study. *Emotion, 6,* 498–510.

Spinrad, T. L., Eisenberg, N., & Gaertner, B. M. (2007). Measures of effortful regulation for young children. *Infant Mental Health Journal, 28,* 606–626.

Stipek, D., & Miles, S. (2008). Effects of aggression on achievement: Does conflict with the teacher make it worse? *Child Development, 79,* 1721–1735.

Tamis-LeMonda, C. S., & Bornstein, M. H. (1989). Habituation and maternal encouragement of attention in infancy as predictors of toddler language, play, and representational competence. *Child Development, 60,* 738–751.

Thomson, E., & Williams, R. (1984). A note on correlated measurement error in wife-husband data. *Journal of Marriage and Family, 46,* 643–649.

U.S. Department of Education. (2004). *The condition of education 2004.* Washington, DC: U.S. Government Printing Office. Retrieved from http://nces.ed.gov/pubs2006/dropout/ref.asp#ed

Valiente, C., & Eisenberg, N. (2008). Emotion regulation. In E. Anderman & L. Anderman (Eds.), *Psychology of classroom learning: An encyclopedia* (pp. 357–360). Detroit, MI: Macmillan Reference.

Valiente, C., Lemery-Chalfant, K., & Castro, K. S. (2007). Children's effortful control and academic competence. Mediation through school liking. *Merrill-Palmer Quarterly, 53,* 1–25.

Valiente, C., Lemery-Chalfant, K. S., & Swanson, J. (2010). Prediction of kindergartners' academic competence from their effortful control and negative emotionality: Evidence for direct and moderated relations. *Journal of Educational Psychology, 102,* 550–560.

Valiente, C., Lemery-Chalfant, K., Swanson, J., & Reiser, M. (2008). Prediction of children's academic competence from their effortful control, relationships, and classroom participation. *Journal of Educational Psychology, 100,* 67–77.

Welsh, M., Parke, R. D., Widaman, K., & O'Neil, R. (2001). Linkages between children's social and academic competence: A longitudinal analysis. *Journal of School Psychology, 39,* 463–482.

Wentzel, K. R., Baker, S., & Russell, S. (2009). Peer relationships and positive adjustment at school. In R. Gilman, E. S. Huebner, & M. J. Furlong (Eds.), *Handbook of positive psychology in schools* (pp. 229–243). New York, NY: Routledge.

West, S. G., Finch, J. F., & Curran, P. J. (1995). Structural equation models with nonnormal variables: Problems and remedies. In R. H. Hoyle (Ed.), *Structural equation modeling: Concepts, issues, and applications* (pp. 56–75). Thousand Oaks, CA: Sage.

Winer, B. J. (1971). *Statistical principles in experimental design.* New York, NY: McGraw-Hill.

Zhou, Q., Hofer, C., Eisenberg, N., Reiser, M., Spinrad, T. L., & Fabes, R. A. (2007). The developmental trajectories of attention focusing, attentional and behavioral persistence, and externalizing problems during school-age years. *Developmental Psychology, 43*, 369–385.

Zhou, Q., Lengua, L. J., & Wang, Y. (2009). The relations of temperament reactivity and effortful control to children's adjustment problems in China and the United States. *Developmental Psychology, 45*, 724–739.

Zhou, Q., Main, A., & Wang, Y. (2010). The relations of temperamental effortful control and anger/frustration to Chinese children's academic achievement and social adjustment: A longitudinal study. *Journal of Educational Psychology, 102*, 180–196.

Zimmerman, B. J. (1998). Developing self-fulfilling cycles of academic regulation: An analysis of exemplary instructional models. In D. H. Schunk (Ed.), *Self-regulated learning: From teaching to self-reflective practice* (pp. 1–19). New York, NY: Guilford Press.

Relations of Children's Effortful Control and Teacher–Child Relationship Quality to School Attitudes in a Low-Income Sample

Kassondra M. Silva and Tracy L. Spinrad

Nancy Eisenberg and Michael J. Sulik

Carlos Valiente

Snjezana Huerta and Alison Edwards

Natalie D. Eggum

Anne S. Kupfer

Christopher J. Lonigan, Beth M. Phillips, and Shauna B. Wilson

Jeanine Clancy-Menchetti

Susan H. Landry, Paul R. Swank, Michael A. Assel, and Heather B. Taylor

School Readiness Consortium

Research Findings: The purpose of this study was to examine the relations of children's effortful control and quality of relationships with teachers to school attitudes longitudinally in an ethnically diverse and economically disadvantaged sample. Data were collected as part of a larger intervention project during mid-fall, winter, and late spring ($ns = 823$, 722, and 758, respectively) for 2 cohorts of 3- to 5-year-olds (collected during 2 different school years). Children's effortful control was assessed in the fall with parents' and teachers' reports and 2 behavioral measures. Teacher–child relationship quality was assessed mid-year with teachers' reports of closeness and conflict. Attitudes toward school were assessed in late spring using teachers' and students' reports of school avoidance and liking. Effortful control, in general, was positively correlated with teacher–child closeness and school liking and negatively correlated with conflict and school avoidance. Using structural equation modeling and controlling for sex and ethnicity, we found that effortful control was positively related to teacher–child relationship quality, which in turn was positively related to school attitudes. Furthermore, the relation of effortful control to school attitudes was mediated by teacher–child relationship quality. *Practice or Policy*: Results provide evidence for the importance of relational processes that take place within the classroom context and have implications for teachers and clinicians working to increase school success in ethnic minority and low-income children.

There has been mounting concern that children belonging to socioeconomically disadvantaged families and/or an ethnic minority group are at risk for difficulties with school adjustment (National Education Goals Panel, 1997). Consequently, researchers have sought to understand how best to prepare children, especially high-risk groups, for success in school as they make the transition from preschool to formal schooling. This issue is especially important given that early risk factors such as low income appear to predict academic problems from first grade through high school

(Gutman, Sameroff, & Cole, 2003), and the gap in academic outcomes between disadvantaged children and their peers grows during the elementary school years (Children's Defense Fund, 1993; Entwisle & Alexander, 1992).

Different forms of school engagement have been studied as possible antecedents of academic achievement. A crucial hypothesis posited in the engagement literature is that to fully benefit from education and ultimately be successful, students must be present and actively engage in the classroom (Fredricks, Blumenfeld, & Paris, 2004). Indeed, a large body of work supports the notion that school engagement is an important predictor of school success (Buhs & Ladd, 2001; Ladd, Buhs, & Seid, 2000; Ladd & Dinella, 2009) and that children from low-income families are more likely to exhibit increasing levels of disengagement from school (Finn, 1989; Hauser-Cram, Warfield, Stadler, & Sirin, 2006). In this article, we focus on components of *emotional school engagement*, defined as children's affective reactions and attitudes toward peers, teachers, academics, and school in general (Fredricks et al., 2004), such as school liking and avoidance. In contrast to behavioral and cognitive forms of engagement, positive school attitudes have been less thoroughly researched, especially in young children. Theoretically speaking, such attitudes are thought to foster students' connection to the larger school environment, influencing motivation to achieve and increasing their active participation in their education (Fredricks et al., 2004). Conversely, a lack of positive attitudes toward school is believed to predict poor school adjustment and achievement, especially if such sentiments are experienced early in children's schooling (Alexander & Entwisle, 1988; Ladd, 1996; Ladd et al., 2000).

Current findings suggest that positive attitudes toward school are related to children's higher achievement (Buhs & Ladd, 2001; Ladd, Birch, & Buhs, 1999; Valiente, Lemery-Chalfant, & Castro, 2007; Valiente, Lemery-Chalfant, Swanson, & Reiser, 2008). In a sample of kindergartners, Ladd et al. (2000) found evidence that school liking promoted classroom participation and achievement. There was, however, less evidence that the reverse causal relation was true (i.e., that school liking was a consequence of participation and achievement). In addition, Ladd et al. (2000) found that early academic achievement was predicted by school attitudes through increasing participation in the classroom and that these associations remained significant when background variables such as family socioeconomic status and child's mental maturity were included in models. In a slightly older sample, school attitudes (e.g., school liking and avoidance) assessed in Grades 1–3 were predictive of long-term academic achievement. Children who consistently had higher propensities to like, rather than avoid, school exhibited more academic progress through the eighth grade compared to peers who had lower levels of engagement (Ladd & Dinella, 2009). Given the importance of school attitudes for students, the purpose of the present study was to examine the associations of both child characteristics (e.g., effortful control) and contextual factors (e.g., teacher–child relationship quality) with positive feelings toward school in a sample of ethnically diverse, low-income preschoolers aged 3 to 5 years old.

THE RELATIONS OF CHILDREN'S EFFORTFUL CONTROL TO SCHOOL ATTITUDES

In understanding the antecedents of children's social and academic success, developmentalists have considered the role of children's temperamentally based qualities, including regulation. A substantial body of work provides evidence that higher levels of regulation in preschool are related to better academic performance (e.g., Blair & Razza, 2007; McClelland et al., 2007). Less work has explicitly examined the relations of regulation to other constructs that are important to academic success, such as attitudes toward school.

Effortful control, the regulatory aspect of temperament, has been defined as "the efficiency of executive attention, including the ability to inhibit a dominant response and/or to activate a subdominant response, to plan, and to detect errors" (Rothbart & Bates, 2006, p. 129). Behavioral measures of effortful control involve skills such as the abilities to focus and shift attention, inhibit or activate a behavior, and delay gratification as well as to execute fine and gross motor control (Kochanska, Murray, & Harlan, 2000; Murray & Kochanska, 2002). Although the subcomponents of effortful control involve different sets of abilities, some researchers have found that the indicators are consistently positively related to one another and generally thought to be indicative of a latent effortful control factor (e.g., Kochanska et al., 2000). In addition, a battery of effortful control tasks measuring a number of aspects of this skill (e.g., slowing down motor behavior, attentional control) exhibited high reliability in a sample of children aged 33 to 42 months (Kochanska & Knaack, 2003). Some questionnaires and behavioral tasks used to assess effortful control likely tap some of these skill sets more than others, but they have been combined as an indicator of effortful control in studies using the same sample of low-income preschoolers in this study (Sulik et al., 2010) as well as in low-risk samples (Kochanska et al., 2000; Spinrad et al., 2007).

Although there is less research on the relations of effortful control to children's feelings about school, there are conceptual reasons for expecting associations. Effortful control allows for adaptive flexibility in attentional processes and for the regulation of behavioral reactivity (Rothbart & Bates, 2006). Children who are well regulated are likely more successful at managing and inhibiting inappropriate behaviors and impulses, feel more comfortable interacting with others, and engage in more positive exchanges with teachers and peers. These positive experiences may include receiving praise from teachers and being well liked by peers, which could further serve to increase children's enjoyment of school. Conversely, children who are not able to self-regulate may encounter difficulty in participating in and completing activities and have less opportunity to form supportive networks in the classroom. These difficulties could potentially lead to frustration, peer rejection, and disciplinary action. Indeed, children's low effortful control has been associated with increased levels of victimization (Deater-Deckard, 2001), externalizing behaviors (Brody & Ge, 2001), and low levels of social competence (Eisenberg et al., 2001). Children who experience these outcomes may feel excluded and lonely, which could contribute to negative attitudes toward school. For example, attentional problems were negatively related to children's school liking in kindergarten and first grade (Ladd & Burgess, 2001), whereas effortful control positively predicted school liking in older samples (e.g., 7- to 12-year olds; Valiente et al., 2007). In addition, researchers have demonstrated the importance of effortful control in children's academic competencies (Blair & Razza, 2007; McClelland et al., 2007). Thus, children who have better academic skills may also find school more enjoyable.

Although it is not currently clear whether the relation between effortful control and school attitudes is present in preschool, school attitudes have been shown to be moderately stable from first to third grade (Ladd & Dinella, 2009). Early school attitudes are arguably crucial, as children who started kindergarten with negative feelings about school had lower levels of academic achievement in the fifth grade (Hauser-Cram, Durand, & Warfield, 2007). It is likely that children's earliest attitudes about school are related to later feelings as they continue their education. Thus, it is important to investigate the relations of effortful control with children's attitudes in preschool and, in addition, to examine what role is played by teacher–child relationship quality.

THE RELATIONS OF TEACHER–CHILD RELATIONSHIP QUALITY TO SCHOOL ATTITUDES

Although the evidence suggests that effortful control plays a role in the formation of children's attitudes toward school, contextual factors also may be related to school attitudes. A particularly relevant contextual factor may be the quality of the teacher–child relationship. The quality and nature of children's relationships with their teachers can be highly variable and can be characterized by closeness (e.g., reciprocal support and warmth) or conflict (e.g., overt struggle between child and teacher; Howes & Matheson, 1992; Pianta, Steinberg, & Rollins, 1995). Individual differences in relationship quality may influence the support received by children as they make the transition to school and thus may be related to differences observed in children's attitudes toward school.

The quality of teacher–child relationships has been consistently related to children's functioning across social and academic domains, including academic achievement and motivation, externalizing behaviors, disciplinary problems, and peer relations, across a variety of ages (Birch & Ladd, 1996, 1997; Crosnoe, Johnson, & Elder, 2004; Griggs, Gagnon, Huelsman, Kidder-Ashley, & Ballard, 2009; Hamre & Pianta, 2001; Hughes & Kwok, 2006; Pianta, 1999). However, less work has examined how the quality of teacher–child relationships is related to school attitudes, particularly with young children. As children enter school, teachers become an important resource upon which they can rely as they learn to navigate a new environment. Children who have difficulty making the transition to preschool but are able to form open, close relationships with their teachers may come to enjoy and like school despite initial challenges. In contrast, children who develop relationships with teachers that are characterized by high conflict and low closeness may be more likely to have poor peer relationships as well. Both these relational risk factors may contribute to feelings of loneliness and contribute to less school liking and more school avoidance.

Although this association has not been thoroughly addressed in preschool-age samples, there is some work demonstrating that the quality of teacher–child relationships is related to school attitudes in older children. For example, Birch and Ladd (1997) found that children who had closer relationships with teachers in kindergarten liked school more, and those children who had more conflictual relationships were reported by teachers to like school less and be more school avoidant. We expected children's relationships with their preschool teachers to be related to their school attitudes in ways similar to what has been found for older children. In support of this notion, teacher–child closeness and conflict in preschool were found to be significant predictors of teacher-reported classroom adjustment, which included items that assessed children's attitudes toward school (Garner & Waajid, 2008). Taken together, such findings suggest the importance of examining children's relationships with teachers when predicting children's school attitudes in preschool.

THE RELATIONS OF EFFORTFUL CONTROL TO THE TEACHER–CHILD RELATIONSHIP

According to the conceptual model of student–teacher relationships proposed by Pianta (1999), attributes of the individuals who make up a relationship contribute to the quality of the relationship formed. More specifically, dispositional characteristics, particularly regulation, may contribute to how children are viewed by others. Indeed, children's temperamental qualities, such as attentional and behavioral control, have been related to teachers' expectations of the students, which influence relationship quality (Keogh, 1982, 1994; Myers & Pianta, 2008). Therefore, effortful control may be associated with school attitudes through children's relationships with teachers. Given that children high on effortful control are found to be more socially competent and exhibit less behavioral problems (Eisenberg et al., 1997, 2003), it is likely that these children are viewed by teachers as well-behaved, less disruptive, and more ideal students. Teachers' interactions with these students may unintentionally include behaviors such as rewards and praise. Such exchanges are thought to be more "open" in nature (Keogh, 2003) and to foster more warm, caring relationships with low levels of conflict. Children who lack regulatory abilities may be perceived by teachers as misbehaving intentionally, and this disruptive behavior may result in disciplinary action that leads to negative interactions. In addition, teachers may engage with these children in an entirely instructional way, with less opportunity to facilitate closeness. In fact, effortful control was related to less teacher–child conflict in a sample of low-income preschoolers (Myers & Morris, 2009) as well as to greater teacher–child closeness in first grade (Liew, Chen, & Hughes, 2010; Rudasill & Rimm-Kaufman, 2009). However, the relation of dispositional influences such as children's effortful control with the quality of the teacher–child relationship has not been well examined in preschool.

THE MEDIATING ROLE OF TEACHER–CHILD RELATIONSHIP QUALITY

There are likely multiple influences that affect how children feel about school. As discussed previously, two of these influences may be children's effortful control and children's relationships with teachers. Although research examining these factors during the preschool years is sparse, there is some support for the notion that these factors are related to school attitudes directly and indirectly. In the present study, our first research aim was to examine the direct relations of children's effortful control to teacher–child relationship quality as well as relationship quality to school attitudes. Next we examined whether effortful control was indirectly related to school attitudes through teacher–child relationship quality. If such mediation exists, one would expect effortful control to predict more positive teacher–child relationships (e.g., high closeness and low conflict), which in turn may predict more positive school attitudes. We used a longitudinal design over the course of a school year to test this mediational process using an ethnically diverse and low-income preschool sample.

METHOD

Participants

Data were from a large, two-site intervention project designed to examine the impact of a school readiness curriculum on children's regulation and school-related outcomes. Participants in the present study were 829 children enrolled in 108 preschool classrooms in and surrounding Houston, Texas ($n = 51$ classrooms), and Tallahassee, Florida ($n = 57$ classrooms). Private preschools as well as public Head Start centers participated. A majority of these centers were full-day programs. At least 60% of students in each preschool had to qualify for free or reduced lunch in order to be eligible for the intervention project. Preschools that were eligible in Texas were identified by directors of Head Start schools and independent school districts and by a website for the Florida Department of Children and Families. The sample included all eligible preschools that agreed to participate in the study. Typically only one classroom was selected at each preschool. If more than one classroom met the eligibility requirement, one classroom was chosen for participation based on recommendations from directors and agency leaders. Parents of all children in a classroom were invited to participate. Then 8 to 10 children per classroom ($M = 7.56$) between the ages of 3 and 5, none of whom had any significant visual/auditory impairments or cognitive/language deficits, were randomly selected to participate. There were 3 participating classrooms in Texas and 17 classrooms in Florida with fewer than eight children.

Data collection took place over a span of 2 years; one cohort was assessed in 2006 and the other in 2007. Different schools participated in each year. Although there were comparable numbers of African American participants across sites, nearly all Euro-American participants were enrolled in Florida preschools, whereas nearly all Hispanic participants were enrolled in Texas preschools. Participants in Texas included 5 Euro-American participants, 182 Hispanic participants, 204 African American participants, and 14 participants classified as "other." The Florida sample included 207

Euro-American participants, 11 Hispanic participants, 188 African American participants, and 18 participants reported as "other." The highest level of parental education was reported by the primary caregiver, in most cases the mother, on a 10-point scale: $1 =$ middle school, $2 =$ some high school, $3 =$ high school diploma, $4 =$ vocational training, $5 =$ some college, $6 =$ associate's degree, $7 =$ bachelor's degree, $8 =$ graduate school but no degree, $9 =$ master's degree, $10 =$ doctorate. The mean level of education at both sites was low, but it was higher in Florida ($M = 4.41$, $SD = 1.74$) than in Texas ($M = 3.66$, $SD = 1.68$), $t(611) = -5.43$, $p < .001$. Although 829 students had data from at least one time point, fewer students were observed at each wave. At Time 1 (T1), data were available for 823 students (404 Texas, 215 girls, M age $= 4.66$ years, $SD = 0.40$; 419 Florida, 217 girls, M age $= 4.57$ years, $SD = 0.48$). At Time 2 (T2), there were data for 722 students (393 Texas, 207 girls, M age $= 4.80$ years, $SD = 0.41$; 329 Florida, 169 girls, M age $= 4.69$ years, $SD = 0.53$). At Time 3 (T3), there were data for 758 students (386 Texas, 205 girls, M age $= 5.09$ years, $SD = 0.40$; 372 Florida, 195 girls, M age $= 5.09$ years, $SD = 0.40$). To assess attrition effects, we conducted t tests to investigate differences between students who had data at T1 and either T2 or T3 ($n = 795$) and those with only data at T1 ($n = 34$) on all study variables. There were no differences on T1 variables.

Teachers who participated in this study had an average of 10.27 ($SD = 6.44$) years of preschool teaching experience. Across all sites, 71 lead teachers were African American, 43 were Euro-American, 11 were Hispanic, 2 were of other ethnicities, and 5 did not report ethnicity. Lead teachers also reported their education level. Four lead teachers had graduate-level degrees, 30 had received a 4-year college degree, 56 had received a 2-year college degree, 41 had received high school diplomas, and 1 did not report education level.

Procedure

For this study, 132 teachers completed questionnaires at three time points during the school years of 2006 and 2007: mid-fall, winter, and late spring. In a few cases, there was a change in the lead teacher over the course of the academic year; therefore, there are more teachers than individual classrooms. In addition, 632 (332 Texas) parents completed questionnaires at one time (fall to winter). Behavioral assessments of effortful control were conducted in the preschools by teams of experimenters consisting of both university personnel and staff members drawn from the community who were trained by expert staff. Because of the large percentage of Hispanic children, bilingual experimenters who spoke Spanish were available as needed. Parents reported in the consent packet whether their children had exposure to Spanish. If parents indicated yes, they received a follow-up phone call and were asked about the language spoken at home. Assessments were conducted in Spanish for children whose parents indicated that the child used Spanish more than 50% of the time. At T1, 52% of the Hispanic children ($n = 106$) were assessed fully or partially in Spanish. Instruments were translated and back-translated if used for an assessment conducted in Spanish.

The intervention program involved five conditions. In addition to a control group, there were two treatment groups that received an explicit regulation curriculum with elements targeting socioemotional outcomes, and two treatment groups that received an implicit curriculum that used professional development and general guidance for teachers (Lonigan, Phillips, Clancy-Menchetti, Klein, & Landry, 2009). Because of our focus on socioemotional variables, we combined groups into three categories: control, regulation curriculum, and no regulation curriculum. Because the efficacy of the intervention was not a focus of the current study, we did not examine intervention treatment effects in relation to the outcome variables for this study. Rather, treatment group was considered a control variable and was included only when significant.

In most cases, children were administered the behavioral assessments in one videotaped session and in the same order. For each behavioral assessment, there was a main coder and a reliability coder trained by graduate students (with the input of faculty) who coded data from videotapes. Coders underwent training together until they reached acceptable levels of agreement. Main coders were responsible for coding 100% of the data, and reliability coders scored approximately 25% of the data independently. Reliability was assessed by calculating intraclass correlation coefficients (ICCs) on the overlapping coded data.

Missing Data

To assess whether ethnicity and sex were related to missing data, we conducted three one-factor multivariate analyses of variance (MANOVAs) to predict missingness on the study variables. In the first MANOVA, gender was used as a predictor for the entire sample of missing data. In the next MANOVAs, ethnicity was used as a predictor of missing data in separate runs by site (site differences could be confounded with ethnic differences) of missing data. The MANOVAs for gender and ethnicity in Florida were not significant. The MANOVA for ethnicity in Texas was significant, $F(3, 401) = 2.68$, $p < .05$. Follow-up analyses showed that African Americans were more likely to be missing parent-reported effortful control data. A follow-up analysis of variance showed that there were no mean-level differences in parent-rated effortful control across ethnic groups on this measure within Texas, suggesting that ethnicity was not related to the values of the missing data. In addition, children with parental data were compared to children without parental data at T1 on all study variables. There were no significant differences.

Measures

Reported effortful control. At T1 the primary caregiver, usually the mother, and teachers reported on two scales from the Children's Behavior Questionnaire (Rothbart, Ahadi, Hersey, & Fisher, 2001). Although the Children's Behavior Questionnaire was created as a parent-report measure of temperament, it has been used with teachers in numerous studies, and good internal consistency has been found using teacher-reported data (Eisenberg, Fabes, Guthrie, & Murphy, 1996; Eisenberg et al., 2001, 2009). In addition, parents' and teachers' reports show correlational stability over time (Murphy, Eisenberg, Fabes, Shepard, & Guthrie, 1999), and teachers' reports tend to correlate positively with behavioral measures of effortful control (Eisenberg, Fabes, Guthrie, & Reiser, 2000; Eisenberg et al., 2010; Spinrad et al., 2007). Adults responded to a 14-item attention-focusing scale (e.g., "When building or putting something together, becomes very involved in what s/he's doing, and works for long periods"; teacher $\alpha = .86$, parent $\alpha = .76$) and a 13-item inhibitory control scale (e.g., "Can wait before entering into new activities if s/he is asked to"; teacher $\alpha = .86$, parent $\alpha = .76$). Items were rated on a 7-point scale ($1 = never$, $7 = always$). The two scales were highly correlated, $rs(630, 802) = .68$ and $.82$, $ps < .001$, for mothers and teachers, respectively, and were averaged to create a composite for each reporter.

Observed effortful control. Two tasks were used to assess effortful control. First, the *knock tap* task of executive functioning was used. For this task, the experimenter either tapped the table with an open, flat hand or knocked with a closed fist (Luria, 1966; Perner & Lang, 2000). During the first eight trials, the child was instructed to imitate the experimenter. When the experimenter tapped the child also tapped, and when the experimenter knocked the child also knocked. After the imitation trials, the child was instructed to reverse his or her actions and knock when the experimenter tapped or tap when the experimenter knocked. The proportion of correct trials during the reversed trials was used (ICC = .99).

Second, the *gift wrap* procedure was used (Kochanska et al., 2000). Children were instructed to remain seated, face forward, and not peek while the experimenter noisily wrapped a gift behind the child. A latency to peek score was created by calculating the number of seconds elapsed from when the experimenter finished the instructions and began wrapping the gift to the child's first attempt to peek or the end of the minute, depending on which came first. Latency scores were divided by 60 to calculate a score representative of the proportion of the 1-min maximum (ICC = .96).

Teacher–child relationship. At T2, the quality of the teacher–child relationship was assessed using the Student–Teacher Relationship Scale (Pianta, 2001). Because of time constraints and the large number of participants, a shortened version of the original 28-item Student–Teacher Relationship Scale was used. The shortened version has been used in other large-scale investigations such as the National Institute of Child Health and Human Development Study of Early Child Care (see Pianta & Stuhlman, 2004). This measure was designed to assess teachers' perceptions of their relationships with students. Teachers rated how accurately each statement described their relationship with a specific child ($1 = $ *definitely does not apply*, $5 = $ *definitely applies*). Scores for two subscales were created: an 8-item (the original scale includes 11 items) closeness scale (e.g., "I share an affectionate, warm relationship with this child"; $\alpha = .80$) and a 7-item (the original scale includes 12 items) conflict scale (e.g., "This child and I always seem to be struggling with each other"; $\alpha = .87$). Higher scores on the closeness subscale and lower scores on the conflict subscale indicate more positive teacher–child relationship quality.

School attitudes. At T3, teachers and students reported on children's liking and avoidance of school on the School Liking and Avoidance Questionnaire (Ladd & Price, 1987). Teacher rated items on a 5-point Likert-type scale ($1 = $ *almost never*, $5 = $ *almost always*; e.g., "Makes up reasons to go home from school"). Two subscale scores were created: a 6-item school avoidance scale ($\alpha = .85$) and a 7-item school liking scale ($\alpha = .88$). A child-report version of this measure has been used with young children soon after entering kindergarten and has demonstrated good reliability and convergent validity (Ladd et al., 2000). Students rated items that were read by an experimenter. Students were instructed to answer questions with "no," "sometimes," or "yes" ($1 = no$, $2 = sometimes$, $3 = yes$). Practice items were used until it was clear the child understood how to use the answers correctly. The school avoidance subscale for students consisted of five items (e.g., "Do you ask your Mommy or Daddy to let you stay home from school?"; $\alpha = .63$), and the school liking subscale consisted of nine items (e.g., "Are you happy when you're at school?"; $\alpha = .84$). For both teachers and students, average school avoidance scores were subtracted from average school liking scores to create one difference score for each reporter, such that higher scores reflect more positive attitudes toward school. Teacher- and student-reported school attitude scores were positively correlated, $r(827) = .61, p < .001$.

RESULTS

Descriptive statistics are presented in Table 1. In tests of sex differences, parents and teachers rated girls higher than boys on effortful control, and girls scored higher than boys on effortful control during the observed gift wrap task. In addition, teachers reported more closeness, less conflict, and greater school liking for girls than for boys (see Table 1).

Analyses of variance were also conducted to examine ethnic differences among Euro-Americans (EA), African Americans (AA), and Hispanics using Tukey adjustment post hoc tests to ensure that a .05 Type I error rate was maintained. There were significant differences on T1 teacher-reported effortful control, $F(2, 772) = 3.04, p < .05$. Teachers reported that Hispanic students had higher levels of effortful control ($M = 4.63$) than did AA students ($M = 4.42$). EA students did not differ from the other groups ($M = 4.51$). On the behavioral measures, EA students had higher scores on the gift wrap task ($M = 0.70$) compared to Hispanics ($M = 0.51$) and

TABLE 1
Means and Standard Deviations for Study Variables

Variable	Total		Boys		Girls	
	M	SD	M	SD	M	SD
Teacher EC	4.49[a]	.94	4.27	.90	4.69	.92
Parent EC	4.77[b]	.76	4.61	.74	4.91	.75
Knock tap	0.59	.36	0.56	.36	0.61	.35
Gift wrap	0.57[c]	.41	0.51	.41	0.63	.41
Teacher closeness	4.38[d]	.56	4.29	.57	4.45	.54
Teacher conflict	1.81[e]	.83	1.94	.86	1.70	.78
Teacher avoidance	1.41	.56	1.43	.57	1.40	.55
Student avoidance	2.43	.53	2.47	.51	2.40	.55
Student liking	2.53	.53	2.52	.55	2.55	.52
Teacher liking	4.42[f]	.61	4.34	.63	4.49	.59

Note. EC = effortful control.
[a]Sex difference, $t(802) = 6.54, p < .001$.
[b]Sex difference, $t(630) = 5.06, p < .001$.
[c]Sex difference, $t(785) = 4.09, p < .001$.
[d]Sex difference, $t(720) = 3.81, p < .001$.
[e]Sex difference, $t(692) = 3.88, p < .001$.
[f]Sex difference, $t(678) = 3.20, p < .01$.

AA students ($M = 0.52$), $F(2, 758) = 17.55$, $p < .001$. Teachers reported more closeness with EA students ($M = 4.46$) than AA students ($M = 4.31$), $F(2, 693) = 4.86$, $p < .01$. Teachers' reports of closeness with Hispanic students did not differ from those for other groups ($M = 4.41$). Teachers reported less conflict with Hispanic students ($M = 1.57$) than EA students ($M = 1.81$) and AA students ($M = 1.94$), $F(2, 691) = 12.37$, $p < .001$. EA students reported less school liking at T3 ($M = 2.44$) than Hispanic students ($M = 2.58$) and AA students ($M = 2.55$), $F(2, 707) = 3.70$, $p < .05$. EA students reported less school avoidance at T3 ($M = 2.35$) than Hispanic students ($M = 2.54$) and AA students ($M = 2.42$), $F(2, 707) = 6.19$, $p < .01$. Based on these findings, we controlled for sex and ethnicity in structural equation models.

Relations Within Constructs

Correlations among the study variables are presented in Table 2. Teachers' and parents' reports of effortful control were positively related to each other and to observed measures of effortful control. Teacher-reported conflict was negatively correlated with closeness. School avoidance and liking were significantly negatively correlated with each other within reporters. In addition, teachers' reports of school avoidance and liking were significantly correlated in the expected directions with students' reports. These patterns of correlations suggested that latent constructs could be created in structural equation modeling.

Relations Across Constructs

Reported effortful control was positively related to teacher–child closeness and school liking and negatively related to conflict and teacher-reported school avoidance (see Table 2). Parent-reported effortful control was marginally negatively related to student-reported avoidance. Teacher-reported effortful control was not related to students' reports of avoidance. Closeness was significantly related to teacher-reported avoidance and liking and marginally correlated with student-reported liking and avoidance in the expected directions. Conflict was negatively related to teacher- and student-reported school liking, positively related to teacher-reported school avoidance, and marginally positively related to student-reported school avoidance.

Measurement Model

Before testing structural equation models, we computed a measurement model using confirmatory factor analysis to test whether latent variables could be created and observed variables related to one another in expected

TABLE 2
Correlations Among the Study Variables

Variable	1	2	3	4	5	6	7	8	9	10
1. T effortful control T1	—	.28***	.18***	.28***	.28***	−.44***	−.22***	−.05	.11**	.32***
2. P effortful control T1		—	.11**	.18***	.11**	−.24***	−.18***	−.07†	.11**	.21***
3. Knock tap T1			—	.26***	.05	−.07†	−.08*	−.08*	.01	.09*
4. Gift wrap T1				—	.11**	−.17***	−.09*	−.07†	.06	.12**
5. T closeness T2					—	−.38***	−.14***	−.06†	.06†	.32***
6. T conflict T2						—	.30***	.07†	−.09*	−.41***
7. T school avoidance T3							—	.09*	−.10*	−.75***
8. S school avoidance T3								—	−.19***	−.08*
9. S school liking T3									—	.08*
10. T school liking T3										—

Note. T = teacher report; T1 = Time 1; P = parent report; T2 = Time 2; T3 = Time 3; S = student report.
†*p* < .10. **p* < .05. ***p* < .01. ****p* < .001.

ways. All models, including confirmatory factor analysis, used standard errors and fit statistics that accounted for the nested data structure (MacKinnon, 2008). The measurement model included eight measured variables on three latent constructs: effortful control, teacher–child relationship quality, and school attitudes. There were four indicators for effortful control: both parent- and teacher-reported effortful control composites (an average of attention focusing and inhibitory control), proportion of correct responses during the knock tap task, and latency to peek during the gift wrap task (in seconds). Teacher-reported closeness and conflict were indicators of teacher–child relationship quality. The two indicators of school attitudes were teacher- and student-reported positive school attitudes. We allowed latent factors and errors of study variables to covary as indicated by modification indices. In order to account for missing data, we tested models using Mplus Version 5.2 (Muthén & Muthén, 2007), which uses full information maximum likelihood estimation. This method produces unbiased parameter estimates when data are missing at random (Schafer & Graham, 2002). Because the significance of the chi-square statistic is affected by sample size (Hu & Bentler, 1999; Kline, 1998), model fit was assessed using three alternative fit indices: the comparative fit index (CFI), the root mean square error of approximation (RMSEA), and the standardized root-mean-square residual (SRMR). CFI values greater than .90 and SRMR values less than .08 indicate an adequate fit (Kelloway, 1998). Values less than .05 for the RMSEA indicate a good fit, and values between .05 and .08 are considered acceptable (Browne & Cudeck, 1993).

The measurement model initially had adequate fit: CFI = .95, RMSEA = .04 (90% confidence interval [CI] = .02, .06), SRMR = .03. Modification indices, however, showed that the model fit could be improved by estimating a covariance between the error terms of observed effortful control on the knock tap task and the gift wrap task. The revised model had a good fit to the data: CFI = 1.00, RMSEA = .000 (90% CI = .00, .03), SRMR = .02. Model-estimated loadings of all indicator variables were significant in the expected directions. Relations among the latent constructs were in the expected directions. T1 effortful control was positively correlated with T2 teacher–child relationship quality ($r = .73$, $p < .001$) and positively correlated with T3 positive school attitudes ($r = .65$, $p < .001$). Teacher–child relationship quality at T2 was also positively related to school positive school attitudes ($r = .80$, $p < .001$).

Structural Equation Model

After assessing the measurement model, we added paths among the latent factors in order to address the proposed research questions, and standard errors and fit statistics adjusted for nested data were used. The model included direct paths from T1 effortful control to T2 teacher–child relationship quality and from T2 teacher–child relationship to T3 school attitudes. The same covariance between errors that were estimated in the measurement model were estimated in the structural model. Sex and ethnicity were included as covariates in the model. Ethnicity was dummy coded, with EA status as the reference group. Intervention status was also included as a covariate with direct paths to each factor estimated.

This model had an adequate fit to the data: CFI = .93, RMSEA = .03 (90% CI = .02, 04), SRMR = .04. Model-estimated loadings of the indicator variables displayed in Table 3 were significant in the expected directions. As shown in Figure 1, the significant negative path from child sex to effortful control indicated that boys had lower levels of effortful control at T1. Based on the significant paths from the ethnicity variables to the latent constructs, Hispanic students had more positive relationships with teachers than EA students. Intervention status was not related to any of the latent constructs. Results from the structural equation model were consistent with our hypotheses: Effortful control was positively related to more positive teacher–child relationship quality, and teacher–child relationship quality was related to more positive school attitudes. A formal test of mediation was conducted with the CI method to address the nonnormal distribution of the indirect effects (MacKinnon, Lockwood, Hoffman, West, & Sheets, 2002). A CI that does not include zero indicates significant mediation. The 95% CI based on unstandardized estimates was .11 and .90, providing evidence that teacher–child relationship quality significantly mediated the

TABLE 3
Standardized and Unstandardized Loadings for Latent Constructs

Construct	Unstandardized	Standardized
Effortful control, Time 1		
Teacher reported	1.00	.75
Parent reported	0.44***	.40
Knock tap score	0.11***	.22
Gift wrap latency	0.22***	.37
Teacher–child relationship, Time 2		
Teacher-reported closeness	1.00	.50
Teacher-reported conflict	−2.25***	−.76
School avoidance, Time 3		
Teacher-reported attitudes	1.00	.61
Student-reported attitudes	0.24**	.20

$**p < .01.$ $***p < .001.$

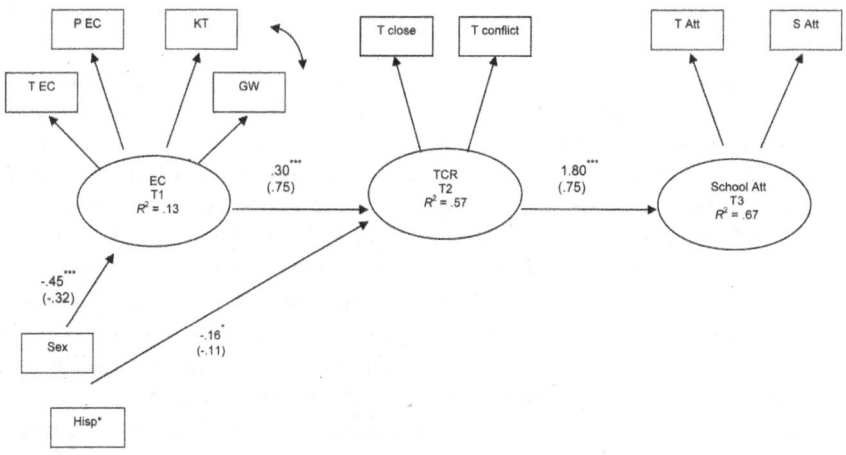

FIGURE 1 Final SEM model with standardized and unstandardized estimates (in parentheses). Asterisks indicate that a variable is dummy coded, with Euro-Americans as the reference group for ethnicity. Variables are as follows: Hispanic (Hisp; Hispanic = 1, other ethnicity = 0). Only significant paths are shown. T = teacher; P = parent; EC = effortful control; KT = knock tap proportion correct score; GW = gift wrap latency to peek score; TCR = teacher–child relationship; close = closeness; S = student; Att = attitudes; T1 = Time 1; T2 = Time 2; T3 = Time 3. *$p < .05$. ***$p < .001$.

association between effortful control and children's negative school attitudes.

DISCUSSION

Researchers have argued that children's attitudes toward school, a component of emotional engagement in school, are an important antecedent of children's academic achievement (Fredricks et al., 2004). Thus, researchers have sought to identify which factors, both dispositional and contextual, facilitate children's positive feelings about school. A lack of positive attitudes toward school early in education may be especially problematic for children already at risk for low school success. Relatively few studies have examined predictors of school attitudes in preschool, especially in children from low-income and ethnic minority families. In addition, there has been little work on the mechanisms by which effortful control may influence school attitudes. Our findings provide evidence that the relation between effortful control and children's school attitudes is mediated by the quality of the teacher–child relationship, even after the nested structure of the data is accounted for and the effects of sex, ethnicity, and intervention status are controlled.

The results of this study provide support for the fact that child characteristics predict the quality of children's relationships with their teachers (Myers & Pianta, 2008; Pianta, 1999). Children who had higher levels of effortful control developed closer, less conflictual relationships with their teachers. These findings are consistent with research that has investigated direct relations among these constructs in older children (Birch & Ladd, 1997). It is thought that children with high effortful control are better able to attend to tasks and follow directions than their less regulated peers— behaviors that are of high priority to teachers in the preschool classroom. Thus, it is likely that well-regulated children are viewed positively and engage in pleasant interactions with teachers. Teachers are also more likely to offer encouraging feedback to, and engage in more positive interaction time with, well-regulated children; such exchanges afford more opportunities to form a warm, supportive teacher–child relationship and decrease the likelihood of conflict. Less-regulated children potentially engage with teachers mainly for disciplinary reasons, are singled out for poor behavior, or interact for purely instructional reasons, leading to relationships characterized by conflict and less closeness.

The findings also provide support for the notion that teacher–child relationship quality predicts school attitudes in preschool. Within the contexts of high-quality relationships, children likely feel more confident in their abilities to do well in school, increasing their motivation to participate in activities and contributing to positive school attitudes. Children who experience low-quality relationships with important school figures such as teachers may develop lower levels of school liking and higher levels of school avoidance because school is perceived to be an aversive, unsupportive environment.

In this study, effortful control measured at the beginning of the school year longitudinally predicted attitudes toward school at the end of the school year. Well-regulated children likely have the attentional skills and behavioral control to participate in and stay focused on classroom activities (Coplan, Barber, & Lagacé-Séguin, 1999) as well as to interact competently with peers (Fabes, Hanish, Martin, & Eisenberg, 2002). Such experiences likely contribute to the formation of children's positive perceptions of school as an enjoyable environment. In contrast, children low in effortful control may have difficulty regulating behavior and may be at risk for poor peer relationships (Deater-Deckard, 2001). These less socially competent children may develop the perception of school as a frustrating, hostile, and lonely place, a perception that inhibits the formation of positive school attitudes. Findings from our study further add to the literature by providing evidence that effortful control is associated with affective processes such as sentiments toward school in preschool, as well as academic competence (Fabes, Martin, Hanish, Anders, & Madden-Derdich, 2003; Valiente et al., 2007).

Although direct relations of effortful control and teacher–child relationship quality to school attitudes were examined, another goal of this study was to determine whether teacher–child relationship quality serves as a mediator of this relation and to begin to elucidate the mechanisms by which children's effortful control contributes to positive feelings in school. Indeed, we found that teacher–child relationship quality mediated the relation of effortful control to school attitudes. Thus, this study provides evidence that children's effortful control may be linked to increased school success through children's social relationships.

There probably are multiple mechanisms by which effortful control influences children's attitudes toward school. Future research should also investigate other potential mediators. For example, it is likely that children's social competence also plays an important role in the relations between effortful control and children's attitudes. Effortful control has been consistently related to higher social competence in young children (Eisenberg et al., 1997, 2000; Spinrad et al., 2007), including popularity (Eisenberg et al., 2003; Spinrad et al., 2006) and low levels of problem behaviors (Kochanska, Barry, Aksan, & Boldt, 2008; Rydell, Berlin, & Bohlin, 2003). Thus, children's social competence may also mediate the relations between their effortful control and school attitudes and perhaps effortful control and the teacher–child relationship; however, to our knowledge, these relations have not yet been examined.

Although not the main focus of this study, it should be noted that there were sex and ethnic differences for some variables. These differences are consistent with other studies that have demonstrated risk in minority samples (e.g., Aikens, Coleman, & Barbarin, 2008; Loukas & Roalson, 2006). Ethnic differences in regulation may be due in part to ethnic differences in negative emotionality (e.g., Ispa et al., 2004) as well as partially accounted for by differences in socioeconomic status and the risks associated with such disparities. However, it is also important to note that Sulik et al. (2010), using the same sample, demonstrated measurement equivalence in effortful control across sex and ethnicity. Thus, although some mean differences exist, the constructs appear to function in the same way.

This study has several strengths. Measures of effortful control at T1 and school attitudes at T3 included data from two different reporters (i.e., parents and teachers, and teachers and students) to minimize common source variance. Observational assessments of children's regulation that have been found to be valid and reliable were also used as indicators of effortful control. Furthermore, the sample for this study was ethnically diverse, with large percentages of Hispanic and African American children, which increases the generalizability of our findings. In addition, these relations were tested longitudinally over the course of a school year. Finally, our focus on the mechanisms that underlie the relations between children's regulation and school attitudes in preschool is a strength. Identifying direct as well as indirect relations among factors associated with academic achievement is important, particularly for ethnic minority students, who have a greater likelihood of not graduating from high school (Kaufman, Alt, & Chapman, 2004; U.S. Census Bureau, 2004).

Limitations and Future Directions

Despite these strengths, this study does have limitations. Because of the design of the larger project, measures of all of the variables could not be attained at every wave. Therefore, the stability of all constructs could not be taken into account. In future investigations, it would be useful to test whether these relations remain after the stability of all of the constructs over time is controlled. Work that also examines the transactional nature of these variables will be important. An assumption of transactional models is that development at the individual level is affected by the constant interplay between the individual and context (Sameroff & MacKenzie, 2003; Sutherland & Oswald, 2005). There is preliminary evidence to suggest that there are bidirectional effects between children's behavior and teacher–child relationship quality. Using a longitudinal research design, Doumen and colleagues (2008) found that children's aggression at the beginning of kindergarten predicted more teacher–child conflict during the middle of the school year, which in turn was predictive of more aggression by the end of the school year, even after across- and within-time associations were controlled. Another avenue of research to pursue is examining whether these bidirectional effects are observed for effortful control and teacher–child relationship quality in preschool children.

Although this study used data from three different time points during the school year, work that examines these relations over several years will be important to assess whether children's attitudes in preschool are related to other forms of school engagement and academic achievement in elementary school. Ladd and Dinella (2009) found that engagement, including school liking and avoidance, was moderately rather than highly stable throughout the primary grades and that there was variability in children's consistency in school engagement. Some children had early patterns of school engagement that continued to stabilize over time, whereas other children demonstrated greater levels of variability in school engagement over time. Our findings suggest that children's relationships with teachers may explain why some children experience changes in attitudes toward school over time. Given that school attitudes do change over time for some children, those who are at risk for having stable low school engagement across multiple years may benefit from a warm, close relationship with a teacher, even if this occurs relatively late in the elementary school years.

Applied Implications

This work has important implications for researchers and policymakers seeking to foster more positive attitudes about school in young children, especially those who are at risk for low academic achievement. Children's regulation and relationships within the classroom play important roles in their formation of attitudes toward school and, thus, their later academic success. Findings from this study suggest that children's attitudes toward school may be improved by focusing on increasing children's self-regulatory abilities and the quality of teacher–child relationships. With increased concerns about children's school readiness there has been a focus on improving academic skills and the quality of teachers' instructional styles. Our findings suggest that children's socioemotional skills also play an important role in children's school adaptations. Consistent with prior research, policymakers and educators should implement training programs that educate teachers about the importance of regulatory skills in preschool and fostering positive relationships with students. Furthermore, teachers should be aware that early conflictual relationships may have long-term consequences for how children feel about school and that conflict may be more likely with some children (e.g., less regulated children). Continued research on the associations of children's regulation, as well as other dispositional characteristics, to relational processes in the classroom context is warranted.

ACKNOWLEDGMENT

This research was supported by a grant to Nancy Eisenberg (principal investigator), Tracy Spinrad, Carlos Valiente, and the School Readiness Consortium from the National Institute of Child Health and Human Development.

REFERENCES

Aikens, N. L., Coleman, C. P., & Barbarin, O. A. (2008). Ethnic differences in the effects of parental depression on preschool children's socioemotional functioning. *Social Development, 17,* 137–160.

Alexander, K. L., & Entwisle, D. R. (1988). Achievement in the first 2 years of school: Patterns and processes. *Monographs of the Society for Research in Child Development, 53*(2), 157.
Birch, S., & Ladd, G. (1996). *Interpersonal relationships in the school environment and children's early school adjustment: The role of teachers and peers.* New York, NY: Cambridge University Press.
Birch, S. H., & Ladd, G. W. (1997). The teacher–child relationship and children's early school adjustment. *Journal of School Psychology, 35*(1), 61–79.
Blair, C., & Razza, R. P. (2007). Relating effortful control, executive function, and false belief understanding to emerging math and literacy ability in kindergarten. *Child Development, 78,* 647–663.
Brody, G. H., & Ge, X. (2001). Linking parenting processes and self-regulation to psychological functioning and alcohol use during early adolescence. *Journal of Family Psychology, 15*(1), 82–94. doi:10.1037/0893-3200.15.1.82
Browne, M. W., & Cudeck, R. (1993). Alternative ways of assessing model fit. In K. A. Bollen & S. J. Long (Eds.), *Testing structural equation models.* Newbury Park, CA: Sage.
Buhs, E. S., & Ladd, G. W. (2001). Peer rejection as antecedent of young children's school adjustment: An examination of mediating processes. *Developmental Psychology, 37,* 550–560. doi:10.1037/0012-1649.37.4.550
Children's Defense Fund. (1993). *Progress and peril: Black children in America.* Washington, DC: Author.
Coplan, R. J., Barber, A. M., & Lagacé-Séguin, D. G. (1999). The role of child temperament as a predictor of early literacy and numeracy skills in preschoolers. *Early Childhood Research Quarterly, 14,* 537–553. doi:10.1016/S0885-2006(99)00025-3
Crosnoe, R., Johnson, M. K., & Elder, G. H., Jr. (2004). School size and the interpersonal side of education: An examination of race/ethnicity and organizational context. *Social Science Quarterly, 85,* 1259–1274. doi:10.1111/j.0038-4941.2004.00275.x
Deater-Deckard, K. (2001). Annotation: Recent research examining the role of peer relationships in the development of psychopathology. *Journal of Child Psychology and Psychiatry, 42,* 565–579. doi:10.1111/1469-7610.00753
Doumen, S., Verschueren, K., Buyse, E., Germeijs, V., Luyckx, K., & Soenens, B. (2008). Reciprocal relations between teacher-child conflict and aggressive behavior in kindergarten: A three-wave longitudinal study. *Journal of Clinical Child and Adolescent Psychology, 37,* 588–599. doi:10.1080/15374410802148079
Eisenberg, N., Fabes, R. A., Guthrie, I. K., & Murphy, B. C. (1996). The relations and emotionality to problem behavior in elementary school children. *Development and Psychopathology, 8*(1), 141–162.
Eisenberg, N., Fabes, R. A., Guthrie, I. K., & Reiser, M. (2000). Dispositional emotionality and regulation: Their role in predicting quality of social functioning. *Journal of Personality and Social Psychology, 78,* 136–157.
Eisenberg, N., Gershoff, E. T., Fabes, R. A., Shepard, S. A., Cumberland, A. J., Losoya, S. H., ... Murphy, B. C. (2001). Mothers' emotional expressivity and children's behavior problems and social competence: Mediation through children's regulation. *Developmental Psychology, 37,* 475–490. doi:10.1037/0012-1649.37.4.475
Eisenberg, N., Guthrie, I. K., Fabes, R. A., Reiser, M., Murphy, B. C., Holgren, R., ... Losoya, S. (1997). The relations of regulation and emotionality to resiliency and competent social functioning in elementary school children. *Child Development, 68,* 295–311.
Eisenberg, N., Valiente, C., Fabes, R. A., Smith, C. L., Reiser, M., Shepard, S. A., ... Cumberland, A. J. (2003). The relations of effortful control and ego control to children's resiliency and social functioning. *Developmental Psychology, 39,* 761–776. doi:10.1037/0012-1649.39.4.761

Eisenberg, N., Valiente, C., Spinrad, T. L., Cumberland, A., Liew, J., Reiser, M., ... Lasoya, S. H. (2009). Longitudinal relations of children's effortful control, impulsivity, and negative emotionality to their externalizing, internalizing, and co-occurring behavior problems. *Developmental Psychology, 45*, 988–1008.

Eisenberg, N., Vidmar, M., Spinrad, T. L., Eggum, N. D., Edwards, A., Gaertner, B., & Kupfer, A. (2010). Mothers' teaching strategies and children's effortful control: A longitudinal study. *Developmental Psychology, 46*, 1294–1308.

Entwisle, D., & Alexander, K. (1992). Summer setback: Race, poverty, school composition, and mathematics achievement in the first two years of school. *American Sociological Review, 57*, 72–84.

Fabes, R. A., Hanish, L. D., Martin, C. L., & Eisenberg, N. (2002). Young children's negative emotionality and social isolation: A latent growth curve analysis. *Merrill-Palmer Quarterly, 48*, 284–307. doi:10.1353/mpq.2002.0012

Fabes, R. A., Martin, C. L., Hanish, L. D., Anders, M. C., & Madden-Derdich, D. A. (2003). Early school competence: The roles of sex-segregated play and effortful control. *Developmental Psychology, 39*, 848–858.

Finn, J. D. (1989). Withdrawing from school. *Review of Educational Research, 59*(2), 77–92.

Fredricks, J. A., Blumenfeld, P. C., & Paris, A. H. (2004). School engagement: Potential of the concept, state of the evidence. *Review of Educational Research, 74*(1), 59–109. doi:10.3102/00346543074001059

Garner, P. W., & Waajid, B. (2008). The associations of emotion knowledge and teacher-child relationships to preschool children's school-related developmental competence. *Journal of Applied Developmental Psychology, 29*(2), 89–100. doi:10.1016/j.appdev.2007.12.001

Griggs, M. S., Gagnon, S. G., Huelsman, T. J., Kiddler-Ashley, P., & Ballard, M. (2009). Student-teacher relationships matter: Moderating influences between temperament and preschool social competence. *Psychology in the Schools, 46*, 553–567. doi:10.1002/pits.20397

Gutman, L. M., Sameroff, A. J., & Cole, R. (2003). Academic growth curve trajectories from 1st grade to 12th grade: Effects of multiple social risk factors and preschool child factors. *Developmental Psychology, 39*, 777–790. doi:10.1037/0012-1649.39.4.777

Hamre, B., & Pianta, R. (2001). Early teacher-child relationships and the trajectory of children's school outcomes through eighth grade. *Child Development, 72*, 625–638.

Hauser-Cram, P., Durand, T. M., & Warfield, M. E. (2007). Early feelings about school and later academic outcomes of children with special needs living in poverty. *Early Childhood Research Quarterly, 22*(2), 161–172. doi:10.1016/j.ecresq.2007.02.001

Hauser-Cram, P., Warfield, M. E., Stadler, J., & Sirin, S. R. (2006). School environments and the diverging pathways of students living in poverty. In A. C. Huston & M. N. Ripke (Eds.), *Developmental contexts in middle childhood: Bridges to adolescence and adulthood*, (pp. 198–216). New York, NY: Cambridge University Press.

Howes, C., & Matheson, C. C. (1992). School of the future: Contextual constraints on the concordance of mother-child and teacher-child relationships. *New Directions for Child and Adolescent Development, 57*, 25–90.

Hu, L., & Bentler, P. M. (1999). Cutoff criteria for fit indexes in covariance structure analysis: Conventional criteria versus new alternatives. *Structural Equation Modeling, 6*, 1–55.

Hughes, J. N., & Kwok, O. (2006). Classroom engagement mediates the effect of teacher-student on elementary students' peer acceptance: A prospective analysis. *Journal of School Psychology, 43*, 465–480.

Ispa, J. M., Fine, M. A., Halgunseth, L. C., Harper, S., Robinson, J., Boyce, L., ... Brady-Smith, C. (2004). Maternal intrusiveness, maternal warmth, and mother-toddler relationship outcomes: Variations across low-income ethnic and acculturation groups. *Child Development, 75,* 1613–1631. doi:10.1111/j.1467-8624.2004.00806.x

Kaufman, P., Alt, M. N., & Chapman, C. D. (2004). *Dropout rates in the United States: 2001* (Publication No. NCES 2005046). Washington, DC: U.S. Government Printing Office.

Kelloway, E. K. (1998). *Using LISREL for structural equation modeling: A researcher's guide.* Thousand Oaks, CA: Sage.

Keogh, B. K. (1982). Children's temperament and teachers' decisions. In R. Porter & G. M. Collins (Eds.), *Temperament differences in infants and young children* (pp. 269–285). London, England: Pitman.

Keogh, B. K. (1994). Temperament and teachers' views of teachability. In W. B. Carey & S. C. McDevitt (Eds.), *Prevention and ear intervention: Individual differences as risk factors for the mental health of children* (pp. 246–256). New York, NY: Brunner/Mazel.

Keogh, B. K. (2003). *Temperament in the classroom: Understanding individual differences.* Baltimore, MD: Brookes.

Kline, R. B. (1998). *The principles and practice of structural equation modeling.* New York, NY: Guilford Press.

Kochanska, G., Barry, R. A., Aksan, N., & Boldt, L. J. (2008). A developmental model of maternal and child contributions to disruptive conduct: The first six years. *Journal of Child Psychology and Psychiatry, 49,* 1220–1227.

Kochanska, G., & Knaack, A. (2003). Effortful control as a personality characteristic of young children: Antecedents, correlates, and consequences. *Journal of Personality, 71,* 1087–1112. doi:10.1111/1467-6494.7106008

Kochanska, G., Murray, K. T., & Harlan, E. T. (2000). Effortful control in early childhood: Continuity and change, antecedents, and implications for social development. *Developmental Psychology, 36,* 220–232.

Ladd, G. W. (1996). Shifting ecologies during the 5 to 7 year period: Predicting children's adjustment during the transition to grade school. In A. J. Sameroff & M. M. Haith (Eds.), *Reason and responsibility: The passage through childhood* (pp. 363–386). Chicago, IL: University of Chicago Press.

Ladd, G. W., Birch, S. H., & Buhs, E. S. (1999). Children's social and scholastic lives in kindergarten: Related spheres of influence? *Child Development, 70,* 1373–1400.

Ladd, G. W., Buhs, E. S., & Seid, M. (2000). Children's initial sentiments about kindergarten: Is school liking an antecedent of early classroom participation and achievement? *Merrill-Palmer Quarterly, 46,* 255–279.

Ladd, G. W., & Burgess, K. B. (2001). Do relational risks and protective factors moderate the linkages between childhood aggression and early psychological and school adjustment? *Child Development, 72,* 1579–1601.

Ladd, G. W., & Dinella, L. M. (2009). Continuity and change in early school engagement: Predictive of children's achievement trajectories from first to eighth grade? *Journal of Educational Psychology, 101,* 190–206. doi:10.1037/a0013153

Ladd, G. W., & Price, J. M. (1987). Predicting children's social and school adjustment following the transition from preschool to kindergarten. *Child Development, 58,* 1168–1189.

Liew, J., Chen, Q., & Hughes, J. N. (2010). Child effortful control, teacher–student relationships, and achievement in academically at-risk children: Additive and interactive effects. *Early Childhood Research Quarterly, 25,* 51–64. doi:10.1016/j.ecresq.2009.07.005

Lonigan, C., Phillips, B. M., Clancy-Menchetti, J., Klein, A. S., & Landry, S. H. (2009, April). *Effects of a comprehensive preschool curriculum: Overall impacts and relative impacts of explicit versus implicit socio-emotional variations.* Paper presented at the 2009 Biennial Meeting of the Society for Research in Child Development, Denver, CO.

Loukas, A., & Roalson, L. A. (2006). Family environment, effortful control, and adjustment among European American and Latino early adolescents. *Journal of Early Adolescence, 26,* 432–455.

Luria, A. (1966). *Higher cortical functions in man.* New York, NY: Basic Books.

MacKinnon, D. P. (2008). *Introduction to statistical mediation analysis.* New York, NY: Taylor & Francis Group.

MacKinnon, D. P., Lockwood, C. M., Hoffman, J. M., West, S. G., & Sheets, V. (2002). A comparison of methods to test mediation and other intervening variable effects. *Psychological Methods, 7,* 83–104.

McClelland, M. M., Cameron, C. E., Connor, C. M., Farris, C. L., Jewkes, A. M., & Morrison, F. J. (2007). Links between behavioral regulation and preschoolers' literacy, vocabulary, and math skills. *Developmental Psychology, 43,* 947–959.

Murphy, B. C., Eisenberg, N., Fabes, R. A., Shepard, S., & Guthrie, I. K. (1999). Consistency and change in children's emotionality and regulation: A longitudinal study. *Merrill-Palmer Quarterly, 46,* 413–444.

Murray, K. T., & Kochanska, G. (2002). Effortful control: Factor structure and relation to externalizing and internalizing behaviors. *Journal of Abnormal Child Psychology, 30,* 503–514. doi:10.1023/A:1019821031523

Muthén, L. K., & Muthén, B. O. (2007). *Mplus user's guide* (5th ed.). Los Angeles, CA: Author.

Myers, S. S., & Morris, A. S. (2009). Examining associations between effortful control and teacher-child relationships in relation to head start socioemotional adjustment. *Early Education & Development, 20,* 756–774.

Myers, S. S., & Pianta, R. C. (2008). Developmental commentary: Individual and contextual influences on student-teacher relationships and children's early problem behaviors. *Journal of Clinical Child and Adolescent Psychology, 37,* 600–608.

National Education Goals Panel. (1997). *Building a nation of learners.* Washington, DC: Author.

Perner, J., & Lang, B. (2000). Theory of mind and executive function: Is there a developmental relationship? In S. Baron-Cohen, H. Tager-Flusberg, & D. J. Cohen (Eds.), *Understanding other minds: Perspectives from developmental cognitive neuroscience* (2nd ed., pp. 150–181). New York, NY: Oxford University Press.

Pianta, R. C. (1999). *The emotional bond between children and adults.* Washington, DC: American Psychological Association. doi:10.1037/10314-004

Pianta, R. C. (2001). *Student-teacher relationship scale.* Odessa, FL: Psychological Assessment Resources, Inc.

Pianta, R., Steinberg, M. S., & Rollins, K. B. (1995). The first two years of school: Teacher-child relationships and deflections in children's classroom adjustment. *Development and Psychopathology, 7*(2), 295–312.

Pianta, R. C., & Stuhlman, M. W. (2004). Teacher-child relationships and children's success in the first years of school. *School Psychology Review, 33,* 444–458.

Rothbart, M. K., Ahadi, S. A., Hersey, K. L., & Fisher, P. (2001). Investigations of temperament at three to seven years: The Children's Behavior Questionnaire. *Child Development, 72,* 1394–1408.

Rothbart, M. K., & Bates, J. E. (2006). Temperament. In W. Damon (Series Ed.) & N. Eisenberg (Vol. Ed.), *Handbook of child psychology: Vol. 3. Social, emotional, and personality development* (6th ed., pp. 105–176). New York: Wiley.

Rudasill, K. M., & Rimm-Kaufman, S. E. (2009). Teacher–child relationship quality: The roles of child temperament and teacher–child interactions. *Early Childhood Research Quarterly, 24*(2), 107–120.

Rydell, A.-M., Berlin, L., & Bohlin, G. (2003). Emotionality, emotion regulation, and adaptation among 5- to 8-year-old children. *Emotion, 3*, 30–47.

Sameroff, A. J., & MacKenzie, M. J. (2003). Research strategies for capturing transactional models of development: The limits of the possible. *Development and Psychopathology, 15*, 613–640.

Schafer, J. L., & Graham, J. W. (2002). Missing data: Our view of the state of the art. *Psychological Methods, 7*, 147–177.

Spinrad, T. L., Eisenberg, N., Cumberland, A., Fabes, R. A., Valiente, C., Shepard, S. A., ... Guthrie, I. K. (2006). Relation of emotion-related regulation to children's social competence: A longitudinal study. *Emotion, 6*, 498–510. doi:10.1037/1528-3542.6.3.498

Spinrad, T. L., Eisenberg, N., Gaertner, B., Popp, T., Smith, C. L., Kupfer, A., ... Hofer, C. (2007). Relations of maternal socialization and toddlers' effortful control to children's adjustment and social competence. *Developmental Psychology, 43*, 1170–1186.

Sulik, M. J., Huerta, S., Zerr, A. A., Eisenberg, N., Spinrad, T. L., Valiente, C., ... Taylor, H. (2010). The factor structure of effortful control and measurement invariance across ethnicity and sex in a high-risk sample. *Journal of Psychopathology and Behavioral Assessment, 32*(1), 8–22. doi:10.1007/s10862-009-9164-y

Sutherland, K. S., & Oswald, D. P. (2005). The relationship between teacher and student behavior in classrooms for students with emotional and behavioral disorders: Transactional processes. *Journal of Child and Family Studies, 14*, 1–14.

U.S. Census Bureau. (2004). *U.S. interim projections by age, sex, race, and Hispanic origin.* Washington, DC: U.S. Government Printing Office.

Valiente, C., Lemery-Chalfant, K., & Castro, K. S. (2007). Children's effortful control and academic competence: Mediation through school liking. *Merrill-Palmer Quarterly, 53*(1), 1–25.

Valiente, C., Lemery-Chalfant, K., Swanson, J., & Reiser, M. (2008). Prediction of children's academic competence from their effortful control, relationships, and classroom participation. *Journal of Educational Psychology, 100*, 67–77.

The Influence of Demographic Risk Factors on Children's Behavioral Regulation in Prekindergarten and Kindergarten

Shannon B. Wanless

Megan M. McClelland, Shauna L. Tominey, and Alan C. Acock

Research Findings: The present study examined the role of demographic risk factors in the development of children's behavioral regulation. We investigated whether being from a low-income family and being an English language learner (ELL) predicted behavioral regulation between prekindergarten and kindergarten. Results indicated that children from low-income families began prekindergarten with significantly lower behavioral regulation than their more economically advantaged peers. Furthermore, English-speaking children from low-income families exhibited a faster rate of behavioral regulation growth than low-income ELLs. English-speaking children from low-income families narrowed the gap with their more economically advantaged English-speaking peers by the end of kindergarten, but ELLs from low-income families did not. *Practice or Policy:* Discussion focuses on the importance of understanding the effects of being an ELL and being from a low-income family for the demands of formal schooling.

Academic achievement gaps that are present at preschool entry have been found to persist, and in some cases to widen, across the transition to formal schooling (Alexander & Entwisle, 1988; Heckman, 2006). Demographic risk factors, such as low family income and being an English language learner (ELL), have been linked to these differences (Duncan & Brooks-Gunn, 1997; Reardon & Galindo, 2006a). In particular, having an accumulation of risk factors has been related to significant academic deficits (Gutman, Sameroff, & Cole, 2003). Although it is important to understand how demographic factors influence early academic skills, it is also critical to consider how these factors relate to behavioral regulation (including working memory, attention, and inhibitory control), which is a key component of school readiness (Lewit & Baker, 1995; National Scientific Council on the Developing Child, 2004). In fact, early behavioral regulation has been found to predict long-term school success as measured by academic achievement and high school and college graduation rates (Blair, 2002; Cooper & Farran, 1988; McClelland, Acock, & Morrison, 2006; McClelland, Piccinin, & Stallings, 2009; Vitaro, Brendgen, Larose, & Tremblay, 2005).

Despite increasing evidence supporting the importance of these skills for school success, few studies have examined how demographic risk factors are related to behavioral regulation development. The present study examined relations between demographic risk factors, including having a low family income and being a Spanish-speaking ELL, and behavioral regulation development between the fall of prekindergarten and the spring of kindergarten.

DEFINING BEHAVIORAL REGULATION

Although definitions vary, in the present study, *behavioral regulation* refers to the behavioral aspects of self-regulation and specifically the ability to integrate attention, working memory, and inhibitory control (McClelland, Cameron, Wanless, & Murray, 2007; Ponitz et al., 2008). *Attentional flexibility* refers to focusing on a task in the presence of distractions and flexibly switching to a new task when needed (Rothbart & Posner, 2005; Rueda, Posner, & Rothbart, 2005). Some researchers suggest that attentional flexibility is the foundation of behavioral regulation (Rueda, Rothbart, McCandliss, Saccomanno, & Posner, 2005). This skill helps children determine what information is important when receiving multiple stimuli. In the classroom, *attention* helps children listen to their teacher and stay on task. *Working memory* refers to a child's ability to remember single and multistep instructions amid distractions (Gathercole & Pickering, 2000). Within the classroom context, working memory is essential for children to understand

and remember instructions when completing a task. Finally, *inhibitory control* refers to stopping a dominant response in favor of a more adaptive behavior (Dowsett & Livesey, 2000). This skill develops particularly rapidly during early childhood (Diamond, 2002) and can be seen when a child has to clean up toys before moving to another activity.

All three of these aspects of behavioral regulation individually and collectively relate to academic skills, including vocabulary, mathematics, and literacy (Baumeister & Vohs, 2004; Blair & Razza, 2007; Dixon & Salley, 2007; Espy et al., 2004). Specifically, these skills may help children pay attention, remember instructions, and persist when working on tasks, and they have been found to significantly predict academic gains (McClelland, Ponitz, Messersmith, & Tominey, in press). Recent research also suggests that attentional flexibility, working memory, and inhibitory control may load on one factor in early childhood and that this factor is consistent across children of different socioeconomic statuses (Wiebe, Espy, & Charak, 2008).

In the present study, we focused on the integration of these skills because it is this integrated behavior that is often called upon in early learning settings. For example, children frequently use these skills in tandem when teachers give instructions, conduct large-group activities, and ask children to wait for a turn. We used a direct measure of behavioral regulation, the Head-to-Toes Task (HTT), which aims to capture this integration and has predicted academic achievement across multiple cultures (Ponitz et al., 2008; Wanless, McClelland, Acock, Chen, & Chen, in press).

THE IMPORTANCE OF EARLY BEHAVIORAL REGULATION

Accumulating research suggests that behavioral regulation is a critical area of development because it has both short- and long-term consequences for children's success. Skills learned in preschool tend to be cumulative, and children who fail to acquire these skills may be faced with increasing difficulty throughout their schooling (Entwisle & Alexander, 1993). Children with poor behavioral regulation skills are at significantly greater risk of academic difficulty in preschool and throughout elementary school (Blair & Razza, 2007; Galindo & Fuller, 2010; McClelland et al., 2006; McClelland, Morrison, & Holmes, 2000; Ponitz, McClelland, Matthews, & Morrison, 2009) and are less likely to graduate from high school and college (McClelland et al., 2009; Pagani et al., 2008; Vitaro et al., 2005). Despite the long-term relevance of behavioral regulation for school success, predictors of growth in behavioral regulation have not been comprehensively studied.

THE CONTRIBUTION OF FAMILY INCOME TO BEHAVIORAL REGULATION

Research has shown that children from economically disadvantaged backgrounds have more difficulty than their more advantaged peers on a variety of achievement, language, and school readiness assessments (Dearing, Berry, & Zaslow, 2006). In fact, the link between family income and child outcomes has been found to be especially strong for children from low-income families and for preschoolers (Turkheimer, Haley, Waldron, D'Onofrio, & Gottesman, 2003). Recent studies suggest that children from low-income families are also significantly more likely to have lower behavioral regulation in prekindergarten and kindergarten than their peers (Evans & Rosenbaum, 2008; Mezzacappa, 2004; Mistry, Benner, Biesanz, & Clark, in press; Sektnan, McClelland, Acock, & Morrison, in press). Research linking low economic status and behavioral regulation, however, has often relied on parent or teacher reports of behavioral regulation (McClelland et al., 2000; Merritt, Wanless, Ponitz, & Rimm-Kaufman, 2010). Adult reports are useful but do not always correlate to direct assessments. For example, in previous research, adult ratings of behavioral regulation and directly assessed behavioral regulation were not always significantly correlated (Mahone et al., 2002; Mahone & Hoffman, 2005; Wanless et al., 2010). This inconsistency was also found in one cross-cultural study, in which differences between cultures were found in teacher reports but not in direct observations (Jose, Huntsinger, Huntsinger, & Liaw, 2000). These researchers suggested that teacher ratings may reflect cultural expectations for children's behavior more so than direct assessments. Environmental and individual factors were also documented as having an influence on teacher ratings in work by Mashburn, Hamre, Downer, and Pianta (2006). Taken together, these studies point to the need to directly assess behavioral regulation in young children.

To explain the link between family income and children's outcomes, some researchers have proposed a cognitive stimulation model, which suggests that families with low incomes have more difficulty investing in the materials and experiences that would stimulate children's learning (Bradley et al., 1989; Chazan-Cohen et al., 2009; Haveman & Wolfe, 1994; Linver, Brooks-Gunn, & Kohen, 2002). The relation between family income and behavioral regulation may reflect the fewer opportunities to practice aspects of behavioral regulation in economically disadvantaged homes. For example, disadvantaged families may not be able to afford activity classes (e.g., dance or music classes) in which children regularly practice paying attention for long periods of time, remembering instructions, and inhibiting impulses during the class. In fact, research indicates that children in less stimulating home environments have significantly lower behavioral regulation than their peers (Howes, 1990; McClelland et al., 2000). The present study examined the relation between family income and behavioral regulation and examined how children from low-income families who were also ELLs fared in terms of early behavioral regulation.

THE CONTRIBUTION OF BEING FROM A FAMILY WITH A LOW INCOME AND BEING AN ELL TO BEHAVIORAL REGULATION

In the United States, young Hispanic children are the largest and fastest growing ethnic minority (García, 2005; Hernández, 2005). According to the most recent census data, 26% of U.S. infants are Hispanic. Moreover, 34% of these Hispanic infants live in homes in which Spanish is the primary language (López & Barrueco, 2006). This finding is similar to reports from the Early Childhood Longitudinal Study–Kindergarten data collection effort that 30% of Hispanic children at entry to kindergarten were not proficient enough in English to be assessed (National Task Force on Early Childhood Education for Hispanics, 2007). In Oregon, where data for the present study were collected, the Hispanic growth rate increased by 144% between 1990 and 2000, and current estimates predict that the Hispanic population will continue to grow at a faster rate than other minority groups (Cai, 2003).

In addition to the increasing number of Hispanic children, census data document that these children are disproportionately from families with low incomes. In 2006, approximately 29% of Hispanic children lived in poverty compared to 11% of non-Hispanic Whites (U.S. Census Bureau, 2006). Of the 30% of Hispanic children who had limited English proficiency upon entry to kindergarten, almost 75% came from families with low socioeconomic status (Reardon & Galindo, 2006b). Overall, young Hispanic ELLs experience a greater number of risk factors compared to their English-speaking counterparts and thus may be at significant risk for difficulties in school.

Despite these rapid demographic changes and the greater number of risk factors they face, there is relatively little research on the school readiness of Hispanic ELLs. The majority of research that is available focuses on academic skills, and findings suggest that limited English proficiency at kindergarten entry is significantly related to lower math and reading skills in kindergarten (Reardon & Galindo, 2006b). Although these children make steep gains in math and reading from kindergarten to fifth grade, they still have significantly lower math and reading scores than their English-speaking counterparts in fifth grade.

There is reason to believe that young ELLs may also struggle with behavioral regulation. Children from Hispanic families are disproportionately more likely to be from low-income families (U.S. Census Bureau, 2006), suggesting that the effects of poverty, such as fewer opportunities to practice behavioral regulation at home, are also likely to be evident in this population. Although research is sparse, a few studies have begun to look at behavioral regulation in Hispanic children. One study found that Hispanic children had significantly lower behavioral regulation in prekindergarten and kindergarten than their peers (Sektnan et al., in press). That study, however, did not specifically investigate ELLs. Two additional studies that did examine ELLs from low-income families found that Hispanic children who were ELLs had more difficulty with teacher-reported self-regulation. One study of children in Head Start demonstrated less improvement in behavioral regulation compared to Hispanic children who spoke English (California Head Start Association, 2010). This study analyzed teacher ratings of more than 6,000 children enrolled in Head Start grantee center-based preschool programs in California. Although the study supports the importance of examining behavioral regulation in ELL children, it is limited because it only measured children's behavioral regulation twice (over one school year) and it combined behavioral regulation with safety/health scores to create one factor for analyses. The other study found significant deficits in self-control (which is similar to behavioral regulation) for ELLs who spoke Spanish and who were from the poorest families. This study also used teacher-reported measures and assessed self-control at the beginning and end of the kindergarten year (Galindo & Fuller, 2010).

Another study that included disadvantaged Hispanic ELLs found that they had significantly lower behavioral regulation than their English-speaking counterparts in the fall and spring of prekindergarten (McClelland, Cameron, Connor, et al., 2007). Using the same sample of children during their kindergarten year, a related study found that being an ELL was significantly related to lower behavioral regulation on a direct measure at the end of kindergarten but not to teacher ratings of these skills (Ponitz et al., 2009). Although the reason for this discrepancy is difficult to isolate, it suggests that direct assessments and teacher ratings may capture different aspects of behavioral regulation. To further demonstrate this point, parent education level in this study was significantly related to the direct measure of behavioral regulation but not to teacher ratings. It is unclear, however, how being both economically disadvantaged and an ELL is related to children's behavioral regulation over time, because these studies did not analyze growth in behavioral regulation over both years.

Differences in parenting may be one reason that Hispanic children demonstrate lower behavioral regulation, although the research on this issue is mixed. Some research has found that Hispanic parents are no more controlling than non-Hispanic parents, whereas other research has found evidence to the contrary. In support of the former argument, one study found that although Puerto Rican parents had different socialization goals for their children than their Anglo counterparts, these differences did not translate into a difference in parents' emphasis on child compliance (Harwood, Miller, & Irizarry, 1995). In fact, a recent review of the literature described two studies in which Hispanic mothers used lower or similar levels of control than Euro-American mothers in teaching tasks with their 2- to 5-year-olds (Halgunseth, Ispa, & Rudy, 2006; Laosa, 1980; Moreno, 1997). Furthermore, studies of Mexican American families suggested that these mothers were less likely to correct their children's narratives than Euro-American mothers (Eisenberg, 1985; Melzi, 2000). It is possible that a lack of directiveness would allow the children to practice regulating their speech themselves (Martínez, 1988). Other studies, however, support the latter argument and have found that Hispanic parents are more likely to emphasize strictness and child compliance (Brooks-Gunn & Markman, 2005; Wasserman, Rauh, Brunelli, Garcia-Castro, & Necos, 1990).

Research with non-Hispanic samples has found that an emphasis on child compliance is related to children's low levels of behavioral regulation (Kochanska & Knaack, 2003; Wachs, Gurkas, & Kontos, 2004). This research suggests that increased control from parents may not allow children the opportunity to practice behavioral regulation, which is needed when they enter school (Grolnick & Ryan, 1989). Thus, research presents a mixed picture of parenting practices among Hispanic parents, and different parenting practices may be related to different outcomes for children. In the present study, we examined differences in children's behavioral regulation based on demographic factors such as being a Hispanic ELL.

GROWTH IN BEHAVIORAL REGULATION ACROSS PREKINDERGARTEN AND KINDERGARTEN

Although there are reasons to believe that children from low-income families and ELLs are more likely to start prekindergarten with low behavioral regulation, evidence suggests that they may experience growth similar to that of their peers during the prekindergarten and kindergarten years. For example, high-quality stimulation provided at school combined with rapid growth in the prefrontal cortex during prekindergarten and kindergarten may play a role in helping ELLs and children from low-income families increase their behavioral regulation. In recent research, high-quality experiences in prekindergarten classrooms have been linked to better outcomes related to behavioral regulation, such as children's ability to complete work, and to decreases in problem behaviors, such as difficulty following directions and being disruptive in class (Curby et al., 2009; Mashburn et al., 2008). Research on ELLs specifically showed that having a teacher who spoke Spanish, another aspect of some prekindergarten and kindergarten classrooms, related to stronger social skills development (Rolstad, Mahoney, & Glass, 2005).

In addition, dramatic improvement in children's performance on tasks that assess attentional flexibility, working memory, and inhibitory control is often seen during the prekindergarten and kindergarten years (Diamond, 2002). Performance on these tasks depends on the prefrontal cortex and reflects the rapid organization, maturation, and fine-tuning that occurs in this area of the brain during the early years of schooling, particularly once children reach 4 years of age (Tsujimoto, 2008). This research suggests that once children enter prekindergarten, increased classroom supports for regulation and children's increased capacity for regulation may translate into more opportunities to practice and develop behavioral regulation.

GOALS OF THE PRESENT STUDY

The present study had two aims. First, we examined the effect of being from a low-income family and being an ELL on children's behavioral regulation at the beginning of prekindergarten. We hypothesized that being from a low-income family would significantly relate to lower initial behavioral regulation given previous research showing that children from low-income families had significantly lower behavioral regulation than their more advantaged peers (Howse, Lange, Farran, & Boyles, 2003). We also expected that being from a low-income family and being an ELL would have a significant negative effect on behavioral regulation at the beginning of prekindergarten given recent findings showing lower teacher-rated behavioral regulation in ELLs from low-income families (California Head Start Association, 2010). Second, we investigated the relation between being from a low-income family and being an ELL on the rate of development of behavioral regulation across prekindergarten and kindergarten. We hypothesized that English-speaking children from low-income families and ELLs from low-income families would develop at similar rates to children from higher income families because of increased opportunities to practice behavioral regulation in early classroom settings and rapid prefrontal cortex development at this age (Mashburn et al., 2008; Tsujimoto, 2008).

METHOD

Participants

Children and parents participating in the present study were from a rural community in Oregon of mixed socioeconomic status. The sample included children from six preschools that were all accredited by the National Association for the Education of Young Children. The majority of interactions between teachers and children in these preschools occurred in English. Of the families of the 165 prekindergartners in these preschools, 95 (58%) agreed to participate; 2 of the 95 children were excluded from the study because their first language was neither English nor Spanish. The final sample included 93 children from 12 classrooms. Families who participated were given small gift certificates.

The present study examined children (48% boys) from 4.08 to 5.17 years old ($M = 4.62$, $SD = 0.28$) in the fall of their prekindergarten year (Time 1). We followed them longitudinally over the school year and assessed them in the spring (Time 2) and also in the fall (Time 3) and spring (Time 4) of their kindergarten year (see Table 1 for descriptive statistics over all four time points). On average, children had mothers with about an associate's degree, with a range of 4 to 21 years of education. The sample was fairly diverse, with 48% Caucasian, 25% Hispanic, and 19% Asian. The sample size decreased from Time 1 because of attrition to 84 children at Time 2, 62 children at Time 3, and 59 children at Time 4. There were no significant differences between children who participated in Times 2, 3, or 4 and those who did not in terms of child age, gender,

TABLE 1
Descriptive Statistics for Background and Outcome Variables ($N = 93$)

Variable	M	SD	Range
Time 1			
Child age (in years)	4.62	0.63	4.08–5.17
Mother's education (in years)	14.42	3.79	4.00–21.00
Gender (proportion boys)	0.48		
Family income (proportion low income)	0.44		
Primary language (proportion Spanish-speaking)	0.20		
Behavioral regulation (Head-to-Toe Task)			
Time 1	8.86	7.52	0.00–20.00
Time 2	13.23	6.83	0.00–20.00
Time 3	15.12	5.32	0.00–20.00
Time 4	15.63	5.93	0.00–20.00

mother's education, or being an ELL ($ps > .05$; see "Data Analysis" for a description of analyses related to missing data).

Children enrolled in Head Start were identified by their teachers, and this was used as an indicator of low-income status. Classrooms included children funded by Head Start and children not funded by Head Start. In other words, being funded by Head Start was a child-level characteristic and not a classroom-level characteristic. At Time 1, 44% ($n = 41$) of the children were funded by Head Start and thus were considered low income. Children in this low-income group ranged in age from 4.17 to 5.17 years old ($M = 4.71$, $SD = 0.27$), and 56% were boys. Half (50%) of the mothers of these children had less than a high school degree, with a range of 4 to 18 years of education.

At Time 1, 20% ($n = 19$) of the children in the overall sample were identified by their teachers as primarily speaking Spanish and are thus referred to as ELLs in the present study. The ELLs were given vocabulary assessments in Spanish at all four time points (Batería Woodcock-Muñoz-R; Woodcock & Muñoz-Sandoval, 1996). Children's vocabulary performance increased over the course of the present study, suggesting that their Spanish vocabulary skills were improving and their ability to comprehend the direct assessments that were given in Spanish did not change over time. Specifically, Spanish vocabulary scores increased by an age equivalency of 2 years from the fall of prekindergarten to the spring of kindergarten, which documents growth in this skill. Furthermore, Spanish vocabulary standard scores were 45 in the fall of prekindergarten and 79 in the spring of kindergarten, suggesting continued Spanish language development. All but one of the ELLs were from low-income families. The children in the ELL subsample ranged in age from 4.33 to 5.17 years old ($M = 4.72$, $SD = 0.23$), and 63% were boys. The majority (75%) of mothers in this group had less than a high school degree (50% had six or fewer years of education), with a range of 4 to 16 years of education.

Procedure

Research assistants administered the behavioral regulation assessment at all four time points using the HTT. The HTT was part of a larger battery of four tests given over two sessions. Each session lasted 10–15 min and was conducted in a quiet hallway or multipurpose room. Teachers of the participants identified the children who primarily spoke Spanish (the ELLs). These children were given the behavioral regulation task in Spanish by native Spanish speakers.

Measures

Background questionnaire. Parents completed a background questionnaire in English or Spanish. Items included the child's age, the child's gender, the mother's education level, and child's ethnicity. This questionnaire was translated into Spanish and back-translated into English by two native Spanish speakers.

Behavioral regulation. The HTT was used to directly assess behavioral regulation (Ponitz et al., 2008). This 5-min task assesses children's ability to integrate inhibitory control, attention, and working memory skills in a game that is similar to those that are used in early childhood settings. Research assistants began by instructing the children to do the opposite of commands, and they completed four practice questions to make sure that the children understood the instructions. Children were given the following instructions by the research assistants:

> When I say to touch your head, *instead* of touching your head, I want you to touch your toes. When I say to touch your toes, I want you to touch your head, so you're not doing the same thing that I say to do. So what do you do if I say, "Touch your head"?

The research assistant initially modeled the correct response but did not model responses during the following 4 practice items or during the 10 testing items. If children answered a practice question incorrectly, they were reminded of the instructions up to three times. Then the research assistant administered the test items whether or not the child answered the practice questions correctly. Reliability in the present sample was examined, and no significant differences in HTT scores by research assistant were found ($ps > .05$). This finding is consistent with previous studies that have found the HTT to be administered reliably in samples of diverse ages and cultures (Connor et al., in press; Wanless et al., 2009).

The HTT includes a total of 10 items given in a random order. Children were assigned 0 (incorrect), 1 (self-correct), or 2 (correct) points for each item, with higher scores indicating higher behavioral regulation. A self-correct was defined as any discernable motion toward the incorrect response followed by the child stopping and correcting himself or herself. The scores were summed at each time point, and possible scores ranged from 0–20 points (see Table 1). One version of the HTT, the Head–Toes version, was given at Times 1 and 2, and two versions of the task were given at Times 3 and 4 (the Head–Toes version and the Knees–Shoulders version). In the Head–Toes version, children are asked to touch their head (or their toes) but instead are instructed to do the opposite and touch their toes (or their head). In the Knees–Shoulders version, children are asked to touch their knees (or their shoulders) but should instead do the opposite and touch their shoulders (or their knees). In the present study, there were no significant differences between the two versions of the task at Times 3 or 4 after child age was controlled ($ps > .05$; only one form was used at Times 1 and 2). Previous research has also found no significant differences between the two forms of the task (Ponitz et al., 2009; Wanless, McClelland, Acock, Chen, & Chen, in press; Wanless et al., 2010).

The HTT was translated into Spanish and back-translated into English by two Spanish speakers, including a professor of Spanish. In previous analyses with the same sample of children, the HTT was significantly correlated to teacher-rated behavioral regulation (McClelland, Cameron, Connor, et al., 2007). Other research with different samples of children also found that the task significantly correlated to parent and teacher ratings of behavioral regulation (Ponitz et al., 2009; Wanless et al., 2010).

Data Analysis

In the present study, analyses examined the contribution of demographic risk factors (being from a low-income family and being an ELL) on behavioral regulation at the beginning of the prekindergarten year and changes in behavioral regulation over four time points (fall and spring of prekindergarten and fall and spring of kindergarten). We analyzed an additive model as opposed to examining interaction effects, because all but one of the ELLs were from low-income families. Descriptive statistics were calculated and followed by multilevel models with behavioral regulation at each time point nested within children. We calculated the intraclass correlation coefficient (ICC) using an unconditional model analyzed in Stata (StataCorp, 2007). The ICC indicated that 46.70% of the total variance in behavioral regulation was attributable to between-children differences. Because the ICC was relatively high and significant, and the Level 2 sample size was sufficient to obtain unbiased estimates at all time points, we conducted all additional analyses with multilevel models (Maas & Hox, 2005; Raudenbush & Bryk, 2002). Using ordinary least squares (OLS) regressions at each time point, we determined that multicollinearity between primary language, family income, and mother's education was not problematic based on the variance inflation factor statistic (all values were less than 3; Kline, 2005), and all three variables could be included in the present models. Child gender and mother's education were trimmed from our final models, however, because they did not reach statistical significance (Raudenbush & Bryk, 2002).

Because of attrition, the sample size decreased from 93 at Time 1 to 59 at Time 4. In order to maximize power and appropriately deal with missing data, we analyzed our data using maximum likelihood estimation in Stata with the xtmixed commands (StataCorp, 2007). Growth curve analyses with maximum likelihood estimation were particularly useful for these data because a simple examination of mean scores over time would not have accurately accounted for the children with missing data. A missing data pattern analysis indicated that there were 10 patterns of missing data, including a pattern for 46 children with no missing data at any time point. Our main predictors of interest (family income and primary language) were not missing for any children. Initial behavioral regulation and each child's individual OLS estimated behavioral regulation slope over the four time points were not significantly related to patterns of missingness.

RESULTS

Descriptive Analyses

Descriptive statistics for behavioral regulation at each time point are provided in Table 1, and correlations with background variables are in Table 2. Behavioral regulation means indicated a pattern of increasing scores over time. Initial correlations indicated that having a low family income was significantly related to lower behavioral regulation at the first three time points ($rs = -.24, -.31$, and $-.29$, respectively, for Times 1, 2, and 3) and being an ELL (as indicated by teacher report) was significantly related to lower behavioral regulation ($rs = -.20$ to $-.46$) at all four time points. Moreover, the absolute correlation between being an ELL and having lower behavioral regulation consistently increased over time (see Table 2).

How Do Demographic Risk Factors Influence Behavioral Regulation in the Fall of the Prekindergarten Year?

To investigate within-person change in behavioral regulation over prekindergarten and kindergarten, we began with descriptive analyses, including creating empirical growth records for each participant (Singer & Willett, 2003). Empirical growth records are individual growth models using multilevel modeling techniques. They allowed us to look at individual trajectories before running multilevel models for the entire sample. We fit each child's trajectory using a within-person regression model and examined the estimated intercepts, slopes, and R^2s for each child. Based on initial OLS exploratory models there was substantial variability in initial scores.

TABLE 2
Correlations Between Background, Predictor, and Outcome Variables (N=93)

Variable	1	2	3	4	5	6	7	8	9
1. Time 1 behavioral regulation	—								
2. Time 2 behavioral regulation	.54***	—							
3. Time 3 behavioral regulation	.35**	.29*	—						
4. Time 4 behavioral regulation	.51***	39**	.71***	—					
5. Child age (in years)	.18	.03	.22	.20	—				
6. Child gender (1 = male)	−.11	−.14	−.10	−.02	.01	—			
7. Mother's education level (years)	.24*	.36**	.32*	.35*	−.08	−.19	—		
8. Family income (1 = low income)	−.24*	−.31**	−.29*	−.18	.29**	.14	−.68***	—	
9. Primary language (1 = Spanish)	−.20†	−.30**	−.35**	−.46***	.20†	.15	−.68***	.52***	—

†$p < .07$. *$p < .05$. **$p < .01$. ***$p < .001$.

After examining the descriptive statistics, we built our multilevel model. The results suggested that being from a low-income family was significantly related to lower HTT scores in the fall of prekindergarten (see Table 3). Specifically, multilevel model estimates indicated that children from low-income families began prekindergarten, on average, more than 6 points (0.80 *SD*) behind their peers on the HTT (out of 20 possible points). Furthermore, younger children began prekindergarten with significantly lower HTT scores. Being an ELL, in contrast, did not relate significantly to initial HTT scores.

How Do Demographic Risk Factors Influence Growth in Behavioral Regulation across Prekindergarten and Kindergarten?

We next examined descriptive statistics of growth in sample scores of behavioral regulation across each time point for subgroups defined by family income and language (see Table 4). Our sample data showed that the greatest gains in behavioral regulation for all subgroups occurred during the prekindergarten year. These gains were largest for the two groups not considered at greatest risk (i.e., children who were low-income English

TABLE 3
Results of a Multilevel Model of Growth in Behavioral Regulation (N = 93)

Parameter	Coefficient	Standardized Coefficient	SE	t Ratio
	Fixed effects			
Intercept	12.03		0.79	15.25***
Child age (in months, centered)	0.56	.26	0.24	2.33*
Family income (1 = low income)	−6.04	−.42	1.86	−3.24**
Primary language (1 = Spanish)	0.08	.00	2.21	0.04
Slope				
Child age (in months, centered)	−0.02	−.01	0.09	−0.23
Family income (1 = low income)	1.44	.10	0.68	2.11*
Primary language (1 = Spanish)	−1.72	−.10	0.79	−2.17*
	Random parameters			
Level 2	13.99		3.33	111.02***
Level 1	23.07		2.29	

*$p < .05$. **$p < .01$. ***$p < .001$.

speakers and those who were not low-income English speakers). Over the summer before kindergarten, however, the children who were not low income made smaller gains in behavioral regulation than their low-income English- and Spanish-speaking counterparts. Furthermore, over the kindergarten year, the children from low-income families grew at a faster rate than their more economically advantaged peers.

Inspection of empirical growth plots for each child provided additional evidence that behavioral regulation generally increased over time (Singer & Willett, 2003). There was also substantial variability in children's estimated slopes ($M = 2.96$, $SD = 4.70$). On average, children increased in their HTT scores by almost 3 points every 6 months. Estimated intercepts and slopes were highly correlated ($r = -.84$), indicating that children's initial HTT scores were indicative of how fast they grew over the next 2 years. Overall, children with lower initial estimated HTT scores developed at a faster rate. There was substantial variation in the R^2s for each child when we used an OLS model ($M = .61$, $SD = .38$), with a range from 0% to 100%. The majority of children (53%), however, had R^2s greater than or equal to 60%, indicating that a linear model of growth accounted for at least 60% of the variance in their change in behavioral regulation over time.

Multilevel analyses indicated that being an ELL did not significantly relate to initial HTT scores in the fall of prekindergarten (see Table 3). Moreover, being from a family with a low income and being an ELL was

TABLE 4
Observed Descriptive Statistics for Behavioral Regulation (HTT) by Subgroup, Including Means (SD) and N

Variable	Children Not From Low-Income Families		Children From Low-Income Families	
	English Speakers	All	English Speakers	ELLs
Fall prekindergarten children at Time 1	10.45 (7.64) 51	6.88 (6.95) 41	7.48 (7.16) 23	6.11 (6.79) 18
HTT gain[a]	4.57	3.83	4.68	2.89
Spring prekindergarten children at Time 2	15.02 (6.25) 49	10.71 (6.91) 35	12.16 (7.07) 19	9.00 (6.51) 16
HTT gain[b]	1.34	2.46	3.17	2.00
Fall kindergarten children at Time 3	16.36 (4.29) 38	13.17 (6.23) 24	15.33 (5.18) 12	11.00 (6.65) 12
HTT gain[c]	0.06	1.02	2.07	0.27
Spring kindergarten children at Time 4	16.42 (5.05) 38	14.19 (7.17) 21	17.40 (3.41) 10	11.27 (8.52) 11

Note. One child in this study, an ELL who was not from a low-income family, was excluded from this table. HTT = Head-to-Toes Task; ELL = English language learner.
Difference in HTT scores between.
[a]Time 1 and Time 2.
[b]Time 2 and Time 3.
[c]Time 3 and Time 4.

significantly related to rate of growth in behavioral regulation. Overall, children from low-income families improved in behavioral regulation at a significantly faster rate than their economically advantaged counterparts and improved in behavioral regulation, on average, by about 1.5 points more per 6-month time period (see Figure 1). This enabled them to begin to close the behavioral regulation gap between themselves and their more economically advantaged peers by the end of kindergarten (see Table 4 and Figure 1). It is important to note, however, that the observed gap in behavioral regulation scores by income was 3.66 points in the fall of prekindergarten and 2.23 points in the spring of kindergarten. Although this gap narrowed over time, the low-income children continued to have observed scores below those of their more advantaged peers.

In contrast to English-speaking low-income children, low-income ELLs improved in behavioral regulation at a significantly slower rate. On average, low-income ELLs gained almost 2 fewer points per each 6-month period than low-income children who had English as a primary language. Thus, children who were both low income and ELLs were not able to catch up

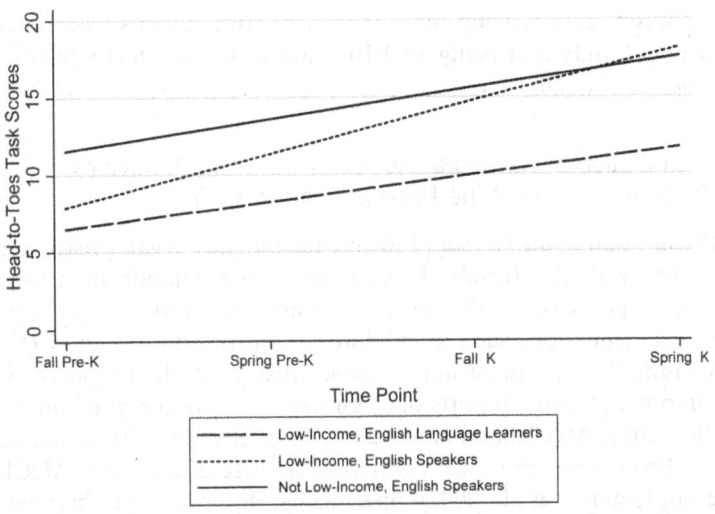

FIGURE 1 Estimated behavioral regulation (Head-to-Toes Task) trajectories ($N = 93$). Pre-K = prekindergarten; K = kindergarten.

in behavioral regulation to their low-income English-speaking peers or to their more advantaged counterparts by the end of kindergarten. In fact, low-income ELLs had observed scores that were on average at least 5.15 points, or almost 1 SD, lower than those of their economically advantaged English-speaking peers at the end of kindergarten.

DISCUSSION

In the present study, we examined how being from a low-income family and being an ELL from a low-income family influenced children's initial level of and growth in behavioral regulation across prekindergarten and kindergarten. We found that at the beginning of prekindergarten, children from low-income families had significantly lower behavioral regulation than more economically advantaged children. Within this low-income group, there were differences in rates of behavioral regulation development based on ELL status. Low-income ELLs developed behavioral regulation at a significantly slower rate than their English-speaking low-income peers. As a result, the English-speaking low-income children narrowed the gap with their English-speaking peers who were not from low-income families. This was not the case for the ELLs from low-income families. These findings suggest that children experiencing both of these risk factors—being from a low-income family and being an ELL—are at the greatest risk for having low behavioral regulation.

The Contribution of Demographic Risk Factors to Behavioral Regulation in the Fall of the Prekindergarten Year

Our finding that children from low-income families began prekindergarten, on average, with significantly lower behavioral regulation than their more advantaged peers fits with previous findings from studies of aspects of behavioral regulation, such as inhibitory control and attention (Evans & Rosenbaum, 2008; Mezzacappa, 2004; Mistry et al., in press; Sektnan et al., in press), teacher reports of classroom behavioral regulation (Galindo & Fuller, 2010; McClelland et al., 2000; Merritt et al., 2010), and research using a direct measure of self-regulation (Howse et al., 2003; McClelland, Cameron, Connor, et al., 2007). Specifically, differences in observed scores in our sample suggest that children from families with low incomes began prekindergarten almost half of one standard deviation behind their economically advantaged peers. These differences may be a function of differences in previous experiences. Research supports the notion that children from low-income families have relatively fewer opportunities to practice paying attention, remembering instructions, or inhibiting impulses (Bradley et al., 1989; Hart & Risley, 1995; Howes, 1990; McClelland et al., 2000). Differences in early behavioral regulation based on economic status may point to later difficulties for children from low-income families, because behavioral regulation has been identified as a key component of school readiness (Rimm-Kaufman, Pianta, & Cox, 2000).

The Contribution of Demographic Risk Factors to Behavioral Regulation Growth Across Prekindergarten and Kindergarten

Overall, children from low-income families experienced significantly faster gains in behavioral regulation than their more economically advantaged counterparts from the beginning of prekindergarten to the end of kindergarten. Despite these rapid gains, however, it is important to note that children from low-income families continued to perform lower than their economically advantaged peers in the spring of the kindergarten year before we accounted for primary language. These findings match previous research documenting the rapid growth in the prefrontal cortex for all children during the preschool years that is partly responsible for advances in behavioral regulation (Calkins, 2007; Diamond, 2002; Rothbart & Posner, 2005; Rueda, Posner, et al., 2005; Tsujimoto, 2008). Thus, the prekindergarten and kindergarten years may be a sensitive period for the development of behavioral regulation. Stimulating preschool environments may also help elicit this growth. Some previous research has shown that experiences in a preschool such as Head Start can serve as a protective factor, helping children in home environments that are relatively less stimulating for certain classroom-relevant skills to be successful in math and reading (Bryant, Burchinal, Lau, & Sparling, 1994; Caughy, DiPietro, & Strobino, 1994; Dearing, McCartney, & Taylor, 2009). For example, typical demands in preschool classrooms, such as waiting for a turn or learning to share a toy, require children to practice paying attention to teachers and peers, remembering classroom rules, and inhibiting impulses to do something immediately or keep a toy for themselves. Research on prekindergarten has found that high-quality teaching is related to more desirable social outcomes in young children, such as positive peer social skills, high frustration tolerance, and focused task orientation, and fewer behavior problems, such as being disruptive in class and being anxious (Curby et al., 2009; Mashburn et al., 2008).

Children from low-income families, however, did not all develop behavioral regulation at the same rate. We found that ELLs from low-income families developed behavioral regulation at a significantly slower rate than English-speaking children from low-income families. Although research is limited, previous work on the development of behavioral regulation in ELLs from low-income families suggests that they consistently score lower than their counterparts during prekindergarten and kindergarten (California Head Start Association, 2010; Galindo & Fuller, 2010). This trend is also evident in studies of academic skills (Reardon & Galindo, 2006b). The results of the present study suggest that the low-income ELLs did not catch up to their more advantaged peers by the end of kindergarten. Specifically, ELLs from low-income families had observed regulation scores that were about 1 *SD* below those of both their low-income and not low-income English-speaking counterparts at the end of kindergarten. The sample of ELLs in the present study, however, was small and largely low income (all but one child), and thus this difference should be interpreted with caution until it can be investigated with a larger and more diverse sample.

Factors that are unique to the experiences of ELLs from low-income families may have played a role in their behavioral development trajectories. For example, it is possible that limited English ability hinders the ability of ELLs to take advantage of the rich learning experiences in their classrooms. Although some of the classrooms in the present study provided general instructions in English and Spanish, the majority of interactions occurred in English. Research suggests that there is often a mismatch between ELLs' language and culture and those of their teachers. Specifically, previous research has found that prekindergartners who are ELLs often experience less than 20% of their interactions with teachers in Spanish, and 23% of ELL prekindergartners have no interactions with teachers in Spanish (Chang et al., 2007). This mismatch has been related to lower expectations and outcomes for ELLs (Rolstad et al., 2005). Unfortunately, these differences were not measured in the present study but should be considered in future research.

In addition, although mother's education level was not a significant predictor in the final models, there were significant differences in mother's education level for the ELLs and English-speaking children. The English-speaking children from low-income families had mothers with 10–18 years of education, with an average of more than 13 years. The ELLs from low-income families had mothers with 4–16 years of education and an average of fewer than 9 years. Most notably, 75% of the mothers of the ELLs had less than a high school degree compared to 33% of the mothers of the English-speaking low-income children. Differences in parent education may translate into even lower outcomes for the ELLs whose parents may have had fewer resources to promote their attention, memory, and inhibitory control. Specifically, previous research has found that less stimulating home environments found in low-income households were related to more behavior problems in young children and lower cognitive outcomes (Linver et al., 2002). Previous research on Hispanic parenting has shown mixed findings regarding culturally specific parenting differences. Some studies have found that Hispanic parents are more controlling and place a greater emphasis on child compliance than Euro-American parents (Brooks-Gunn & Markman, 2005), and some have found similarities between these groups (Halgunseth et al., 2006). Further research on Hispanic parenting styles and their unique relations to child outcomes is needed.

Finally, cultural differences may lead to a mismatch in communication styles between students, teachers, and parents. Research suggests that ELLs and their parents may be perceived as passive, less intelligent, or uninterested in education because of their struggles with the language barrier and the Hispanic culture's emphasis on respect for teachers (Tapia, 1992; Trueba, 1993). This perception may lower their expectations for these children and contribute to ELLs' lower behavioral regulation.

Practical Implications

The findings from the present study emphasize the need for increased access to high-quality preschool programs and increased use of evidence-based behavioral regulation interventions in schools. Overall, when we controlled for ELL status, we found that children from low-income families began prekindergarten with significantly lower behavioral regulation than their economically advantaged peers but developed at a faster rate over prekindergarten and kindergarten. This finding suggests that access to preschool programs such as Head Start may help these children catch up to their non-low-income peers. Increased funding for preschool programs that serve low-income children, including Head Start, may ensure that these children get the high-quality teaching and learning experiences that they need to develop behavioral regulation. For example, research suggests that infusing activities that require children to stop, pay attention, remember instructions, and demonstrate self-regulation into daily teaching practices can help strengthen these skills in young children (McClelland, Cameron, Wanless, et al., 2007; Tominey & McClelland, 2010). There is evidence that behavioral regulation interventions used in schools improve children's skills. One intervention, the Tools of the Mind curriculum, has increased children's attention, working memory, and inhibitory control skills with sociodramatic play, private speech, and drawing strategies (Barnett et al., 2008; Diamond, Barnett, Thomas, & Munro, 2007). In addition, preschool games that help children practice integrating attention, working memory, and inhibitory control skills have been found to significantly improve children's behavioral regulation and early reading skills, especially for children low in these skills (Tominey & McClelland, 2010). Exposure to such activities may help promote the behavioral regulation of all children, and especially those at risk.

One noteworthy finding from the present study is the overall slower rate of growth in behavioral regulation for economically disadvantaged ELLs. Because of the relatively small number of ELLs in our study, however, this finding is preliminary and needs to be examined further with larger samples of ELLs. However, the results are of interest because behavioral regulation is an important predictor of achievement. Thus, starting formal schooling with poor behavioral regulation could have significant implications on later achievement for ELL children. Although the academic gap between Hispanic and White children narrows during kindergarten and first grade, it remains about one half of a standard deviation between first and fifth grades (Reardon & Galindo, 2006b). The results of the present study provide some preliminary evidence that economically disadvantaged ELLs may need more than exposure to high-quality classrooms to close this gap. For example, these children may also benefit from increased classroom interactions in Spanish, teachers' understanding of cultural differences, and increased English competence. Specifically, balanced efforts to make the classroom environment more responsive to low-income ELLs' unique needs and to prepare low-income ELLs to take advantage of stimulating classroom experiences are likely to result in the greatest gains for these children.

Limitations

Although the present study has a number of important findings, there are also limitations. The majority of the variance (62%) in behavioral regulation was attributable to within-child factors. In other words, a substantial amount of behavioral regulation change over time was not captured by child factors such as age, family income, and language. This finding suggests that additional factors, such as parenting practices, classroom quality, and the amount of instruction in Spanish, may also be accounting for changes in behavioral regulation. Future research on behavioral regulation development should assess these time-varying covariates to examine their influence.

The present study is also limited by the small number of ELLs within the sample. Thus, the results of the study are preliminary and need replication. However, we also believe the results are important because there is virtually no research on self-regulation in Hispanic ELLs. Although preliminary, this study can form the foundation for other research with larger samples.

On a related note, all but one of the ELLs included in the sample were from families with low incomes. This sample characteristic limited our ability to understand the developmental trajectories of non-low-income ELLs. However, we were able to separate the effects of income and ELL status in our statistical analyses. Future research should include ELLs from families that do not have low incomes.

Another limitation concerns the determination of ELL status, which we obtained by asking teachers in the fall of prekindergarten (Time 1) to identify children who spoke primarily Spanish. Future studies should use direct assessments of children's English fluency and should take children's degree of English fluency into account in order to more accurately capture the relation between English competence and behavioral regulation skills. Furthermore, including assessments of English and Spanish fluency at all four time points would have allowed us to reevaluate which language version of the behavioral regulation assessment was needed at each time. However, the fact that ELLs continued to improve in Spanish vocabulary scores over the course of the study made us more confident that they were able to continue understanding the HTT in Spanish.

The present study also did not assess teaching and parenting practices that may influence behavioral regulation development. Assessments of the amount of English and Spanish spoken in the classrooms, and the extent to which children have opportunities for behavioral regulation practice at home and at school, may provide information about the reasons why ELLs from low-income families did not catch up to their peers by the end of kindergarten. Finally, although there are benefits to using a direct measure of behavioral regulation, it may be useful to include additional measures, such as teacher reports or assessments of individual components of behavioral regulation such as attention, working memory, and inhibitory control. Assessing behavioral regulation in multiple ways can inform understanding of the developmental changes in these skills over time.

CONCLUSION

In the present study, we examined the development of behavioral regulation over the course of prekindergarten and kindergarten based on children's income and ELL status. Our findings suggest that, on average, children from low-income families entered prekindergarten with significantly lower behavioral regulation than their peers when ELL status was controlled. Furthermore, these children developed behavioral regulation at a significantly faster rate and began to narrow the gap with their more economically advantaged peers by the end of kindergarten. Finally, ELLs from low-income families developed behavioral regulation at a slower rate than English-speaking children from low-income families, and this gap persisted through the end of kindergarten. The results suggest that interventions focusing on ELLs from low-income families may strengthen behavioral regulation in the children who may need these efforts the most.

REFERENCES

Alexander, K. L., & Entwisle, D. R. (1988). Achievement in the first two years of school: Patterns and processes. *Monographs of the Society for Research in Child Development, 53*(2, Serial No. 218).

Barnett, W. S., Jung, K., Yarosz, D. J., Thomas, J., Hornbeck, A., Stechuk, R., & Burns, S. (2008). Educational effects of the Tools of the Mind curriculum: A randomized trial. *Early Childhood Research Quarterly, 23*, 299–313.

Baumeister, R. F., & Vohs, K. D. (2004). *Handbook of self-regulation: Research, theory, and applications.* New York, NY: Guilford Press.

Blair, C. (2002). School readiness: Integrating cognition and emotion in a neurobiological conceptualization of children's functioning at school entry. *American Psychologist, 57*, 111–127.

Blair, C., & Razza, R. P. (2007). Relating effortful control, executive function, and false belief understanding to emerging math and literacy ability in kindergarten. *Child Development, 78*, 647–663.

Bradley, R. H., Caldwell, B. M., Rock, S. L., Ramey, C. T., Barnard, K. E., Gray, C., ... Johnson, D. L. (1989). Home environment and cognitive development in the first 3 years of life: A collaborative study involving six sites and three ethnic groups in North America. *Developmental Psychology, 25*, 217–235.

Brooks-Gunn, J., & Markman, L. B. (2005). The contribution of parenting to ethnic and racial gaps in school readiness. *The Future of Children, 15*(1), 139–168.

Bryant, D. M., Burchinal, M., Lau, L. B., & Sparling, J. J. (1994). Family and classroom correlates of Head Start children's developmental outcomes. *Early Childhood Research Quarterly*, 9, 289–309.

Cai, Q. (2003, December). *Oregon's population change: 1990–2000*. Portland, OR: Population Research Center, Portland State University.

California Head Start Association. (2010). *California Head Start child outcomes bulletin 2010*. Retrieved from http://caheadstart.org/California_Head_Start_Child_Outcomes_Bulletin_2010.pdf

Calkins, S. D. (2007). The emergence of self-regulation: Biological and behavioral control mechanisms supporting toddler competencies. In C. A. Brownell, & C. B. Kopp (Eds.), *Socioemotional development in the toddler years: Transitions and transformations*, (pp. 261–284). New York, NY: Guilford Press.

Caughy, M. O., DiPietro, J. A., & Strobino, D. M. (1994). Day-care participation as a protective factor in the cognitive development of low-income children. *Child Development*, 65, 457–471.

Chang, F., Crawford, G., Early, D. M., Bryant, D., Howes, C., Burchinal, M., ... Pianta, R. (2007). Spanish-speaking children's social and language development in pre-kindergarten classrooms. *Early Education & Development*, 18, 243–269.

Chazan-Cohen, R., Raikes, H. A., Brooks-Gunn, J., Ayoub, C. C., Pan, B. A., Kisker, E. E., ... Fuligni, A. S. (2009). Low-income children's school readiness: Parent contributions over the first five years. *Early Education & Development*, 20, 958–977.

Connor, C. M., Ponitz, C. C., Phillips, B. M., Travis, Q. M., Glasney, S., & Morrison, F. J. (2010). First graders' literacy and self-regulation gains: The effect of individualizing student instruction. *Journal of School Psychology*, 48(5), 433–455.

Cooper, D. H., & Farran, D. C. (1988). Behavioral risk factors in kindergarten. *Early Childhood Research Quarterly*, 3, 1–19.

Curby, T. W., LoCasale-Crouch, J., Konold, T., Pianta, R. C., Howes, C., Burchinal, M., ... Barbarin, O. (2009). The relations of observed pre-K classroom quality profiles to children's achievement and social competence. *Early Education & Development*, 20, 346–372.

Dearing, E., Berry, D., & Zaslow, M. (2006). Poverty during childhood. In K. McCartney & D. Phillips (Eds.), *Handbook of early childhood development* (pp. 399–423). Oxford, UK: Blackwell.

Dearing, E., McCartney, K., & Taylor, B. A. (2009). Does higher quality early child care promote low-income children's math and reading achievement in middle childhood? *Child Development*, 80, 1329–1349.

Diamond, A. (2002). Normal development of prefrontal cortex from birth to young adulthood: Cognitive functions, anatomy, and biochemistry. In D. T. Stuss & R. T. Knight (Eds.), *Principles of frontal lobe function* (pp. 466–503). London: Oxford University Press.

Diamond, A., Barnett, W. S., Thomas, J., & Munro, S. (2007, November 30). Preschool program improves cognitive control. *Science*, 318, 1387–1388.

Dixon, Jr., W. E., & Salley, B. J. (2007). "Shhh! We're tryin' to concentrate": Attention and environmental distracters in novel word learning. *Journal of Genetic Psychology*, 167, 393–414.

Dowsett, S. M., & Livesey, D. J. (2000). The development of inhibitory control in preschool children: Effects of "executive skills" training. *Developmental Psychobiology*, 36(2), 161–174.

Duncan, G. J., & Brooks-Gunn, J. (Eds.). (1997). *Consequences of growing up poor*. New York, NY: Russell Sage Foundation.

Eisenberg, N. (1985). Learning to describe past experiences in conversation. *Discourse Processes*, 8, 177–204.

Entwisle, D. R., & Alexander, K. L. (1993). Entry into school: The beginning school transition and educational stratification in the United States. *Annual Review of Sociology, 19,* 401–423.

Espy, K. A., McDiarmid, M. M., Cwik, M. F., Stalets, M. M., Hamby, A., & Stern, T. E. (2004). The contribution of executive functions to emergent mathematic skills in preschool children. *Developmental Neuropsychology, 26,* 465–486.

Evans, G. W., & Rosenbaum, J. (2008). Self-regulation and the income-achievement gap. *Early Childhood Research Quarterly, 23,* 504–514.

Galindo, C., & Fuller, B. (2010). The social competence of Latino kindergartners and growth in mathematical understanding. *Developmental Psychology, 46,* 579–592.

García, E. (2005). *Teaching and learning in two languages: Bilingualism and schooling in the United States.* New York, NY: Teachers College Press.

Gathercole, S. E., & Pickering, S. J. (2000). Working memory deficits in children with low achievements in the national curriculum at 7 years of age. *British Journal of Educational Psychology, 70,* 177–194.

Grolnick, W. S., & Ryan, R. M. (1989). Parent styles associated with children's self-regulation and competence in school. *Journal of Educational Psychology, 81*(2), 143–154.

Gutman, L. M., Sameroff, A. J., & Cole, R. (2003). Academic growth curve trajectories from 1st grade to 12th grade: Effects of multiple social risk factors and preschool child factors. *Developmental Psychology, 39,* 777–790.

Halgunseth, L. C., Ispa, J. M., & Rudy, D. (2006). Parental control in Latino families: An integrated review of the literature. *Child Development, 77,* 1282–1297.

Hart, B., & Risley, T. R. (1995). *Meaningful differences in the everyday experience of young American children.* Baltimore, MD: Brookes.

Harwood, R. L., Miller, J. G., & Irizarry, N. L. (1995). *Culture and attachment: Perceptions of the child in context.* New York, NY: Guilford Press.

Haveman, R., & Wolfe, B. (1994). *Succeeding generations: On the effects of investments in children.* New York, NY: Russell Sage Foundation.

Heckman, J. J. (2006, June 30). Skill formation and the economics of investing in disadvantaged children. *Science, 312,* 1900–1901.

Hernández, D. (2005). *Young Hispanic children in the U.S.: A demographic portrait based on Census 2000.* Albany: State University of New York Press.

Howes, C. (1990). Can the age of entry into child care and the quality of child care predict adjustment in kindergarten? *Developmental Psychology, 26,* 292–303.

Howse, R. B., Lange, G., Farran, D. C., & Boyles, C. D. (2003). Motivation and self-regulation as predictors of achievement in economically disadvantaged young children. *Journal of Experimental Education, 71*(2), 151–174.

Jose, P. E., Huntsinger, C. S., Huntsinger, P. R., & Liaw, F.-R. (2000). Parental values and practices relevant to young children's social development in Taiwan and the United States. *Journal of Cross-Cultural Psychology, 31,* 677–702.

Kline, R. B. (2005). *Principles and practice of structural equation modeling* (2nd ed.). New York, NY.

Kochanska, G., & Knaack, A. (2003). Effortful control as a personality characteristic of young children: Antecedents, correlates, and consequences. *Journal of Personality, 71,* 1087–1112.

Laosa, L. (1980). Maternal teaching strategies in Chicano and Anglo-American families: The influence of culture and education on maternal behavior. *Child Development, 51,* 759–765.

Lewit, E. M., & Baker, L. S. (1995). School readiness. *The Future of Children, 5,* 128–139.

Linver, M. R., Brooks-Gunn, J., & Kohen, D. E. (2002). Family processes as pathways from income to young children's development. *Developmental Psychology, 38,* 719–734.

López, M., Barrueco, S., & Miles, J. (2006). *Latino infants and families: A national perspective of protective and risk factors for development: A report to the National Task Force on Early Childhood Education for Hispanics.* Tempe, AZ: Arizona State University.

Maas, C. J. M., & Hox, J. J. (2005). Sufficient sample sizes for multilevel modeling. *Methodology: European Journal of Research Methods for the Behavioral and Social Sciences, 1*(3), 86–92.

Mahone, E. M., Cirino, P. T., Cutting, L. E., Cerrone, P. M., Hagelthorn, K. M., Hiemenz, J. R., ... Denckla, M. B. (2002). Validity of the behavior rating inventory of executive function in children with ADHD and/or Tourette syndrome. *Archives of Clinical Neuropsychology, 17*, 643–663.

Mahone, E. M., & Hoffman, J. C. (2005). Behavior ratings of executive function among preschoolers with ADHD [Abstract]. *International Neuropsychological Society, 11*(S1), 129.

Martínez, E. A. (1988). Child behavior in Mexican American/Chicano families: Maternal teaching and child-rearing practices. *Family Relations, 37*(3), 275–280.

Mashburn, A. J., Hamre, B. K., Downer, J. T., & Pianta, R. C. (2006). Teacher and classroom characteristics associated with teachers' ratings of prekindergarteners' relationships and behaviors. *Journal of Psychoeducational Assessment, 24*, 367–380.

Mashburn, A. J., Pianta, R. C., Hamre, B. K., Downer, J. T., Barbarin, O., Bryant, D. M., ... Howes, C. (2008). Measures of classroom quality in pre-kindergarten and children's development of academic, language, and social skills. *Child Development, 79*, 732–749.

McClelland, M. M., Acock, A. C., & Morrison, F. J. (2006). The impact of kindergarten learning-related skills on academic trajectories at the end of elementary school. *Early Childhood Research Quarterly, 21*, 471–490.

McClelland, M. M., Cameron, C. E., Connor, C. M., Farris, C. L., Jewkes, A. M., & Morrison, F. J. (2007). Links between behavioral regulation and preschoolers' literacy, vocabulary, and math skills. *Developmental Psychology, 43*, 947–959.

McClelland, M. M., Cameron, C. E., Wanless, S. B., & Murray, A. (2007). Executive function, self-regulation, and social-emotional competence: Links to school readiness. In O. N. Saracho & B. Spodek (Eds.), *Contemporary perspectives on research in social learning in early childhood education* (pp. 83–107). Charlotte, NC: Information Age.

McClelland, M. M., Morrison, F. J., & Holmes, D. L. (2000). Children at risk for early academic problems: The role of learning-related social skills. *Early Childhood Research Quarterly, 15*, 307–329.

McClelland, M. M., Piccinin, A. M., & Stallings, M. C. (2009). *Relations between preschool attention and sociability and later achievement outcomes.* Manuscript submitted for publication.

McClelland, M. M., Ponitz, C. C., Messersmith, E., & Tominey, S. L. (in press). Self-regulation: The integration of cognition and emotion. In W. F. Overton & R. M. Lerner (Eds.), *Handbook of lifespan human development.* Hoboken, NJ: Wiley.

Melzi, G. (2000). Cultural variations in the construction of personal narratives: Central American and European American mothers' elicitation styles. *Discourse Processes, 30*(2), 153–177.

Merritt, E. G., Wanless, S. B., Ponitz, C. C., & Rimm-Kaufman, S. E. (2010). The contribution of emotional support to social behaviors in first grade. *Manuscript in preparation.*

Mezzacappa, E. (2004). Alerting, orienting, and executive attention: Developmental and sociodemographic properties in an epidemiological sample of young, urban children. *Child Development, 75*, 1373–1386.

Mistry, R. S., Benner, A. D., Biesanz, J., Clark, S., & Howes, C. (2010). Family and social risk, and parental investments during the early childhood years as predictors of low-income children's school readiness outcomes. *Early Childhood Research Quarterly, 25*(4), 432–449.

Moreno, R. (1997). Everyday instruction: A comparison of Mexican American and Anglo mothers and their preschool children. *Hispanic Journal of Behavioral Sciences, 19*(4), 527–539.

National Scientific Council on the Developing Child. (2004). *Children's emotional development is built into the architecture of their brains* (Working Paper No. 2). Retrieved from http://developingchild.harvard.edu/index.php?cID=152

National Task Force on Early Childhood Education for Hispanics. (2007). *The school readiness and academic achievement in reading and mathematics of young Hispanic children in the United States.* Tempe, AZ: Foundation for Child Development.

Pagani, L. S., Vitaro, F., Tremblay, R. E., McDuff, P., Japel, C., & Larose, S. (2008). When predictions fail: The case of unexpected pathways toward high school dropout. *Journal of Social Issues, 64*(1), 175–194.

Ponitz, C. C., McClelland, M. M., Jewkes, A. M., Connor, C. M., Farris, C. L., & Morrison, F. J. (2008). Touch your toes! Developing a direct measure of behavioral regulation in early childhood. *Early Childhood Research Quarterly, 23*, 141–158.

Ponitz, C. C., McClelland, M. M., Matthews, J. S., & Morrison, F. J. (2009). A structured observation of behavioral self-regulation and its contribution to kindergarten outcomes. *Developmental Psychology, 45*, 605–619.

Raudenbush, S. W., & Bryk, A. S. (2002). *Hierarchical linear models: Applications and data analysis methods* (2nd ed.). Thousand Oaks, CA: Sage.

Reardon, S. F., & Galindo, C. (2006a, April). *K-3 academic achievement patterns of Hispanics and other racial/ethnic groups.* Paper presented at the annual conference of the American Education Research Association, April 11, San Francisco, CA.

Reardon, S. F., & Galindo, C. (2006b). *Patterns of Hispanic students' math and English literacy test scores in the early elementary grades.* Tempe, AZ: National Task Force on Early Childhood Education for Hispanics. Retrieved March 10, 2011, from http://ecehispanic.org/work.htm/#briefs

Rimm-Kaufman, S. E., Pianta, R. C., & Cox, M. J. (2000). Teachers' judgments of problems in the transition to kindergarten. *Early Childhood Research Quarterly, 15*, 147–166.

Rolstad, K., Mahoney, K., & Glass, G. V. (2005). The big picture: A meta-analysis of program effectiveness research on English language learners. *Educational Policy, 19*, 572–594.

Rothbart, M. K., & Posner, M. I. (2005). Genes and experience in the development of executive attention and effortful control. *New Directions for Child and Adolescent Development, 109*, 101–108.

Rueda, M. R., Posner, M. I., & Rothbart, M. K. (2005). The development of executive attention: Contributions to the emergence of self-regulation. *Developmental Neuropsychology, 28*, 573–594.

Rueda, M. R., Rothbart, M. K., McCandliss, B. D., Saccomanno, L., & Posner, M. I. (2005). Training, maturation, and genetic influences on the development of executive attention. *Proceedings of the National Academy of Sciences, USA, 102*, 14931–14936.

Sektnan, M., McClelland, M. M., Acock, A. C., & Morrison, F. J. (2010). Relations between early family risk, children's behavioral regulation, and academic achievement. *Early Childhood Research Quarterly, 25*(4), 464–479.

Singer, J. D., & Willett, J. B. (2003). *Applied longitudinal data analysis: Modeling change and event occurrence.* New York, NY: Oxford University Press.

StataCorp. (2007). *Stata statistical software: Release 10.* College Station, TX: Author.

Tapia, M. R. (1992). Motivational orientations, learning, and the Puerto Rican child. In A. N. Ambert & M. D. Alvarez (Eds.), *Puerto Rican children on the mainland* (pp. 109–131). New York: Garland Publishers.

Tominey, S. L., & McClelland, M. M. (2010, this issue). Red light, purple light: Findings from a randomized trial using circle time games to improve behavioral self-regulation in preschool. *Early Education and Development, 22*, 491–522.

Trueba, H. T. (1993). From failure to success: The roles of culture and cultural conflict in the academic achievement of Chicano students. In R. R. Valencia (Ed.), *Chicano school failure and success: Research and policy agendas for the 1990s* (pp. 151–163). Bristol, PA: The Falmer Press.

Tsujimoto, S. (2008). The prefrontal cortex: Functional neural development during early childhood. *Neuroscientist, 14*, 345–358.

Turkheimer, E., Haley, A., Waldron, M., D'Onofrio, B., & Gottesman, I. I. (2003). Socioeconomic status modifies heritability of IQ in young children. *Psychological Science, 14*, 623–628.

U.S. Census Bureau. (2006). Poverty status, food stamp receipt, and public assistance for children under 18 years by race, and hispanic origin of the child for all children: 2006, Table C8. Retrieved April 25, 2011, from http://www.census.gov/population/www/socdemo/hh-fam/cps2006.html

Vitaro, F., Brendgen, M., Larose, S., & Tremblay, R. E. (2005). Kindergarten disruptive behaviors, protective factors, and educational achievement by early adulthood. *Journal of Educational Psychology, 97*, 617–629.

Wachs, T. D., Gurkas, P., & Kontos, S. (2004). Predictors of preschool children's compliance behavior in early childhood classroom settings. *Journal of Applied Developmental Psychology, 25*, 439–457.

Wanless, S. B., McClelland, M. M., Acock, A. C., Chen, F.-M., & Chen, J.-L. (2011). Behavioral regulation and early academic achievement in Taiwan. *Early Education & Development, 22*, 1–28.

Wanless, S. B., McClelland, M. M., Acock, A. C., Ponitz, C. C., Son, S.-H., Lan, X., et al. (2010). Measuring behavioral regulation in four cultures. *Psychological Assessment*. doi: 10.1037/a0021768. Available at http://psycnet.apa.org/psycinfo/2011-04577-001/

Wasserman, G. A., Rauh, V. A., Brunelli, S. A., Garcia-Castro, M., & Necos, B. (1990). Psychosocial attributes and life experiences of disadvantaged minority mothers: Age and ethnic variations. *Child Development, 61*, 566–580.

Wiebe, S. A., Espy, K. A., & Charak, D. (2008). Using confirmatory factor analysis to understand executive control in preschool children: I. Latent structure. *Developmental Psychology, 44*, 575–587.

Woodcock, R. W., & Muñoz-Sandoval, A. F. (1996). *Batería Woodcock-Muñoz-R: Pruebas de aprovechamiento-Revisada* [Batería Woodcock-Muñoz-R: Achievement Tests-Revised], *Supplemental Manual*. Itasca, IL: Riverside.

Red Light, Purple Light: Findings From a Randomized Trial Using Circle Time Games to Improve Behavioral Self-Regulation in Preschool

Shauna L. Tominey and Megan M. McClelland

Research Findings: The present study examined the efficacy of a self-regulation intervention with 65 preschool children. Using circle time games, the study examined whether participating in a treatment group significantly improved behavioral self-regulation and early academic outcomes. Half of the children were randomly assigned to participate in 16 playgroups during the winter of the school year. Behavioral aspects of self-regulation and early achievement were assessed in the fall and spring. Although there was no treatment effect in the overall sample, post hoc analyses revealed that participation in the treatment group was significantly related to self-regulation gains in children who started the year with low levels of these skills. Children in the treatment group also demonstrated significant letter-word identification gains compared to children in the control group. *Practice or Policy:* The findings from this study provide preliminary evidence for the efficacy of the intervention in terms of improving preschoolers' behavioral self-regulation for children low in these skills and improving letter-word identification. Although preliminary, these results have the potential to inform preschool curricula that emphasize behavioral self-regulation as a means of facilitating school readiness.

Every year, many young children transition from preschool to a more structured and academically focused kindergarten environment. Although most children navigate this transition successfully, it can be problematic for those who have not developed the self-regulation critical for success in a classroom setting. In recent years, there has been an increasing emphasis on accountability for children's academic achievement in the U.S. public education system, in part because of legislation such as No Child Left Behind. As a result, pressure is being placed on teachers at all grade levels to adopt a stronger academic focus to ensure that children reach required benchmarks on mandated standardized tests (U.S. Department of Education, 2009). Recent research has documented the fact that children are entering kindergarten and elementary school with varying levels of self-regulation and that these skills are key predictors of children's success in early academic achievement (Blair, 2002; Cooper & Farran, 1988; Eisenberg, Smith, Sadovsky, & Spinrad, 2004; McClelland, Cameron, Wanless, & Murray, 2007; Valiente, Lemery-Chalfant, & Castro, 2007). In particular, children who have difficulty with the behavioral aspects of self-regulation may not have the skills necessary to benefit from classroom learning environments (Howse, Lange, Farran, & Boyles, 2003; McClelland, Morrison, & Holmes, 2000). Academic skills learned in early elementary school tend to be cumulative, so children who lack behavioral self-regulation in early childhood may be at risk for poor academic achievement throughout formal schooling (Entwisle & Alexander, 1993). Studies suggest that self-regulation emerges by preschool as an important predictor of academic outcomes, making preschool an ideal time to introduce interventions aimed at improving the behavioral aspects of self-regulation (Blair & Razza, 2007; McClelland, Cameron, Connor, et al., 2007).

It is clear that behavioral self-regulation is necessary for academic success, but there is relatively little research on how to improve these skills prior to kindergarten entry. Studies have shown that preschool children can improve behavioral self-regulation in individual laboratory training sessions and on computer-based tasks (Dowsett & Livesey, 2000; Rueda, Rothbart, McCandliss, Saccomanno, & Posner, 2005), but few studies have focused on similar interventions using games that are designed for classroom implementation. It is crucial for researchers to develop interventions promoting behavioral self-regulation in preschool that can be easily implemented by teachers to ensure that children enter kindergarten with the skills they need to be academically successful. The present study examined the efficacy of an intervention using circle time games designed to strengthen children's behavioral self-regulation over the prekindergarten year.

DEFINING BEHAVIORAL SELF-REGULATION

The focus of this study is on the behavioral aspects of self-regulation (i.e., attention, working memory, and inhibitory control), skills that are essential for planning and executing goal-directed activities (Blair, 2002). *Attention* is defined as the ability to switch focus from one object or task to another as well as the ability to ignore distractions (Rothbart & Posner, 2005; Rueda, Posner, & Rothbart, 2004). *Working memory* refers to a child's ability to hold information in memory long enough to complete a task (Adams, Bourke, & Willis, 1999). Working memory is an essential component of following through with instructions, especially when completing a multistep task. *Inhibitory control* is the ability to stop a dominant response (e.g., shouting an answer to a question) in order to demonstrate a less automatic but more adaptive behavior (e.g., raising a hand and waiting to be called on; McClelland, Cameron, Wanless, et al., 2007; Rennie, Bull, & Diamond, 2004). The literature supports the notion that the integration of attention, working memory, and inhibitory control is important for success in classroom settings (Baumeister & Vohs, 2004; McClelland, Cameron, Connor, et al., 2007; McClelland, Cameron, Wanless, et al., 2007). The games tested in this study were intended to help children practice integrating these behavioral aspects of self-regulation.

THE IMPORTANCE OF BEHAVIORAL SELF-REGULATION FOR SCHOOL SUCCESS

Research suggests that children's behavioral self-regulation predicts academic outcomes in preschool (Blair & Razza, 2007; McClelland, Cameron, Connor, et al., 2007) and elementary school (Liew, McTigue, Barrois, & Hughes, 2008; McClelland, Acock, & Morrison, 2006; McClelland et al., 2000; Valiente et al., 2007) as well as high school graduation and college completion (McClelland, Piccinin, Acock, & Stallings, 2011; Vitaro, Brendgen, Larose, & Tremblay, 2005). Specifically, studies have shown that attention predicts academic achievement, including math and literacy, in preschool and elementary school (Blair & Razza, 2007; Howse, Lange, et al., 2003). Working memory (Gathercole & Pickering, 2000) and inhibitory control skills (Blair & Razza, 2007) have also been found to predict these same academic outcomes in early elementary school students. Although some studies have found that these specific components of behavioral self-regulation (e.g., attention) predict children's abilities to succeed in a classroom setting (Alexander, Entwisle, & Dauber, 1993; Ladd, 2003), many studies (including the present study) have focused on measures of behavioral self-regulation that integrate attention, working memory, and inhibitory control. For example, in one study, kindergarten behavioral self-regulation (as measured by a composite score of teacher ratings on a questionnaire including impulsivity, planning abilities, and attention) predicted children's academic achievement over the kindergarten year (Howse, Calkins, Anastopoulos, Keane, & Shelton, 2003). Another study found that kindergarten learning-related skills (specifically work-related skills, which include aspects of self-regulation such as paying attention to instructions and complying with teacher requests) predicted children's literacy and math skills between kindergarten and sixth grade and growth in literacy and math from kindergarten to second grade (McClelland et al., 2006, 2000). Moreover, children with poor behavioral self-regulation skills exhibited lower performance than their higher rated peers on reading and math between kindergarten and sixth grade, even after child IQ and parent education level were controlled (McClelland et al., 2006). Taken together, the results from these studies suggest that the integration of the behavioral aspects of self-regulation predicts academic success throughout schooling and that children who have difficulties with these skills may be especially at risk for low academic achievement.

BEHAVIORAL SELF-REGULATION IN THE PRESCHOOL YEARS

The preschool years are an important time for the development of behavioral self-regulation for several reasons. First, for many children, preschool is the first classroom environment in which they are asked to demonstrate behavioral self-regulation (Phillips, McCartney, & Sussman, 2006). Prior to school entry, these skills emerge in the context of the family environment. Throughout early childhood, behavioral self-regulation moves from an external process to an internal process (Kopp, 1991) as children learn to regulate behaviors (e.g., sucking on a thumb to self-soothe or turning away from an unwanted stimuli) that were previously regulated by caregivers (e.g., soothing through rocking and patting). Within a school context, children are continually asked to demonstrate regulation of their own behaviors by paying attention, remembering and following through with instructions, and acting appropriately, even when their impulse is to do otherwise.

Second, it is during preschool that a number of developmental changes occur, including brain maturation in the prefrontal cortex, an area associated with the development of the behavioral aspects of self-regulation (Blair, 2002). Changes in behavioral self-regulation abilities accompany this brain maturation. Children begin to increase the length of time that they are able to pay attention, and their ability to plan and allocate attention to goals improves (Landry, Smith, Swank, & Miller-Loncar, 2000; Wellman, Somerville, & Haake, 1979). Working memory becomes more accurate, and children become more consistent at exhibiting inhibitory control skills in appropriate contexts. Studies have shown that each of these skills can be improved with practice (Ford, McDougall, & Evans, 2009; Landry et al., 2000; St. Clair-Thompson, Stevens, Hunt, & Bolder, 2010). Finding developmentally appropriate and engaging ways to help children practice behavioral self-regulation (e.g., through games in a circle time setting) is critical to helping children who have difficulty with these skills.

Third, research shows that self-regulation in preschool predicts academic achievement in both preschool (Blair & Razza, 2007; McClelland, Cameron, Connor, et al., 2007) and kindergarten (Howse, Lange, et al., 2003). For instance, one study found that preschool children who had difficulty with behavioral self-regulation scored lower on a measure of cognitive achievement than peers with high levels of these skills (Bronson, Tivnan, & Seppanen, 1995). Another study found that behavioral self-regulation, as measured by a direct task, significantly predicted emergent literacy, vocabulary, and math skills over the prekindergarten year. Moreover, gains in preschool behavioral self-regulation significantly predicted gains in these academic measures over the prekindergarten year (McClelland, Cameron, Connor, et al., 2007). Taken together, these studies provide evidence that behavioral self-regulation emerges by preschool as an important predictor of academic success, making preschool an ideal time to introduce interventions aimed at improving these skills prior to kindergarten entry.

Although not all children receive formalized care prior to kindergarten, an estimated 83.2% of children attend early care and education programs before entering kindergarten (Denton Flanagan & McPhee, 2009). Interventions in these settings would reach the majority of children at an important period of behavioral self-regulation development. Furthermore, promoting behavioral self-regulation in preschool may help many children develop the skills needed for the transition to school and for continued success throughout formal schooling.

CHILDREN AT RISK FOR POOR BEHAVIORAL SELF-REGULATION

Numerous studies are showing that children from disadvantaged backgrounds, and especially those experiencing multiple risk factors, perform worse than their more advantaged peers on a variety of language, achievement, and school readiness indicators (Dearing, Berry, & Zaslow, 2006). In particular, research has documented the fact that children from low-income families are less able than their peers to regulate their attention in goal-directed tasks and are especially at risk for entering kindergarten with poor behavioral self-regulation (Evans & Rosenbaum, 2008; Howse, Lange, et al., 2003). In one study, children with an accumulation of risk factors (e.g., children who had low levels of parent education and who were the most economically disadvantaged) were at the highest risk for entering preschool with low levels of behavioral self-regulation, and these low levels persisted through preschool and into kindergarten (Wanless, McClelland, Tominey, & Acock, 2011). These studies provide evidence that children from disadvantaged backgrounds are especially at risk for entering kindergarten without the behavioral self-regulation needed for academic success. Moreover, studies suggest that behavioral self-regulation may serve as a mediating factor between risk and academic achievement. In one study, kindergarten behavioral self-regulation skills (i.e., attention and inhibitory control) mediated the negative effect between risk factors (e.g., high levels of maternal depressive symptoms and economic disadvantage) and children's first-grade achievement in reading, math, and vocabulary (Sektnan, McClelland, Acock, & Morrison, 2010). Thus, children from disadvantaged backgrounds are an especially important population to target for behavioral self-regulation interventions prior to kindergarten entry. The present study included children from economically diverse backgrounds, and high variability in children's behavioral self-regulation abilities was expected.

MEASURING BEHAVIORAL SELF-REGULATION AND THE HEAD–TOES–KNEES–SHOULDERS TASK (HTKS)

Recent research has focused on a relatively new direct measure of behavioral self-regulation, the Head-Toes-Knees-Shoulders task (HTKS), which measures the integration of children's attention, working memory, and inhibitory control (McClelland, Ponitz, Messersmith, & Tominey, 2010; Ponitz, McClelland, Matthews, & Morrison, 2009). The HTKS is a short and relatively simple game that asks children to pay attention, remember up to four rules, and do the opposite (e.g., touch your head when told to touch your toes). Studies supporting the construct validity of the HTKS have found significant relations between children's scores on the HTKS and both parent- and teacher-rated inhibitory control and attention (McClelland, Cameron, Connor, et al., 2007; Ponitz et al., 2009).

Research has also supported the predictive validity of the task. Specifically, children's scores on the HTKS have significantly predicted children's emergent literacy, vocabulary, and math skills in preschool and kindergarten (Matthews, Ponitz, & Morrison, 2009; McClelland, Cameron, Connor, et al., 2007; Ponitz et al., 2009). Moreover, one recent study found that children's HTKS scores in the fall of kindergarten significantly predicted spring literacy, vocabulary, and math skills at the end of the school year and gains children made in math learning skills from fall to spring (Ponitz et al., 2009). Although research has shown that the HTKS is a reliable and valid measure of children's behavioral self-regulation, relatively little research has focused on helping children improve these specific behavioral aspects of self-regulation (i.e., the integration of attention, working memory and inhibitory control). The present study examined the efficacy of a set of circle time games that helped children practice these aspects of behavioral self-regulation (as measured by the HTKS).

INTERVENTION RESEARCH

In recent years, there has been growing interest in the development of school readiness interventions. Interventions targeting specific aspects of self-regulation have focused primarily on individualized training sessions in laboratory settings (Dowsett & Livesey, 2000; Rueda et al., 2005); however, these techniques do not translate easily to a classroom context. In addition, many of the interventions that have been implemented in classroom settings have examined broad constructs of socioemotional skills often in combination with academic intervention, rather than focusing specifically on behavioral self-regulation (Raver, 2002). These interventions often require extensive teacher training and materials for implementation. One example is the Tools of the Mind program, which focuses on social, emotional, and behavioral self-regulation skills in addition to a curricular emphasis on literacy and math in preschool. Children participating in Tools classrooms have shown significant improvement on computer-based executive function tasks (Diamond, Barnett, Thomas, & Munro, 2007) and on a teacher-reported problem behavior scale (Barnett et al., 2008). Another example, the Promoting Alternative Thinking Strategies (PATHS) intervention, targets cooperation, emotional awareness and communication, self-regulation, self-esteem, and problem solving in preschool children. Children participating in the PATHS treatment group were rated more socially competent by parents and teachers than were children in the control group (Domitrovich, Cortes, & Greenberg, 2007). Finally, the Kids in Transition to School program examined the impact of playgroups that focused on a wide range of socioemotional, self-regulation, and early literacy skills on foster children and found that children participating in the treatment group exhibited significantly higher levels of social competence and self-regulatory skills than children in the control group (Pears, Fisher, & Bronz, 2007).

Although each of these interventions included self-regulation as part of broader interventions, none focused specifically on improving behavioral self-regulation as a means of improving academic outcomes. Unlike these previous studies, the intervention presented in this article focused on helping children practice specific behavioral aspects of self-regulation (the integration of attention, working memory, and inhibitory control) that have been shown to predict academic outcomes. In addition, the present study used circle time games that were variations on popular children's games. The games required minimal training for implementation and few materials (e.g., construction paper, children's music CDs, classroom musical instruments), all of which are commonly found in preschool classrooms.

THE PRESENT STUDY

This study investigated whether an intervention using circle time games improved behavioral self-regulation in an economically diverse sample of preschool children. In addition, we examined whether treatment group participation predicted academic gains over the prekindergarten year. The study had two research questions. The first research question was as follows: *Does participation in an intervention lead to greater gains in behavioral self-regulation in a sample of prekindergartners?* Based on research documenting the effectiveness of broader interventions (Diamond et al., 2007; Domitrovich et al., 2007; Pears et al., 2007), we expected that children who were randomly assigned to the treatment group would show significantly greater gains in behavioral self-regulation over the prekindergarten year than children in the control group. The second research question was: *Does intervention treatment group participation relate to academic outcomes over the prekindergarten year?* We hypothesized that participation in the intervention treatment group would predict not only gains in behavioral self-regulation but also gains in academic outcomes. This hypothesis was based on research suggesting that improvements in self-regulation abilities may result in improvements in early achievement (Barnett et al., 2008; Diamond et al., 2007).

METHOD

Participants

Participants were 65 children (out of an initial group of 74 children; see "Attrition") within two child development centers in Oregon. Children were selected based on kindergarten eligibility the following year. Approximately half of the children in the study were from low-income families as measured by enrollment in Head Start ($n = 28$). The average age at the beginning of the study was 54.6 months (range = 44–60 months). Of the children, 39 were female and 26 were male. Mothers of children enrolled in Head Start had an average education level of 12.2 years ($SD = 2.6$) with a range of 6–16 years.

Mothers of children who were not enrolled in the Head Start program had an average education level of 17 years ($SD = 2.7$) with a range of 12–21 years. Three of the children had Spanish as a first language and were administered the tests in Spanish by a native Spanish speaker. Spanish-speaking research assistants translated English instructions into Spanish for children who had Spanish as a first language.

The majority of children in the study ($n = 53$ out of 65) attended preschool in a university child development center and laboratory school. Placement in the center was available to children paying tuition and was also available at no cost to children enrolled in the Head Start program. Approximately half of the children in each classroom paid tuition, and half received care at no cost because of enrollment in Head Start. A small number of children participating in the study ($n = 12$) were attending a program at a second child development center. Across both sites, children were divided among nine classrooms. Information on classroom activities was obtained from classroom teachers. All of the classrooms emphasized play during children's free-choice time, but most of the teacher-facilitated activities were academically focused (e.g., learning letters). Although teachers were familiar with traditional versions of the games used in the intervention, they reported that similar games were rarely implemented in any of the classrooms.

Attrition

Initially, 74 children were recruited for participation in the study. Data were obtained from all 74 children at Time 1 (fall). At Time 2 (spring), data were obtained from only 65 children. The total attrition was nine children: four children moved over the course of the school year, one child left school early for a family vacation, three children declined to participate in the posttest, and one child was withdrawn from the study because of newly diagnosed developmental delays. The children who left the study did not significantly differ from the children who completed the study on age or gender ($ps > .05$). A higher percentage of children who left the study were enrolled in Head Start (67%) as compared to the overall sample (43%), although this difference was not statistically significant ($p > .05$). All analyses were conducted using data from the 65 children who participated in all phases of the study.

Measures

Parent Demographic Questionnaire

In the fall of the prekindergarten year, parents completed a background questionnaire in their native language (English or Spanish) containing questions regarding child age, child gender, whether the child was enrolled in Head Start, and parent education level.

HTKS

In the fall and the spring, the HTKS was used to assess children's behavioral self-regulation (Ponitz et al., 2009). In the HTKS, children play a game where they are asked to touch their head or toes (or knees/shoulders in the alternate version). They are then asked to do the opposite of what the experimenter says. The game requires children to remember up to four rules, pay attention, and demonstrate inhibitory control. The possible score for each item is 0, 1, or 2: 0 denotes an incorrect response, 1 is a self-correct (child makes a motion toward the incorrect response but then stops and gives the correct response), and 2 points is a correct response without movement toward the incorrect response. There are 20 test items, and scores range from 0 to 40, with higher scores indicating higher levels of behavioral self-regulation. Recent research has shown that the HTKS is a reliable and valid measure of children's behavioral self-regulation in diverse populations and cross-culturally (McClelland, Cameron, Connor, et al., 2007; Ponitz et al., 2008, 2009; Wanless, McClelland, Acock, et al., in press). In the present study, interrater reliability on the HTKS was calculated at kappa = 92. Teacher-rated behavioral self-regulation in the fall was correlated with children's fall HTKS scores ($r = .20$, $p = .09$), and teacher-rated behavioral self-regulation in the spring was correlated with children's spring HTKS scores ($r = .24$, $p = .06$).

Academic Outcomes

In the fall and spring, children's academic outcomes were assessed using three subtests of the Woodcock–Johnson Psycho-Educational Battery–III Tests of Achievement (WJ-III).

Letter-Word Identification. Children's letter skills and developing word-coding skills in English or Spanish were assessed using raw scores from the Letter-Word Identification subtest of the WJ-III (Woodcock & Mather, 2000) or the Batería III Woodcock–Muñoz (Muñoz-Sandoval, Woodcock, McGrew, & Mather, 2005). Previous research has shown high reliability for preschool-age children on both the English and Spanish versions of the task (Schrank et al., 2005; Woodcock & Mather, 2000).

Picture Vocabulary. Children's expressive vocabulary skills in English or Spanish were measured using the Picture Vocabulary subtest of the WJ-III or the Batería III Woodcock–Muñoz (Muñoz-Sandoval et al., 2005). Previous research has shown reliability for both versions of the task with preschool-age children at .81 and .89, respectively (Schrank et al., 2005; Woodcock & Mather, 2000).

Applied Problems. Children's mathematical operations needed to solve practical problems, including counting objects, reading numbers, and basic addition and subtraction picture problems, were measured using the Applied Problems subtest of the WJ-III or the Batería III Woodcock–Muñoz (Muñoz-Sandoval et al., 2005). In previous research, both the English and Spanish versions of the task demonstrated reliability for preschool-age children at .94 and .93, respectively (Schrank et al., 2005; Woodcock & Mather, 2000).

Procedure

In the fall of the prekindergarten year (September), an invitation to participate in the study was mailed to parents of all 4-year-olds at the participating preschools. Consent forms were collected from 74 families. The study was divided into three phases: pretest (November–December), intervention (January–March), and posttest (April–May).

Pretest

During this phase, children's behavioral self-regulation and academic outcomes were assessed over 4 weeks. Children received two of the assessments on each of two different days to prevent fatigue, and the order of assessments was randomized. Parents completed questionnaires at this time.

Intervention

During the intervention phase, half of the children in each classroom were randomly assigned to participate in the intervention treatment group. Random assignment at the individual level within classrooms was chosen because of the high variability in class sizes and diversity in child characteristics across classrooms. In addition, the intraclass correlation on the HTKS in the fall was .06 (see Results), showing that limited variance in scores was due to classroom membership and supporting our decision to randomize at the individual level. Children at both sites were frequently taken out of the classroom to participate in individual and small-group activities, so they were accustomed to leaving the classroom and seeing others leave the classroom throughout the school day. Although there were initial concerns regarding potential contamination effects within classrooms, teachers reported that there was no evidence of children sharing intervention activities with other children in the classroom who were assigned to the control group. In addition, research has found that when contamination effects occur because of changes in children's behavior, children assigned to the control group are more likely to act like children in the treatment group, making detection of intervention effects more difficult. These types of contamination effects, however, are often found to be small or negligible (Rhoads, 2009; Torgerson, 2001).

Children in the treatment group participated in a total of 16 playgroups over 8 weeks. The playgroup sessions were held twice weekly, and each session was approximately 30 min. Previous research has found significant improvement in children's self-regulation and social competence in interventions of similar durations (Pears et al., 2007). Each playgroup session had five to eight children and two assistant teachers. The playgroups were held on the same days and times each week as part of the regular preschool day and were scheduled at times chosen by the classroom teachers. The same researcher (Shauna Tominey) led all of the playgroups to ensure fidelity. The playgroup leader developed the games and had previously worked as an early childhood education teacher (Tominey & McClelland, 2008). Playgroup attendance was recorded for each child. Children in the intervention group attended an average of 11.3 sessions (range = 5–16). The most common reason for a child to miss a session was an absence due to illness or vacation. Occasionally, a child would decline to participate on a given day because of involvement in other classroom activities. Other reasons for missing sessions included arriving late for school and lacking transportation (to school).

Posttest

During this phase, behavioral self-regulation and academic assessments were readministered to all children. Research assistants were blind to intervention participation; those who assisted with the intervention phase of the study did not test children from classrooms in which they had previously assisted to prevent researcher bias.

Playgroup Session Format

Playgroup sessions were designed to resemble classroom circle times. At the beginning of each session, children sat on mats in a circle and participated in a greeting song that was intended to help children transition to the playgroup setting. Following the greeting song, the playgroup leader introduced and led children in the playgroup activity. At the end of each playgroup session, children sat on mats in a circle and sang a goodbye song before returning to their classrooms. Six activities were presented over the 16 sessions (omitted for blind review). As the playgroup sessions progressed, additional instructions were added, making the games increasingly complicated. Each game was repeated at subsequent sessions to ensure that children had multiple opportunities to practice and learn both the basic and increasingly complicated versions of the games. Children were also given the opportunity to lead games when appropriate (e.g., select and hold up colors for *Red Light, Purple Light*).

Playgroup Games

In each game, attention and working memory were essential for children to remember and follow through with continually changing multistep instructions. Children practiced inhibitory control by starting and stopping to different cues (oral and visual), performing specific behaviors in response to cues, and performing opposite behaviors. The games used in the present study had been previously piloted in prekindergarten classrooms (Tominey & McClelland, 2008). Teachers reported that these games were easy to implement in a circle time setting with large groups of children with varying developmental levels and self-regulation abilities.

Red Light, Purple Light

Like in the popular children's game *Red Light, Green Light*, a teacher acted as a stoplight by standing at the opposite end of the room from the children and holding up different-colored construction paper circles to represent stop and go. Children responded to specific color cues (e.g., purple is stop and orange is go) and then opposite cues (e.g., purple is go and orange is stop) as well as to different shapes representing stop and go (e.g., any color circle is go and any color square is stop).

The Freeze Game

Children danced when music played and froze when the teacher stopped the music. Children danced slowly to slow songs and quickly to fast songs, alternating between different slow and fast songs. Children were then asked to respond to opposite cues: dancing quickly to slow songs and slowly to fast songs.

Color-Matching Freeze

In this game, which was related to *The Freeze Game*, children danced when music played and froze when the music stopped; however, children were asked to perform an additional step before freezing. Teachers taped different-colored pieces of construction paper to mats placed on the ground.

When the music stopped, the teacher held up a specific color and children were instructed to find and stand on a mat of that color.

Sleeping, Sleeping, All the Children Are Sleeping

Children pretended to sleep when the teacher sang, "Sleeping, sleeping, all the children are sleeping." While children pretended to sleep, the circle leader gave an additional instruction for children to wake up and act out an animal (e.g., "And when they woke up... they were monkeys!"). Additional rules were added to make the game more complicated.

Conducting an Orchestra

The teacher used a dowel rod as a conducting baton to lead children in playing musical instruments (e.g., jingle bells or maracas). When the conductor waved the baton, children played their instruments. When the conductor put the baton down, children stopped. The conductor then instructed children to play their instruments quickly when the baton moved quickly and slowly when the baton moved slowly. Children were also asked to respond to opposite cues. When the conductor waved the baton, children stopped playing their instruments, and when the conductor set the baton down, children played their instruments.

Drum Beats

Children responded to different drum cues with body movements. Teachers chose actions for children to perform while sitting (e.g., clapping or stomping) and while moving around the room (e.g., walking or dancing). For example, children were instructed to walk quickly to fast drumming, walk slowly to slow drumming, and freeze when the drumming stopped. Teachers also asked children to respond to opposite cues (walking slowly to fast drum beats and quickly to slow drum beats) and associated different actions with specific drum cues (e.g., hopping to fast drum beats and crawling to slow drum beats).

RESULTS

Descriptive Statistics

Prior to answering our research questions, we analyzed descriptive statistics and bivariate correlations for the entire sample ($N=65$; see Table 1). As expected, there was high variability in initial behavioral self-regulation scores. At Time 1, the average HTKS score was 11 points ($SD=12$,

TABLE 1
Bivariate Correlations for Children in the Overall Sample (N=65)

Variable	1	2	3	4	5	6	7	8	9	10	11	12	13
1. Child age (months)	—												
2. Child gender[a]	.31*	—											
3. Head Start status[b]	.09	.18	—										
4. Maternal education[c]	-.09	-.31*	-.65***	—									
5. Fall HTKS	-.01	-.17	-.37**	.33*	—								
6. Spring HTKS	-.05	-.02	-.52***	.22	.50***	—							
7. HTKS difference	-.04	.16	-.16	-.12	-.46***	.52***	—						
8. Applied Problems difference	-.20	.03	-.02	.04	.19	-.08	.08	—					
9. Letter-Word Identification difference	-.03	-.12	-.28*	.45***	.29*	.32**	.03	.11	—				
10. Vocabulary difference	-.06	.02	-.15	.14	-.12	-.00	.14	-.03	.06	—			
11. Intervention group[d]	-.11	.05	-.07	.12	.07	.14	.05	.01	.28*	-.04	—		
12. Number of sessions	-.09	.06	-.08	.04	.05	.18	.10	.03	.28*	.01	.94***	—	
13. School absences	-.07	.01	.17	-.13	-.10	-.24†	-.12	-.13	-.05	.01	.07	-.08	—

Note. HTKS = Head–Toes–Knees–Shoulders task.
[a]Child gender: 0 = female, 1 = male.
[b]Head Start status: 0 = not enrolled in Head Start, 1 = enrolled in Head Start.
[c]For correlations including maternal education, n = 55.
[d]Intervention group: 0 = control, 1 = treatment.
†p < .1. *p < .05. **p < .01. ***p < .001.

range = 0–37 points), with skewness of .75 and kurtosis of 2.17. Although the skewness and kurtosis were not indicative of a nonnormal distribution (Kline, 2005), a high number of children scored 0 points on the task at the beginning of the year, indicating likely floor effects. In a previous study examining the HTKS, approximately 30% of children at 48 months had a score of 0 on the task, with this number decreasing to 15% at 54 months (Ponitz et al., 2008). In the present study, 38.5% of children scored at floor level at Time 1 ($n = 25$), and 12.31% of children scored at floor level at Time 2 ($n = 8$). The average HTKS score at Time 2 was 22.3 points ($SD = 13$, range = 0–38). The possibility of ceiling effects on the task was examined but was considered unlikely because no child in the study scored the maximum number of points on the measure at either time point. On average, children gained 11 points on the HTKS over the prekindergarten year ($SD = 13$, range = −10 to 35). Table 2 summarizes the remaining descriptive statistics for the children in the study.

TABLE 2
Means (SD) for Children in the Treatment and Control Groups (N = 65)

Variable	Overall Sample (N = 65)		
	Control (n = 37)	Treatment (n = 28)	Total (N = 65)
Child age (months)	54.9 (3.9)	54.1 (3.2)	54.6 (3.6)
Child gender[a]	0.38	0.43	0.4
Head Start status[b]	0.46	0.4	0.43
Maternal education[c]	15.1 (3.8)	15.9 (3.1)	15.4 (3.5)
School absences	5.5 (4.3)	6.2 (5.6)	5.8 (4.9)
Fall HTKS	10.2 (12.4)	12 (12.1)	11 (12)
Spring HTKS	20.7 (13.5)	24.4 (12.6)	22.3 (13)
Difference in HTKS	10.4 (12.5)	11.7 (13.8)	10.97 (13)
Fall Letter-Word Identification	7.7 (4.3)	8.6 (5.1)	8.1 (4.6)
Spring Letter-Word Identification	9.8 (5.6)*	12.7 (7.3)*	11.1 (6.5)
Difference in Letter-Word Identification	2.1 (2.5)*	4.1 (4.3)*	2.9 (3.5)
Fall Applied Problems	12.2 (4.2)	13.4 (4.9)	12.7 (4.5)
Spring Applied Problems	14.9 (3.7)	16.2 (4.6)	15.5 (4.1)
Difference in Applied Problems	2.76 (2.5)	2.79 (1.7)	2.77 (2.2)
Fall Vocabulary	15.4 (3.2)	16.4 (3.5)	15.8 (3.3)
Spring Vocabulary	16.7 (2.9)	17.5 (3.6)	17.8 (3.2)
Difference in Vocabulary	1.32 (2.4)	1.14 (2.8)	1.25 (2.6)

Note. HTKS = Head–Toes–Knees–Shoulders task.
[a]Child gender: 0 = female, 1 = male.
[b]Head Start status: 0 = not enrolled in Head Start, 1 = enrolled in Head Start.
[c]For descriptive statistics including maternal education, $n = 55$.
*$p < .05$.

Research Question 1: Does Participation in an Intervention Lead to Greater Gains in Behavioral Self-Regulation in a Sample of Prekindergartners?

To ensure that there were no initial differences between the treatment and control groups at Time 1, we used t tests to examine initial differences between children in the two groups on the following variables: maternal education, child age, school absences, academic achievement scores (letter-word identification, picture vocabulary, and applied problems), and fall HTKS scores. In addition, tests of proportion were used to examine differences between the proportion of children enrolled in Head Start in each group and the proportion of gender in each group. No statistically significant differences were found between the treatment and control group in the overall sample on any of these variables in the fall (see Table 2).

Multiple regression analysis was then used to answer the first research question. The regression analysis examined predicted gains in behavioral self-regulation scores (spring HTKS score minus fall HTKS score) for children based on group assignment (treatment or control). In addition to treatment group, we controlled for the following variables: Head Start status (enrolled in Head Start/not enrolled in Head Start), child age (in months), child gender, and initial HTKS score. We then added an interaction term between initial HTKS score and group assignment to test whether intervention effects varied based on children's initial behavioral self-regulation scores. Previous studies of children's self-regulation have found significantly different intervention effects based on children's initial levels of self-regulation (Bierman, Nix, Greenberg, Blair, & Domitrovich, 2008; Connor et al., 2010). Maternal education level was not included as a control variable because of the high correlation between maternal education and Head Start status ($r = .66$). Although children were nested in nine classrooms, the intraclass correlation for the difference in HTKS scores was 0.06, so multilevel modeling was not used in the analyses.

The results of the regression analysis were significant, $F(5, 59) = 6.58$, $p < .01$, $r^2 = .36$. Treatment group participation, however, was not a significant predictor of HTKS gains, $t(59) = 0.49$, $p > .05$. Although not significant, the regression coefficient for intervention group was in the expected direction, showing small gains in behavioral self-regulation for children participating in the playgroups (intervention: $B = 1.34$, $\beta = .06$). Of the control variables, Head Start enrollment was the strongest predictor for HTKS gains, $t(59) = -3.49$, $p < .01$, contributing .21 to the explained variance (r^2). The second strongest predictor was initial HTKS score, $t(59) = -5.17$, $p < .001$. Having a higher HTKS score at the beginning of the year predicted smaller gains over the course of the year ($\beta = -.59$), contributing .13 to the explained variance. The interaction between initial HTKS score and group assignment was not significant, $t(58) = -0.94$, $p > .05$.

Although the interaction was not significant, the high number of children scoring 0 on the task (floor effect) likely contributed to our inability to detect an interaction if one did exist (Lewis-Beck, Bryman, & Liao, 2004). In addition, previous studies have found significant intervention effects for children with poor behavioral self-regulation when no effects were found in the overall sample (Bierman et al., 2008; Connor et al., 2010), so we wanted to investigate this possibility further in our sample. Thus, we conducted post hoc analyses to test for a treatment effect in a subsample of children with low initial HTKS scores ($n = 31$). We selected the 50th percentile (children with HTKS scores less than 6 points) as a cutoff point to maximize our sample size. It was also above this cutoff that negative gain scores appeared on the HTKS, which indicated the possibility of regression to the mean effects and may have contributed to lower overall gain scores experienced by children scoring above the 50th percentile.

The average age of children in the low subgroup was 54.6 months ($SD = 4$). Within this group there were 17 girls and 14 boys. Of the children with low HTKS scores, 19 were in the control group and 12 were in the treatment group. There was little variability in HTKS scores within the low subsample at Time 1 ($M = 0.5$, $SD = 1.3$, range $= 0-5$). At Time 2, however, there was substantial variability in HTKS scores. Specifically, the average HTKS score at Time 2 was 16.9 points ($SD = 13.6$, range $= 0-35$), with skewness of .04 and kurtosis of 1.4, indicating a normal distribution (Kline, 2005). Over the course of the year, children with low initial behavioral self-regulation gained an average of 16.3 points ($SD = 13.3$, range $= 0-35$). In contrast, children scoring above the 50th percentile on the HTKS in the fall gained an average of 6.1 points ($SD = 10.8$, range $= -10$ to 25).

Results of a regression model examining intervention participation as a predictor of HTKS gains for the low subgroup were statistically significant, $F(4, 26) = 5.26$, $p < .01$, $r^2 = .45$ (see Table 3). In addition to intervention group assignment, we controlled for Head Start enrollment status, child gender, and age. The results suggested that for children with low initial HTKS scores, treatment group participation significantly predicted HTKS gains over the prekindergarten year, $t(26) = 2.23$, $p < .05$, $\beta = .34$, accounting for 11% of the explained variance in HTKS gains. Within this subgroup, children in the treatment group were predicted to gain 9.2 more points over the year on the HTKS than children in the control group, which was a difference of approximately 1 SD. Of the control variables, Head Start status was the only statistically significant variable, $t(26) = -3.90$, $p < .01$, $\beta = -.58$, and accounted for 33% of the explained variance.

TABLE 3
Multiple Regression Results Examining Intervention Group and Number of Intervention Sessions to Predict Change in HTKS Score Over the Prekindergarten Year in the Subgroup of Children With Low Initial HTKS Scores ($n=31$)

Variable	Analysis 1 (Intervention Group)			Analysis 2 (Dosage)		
	B	SE B	β	B	SE B	β
Child age (months)	0.82	0.59	.25	0.73	0.56	.22
Child gender[a]	−7.58	4.73	−.29	−7.14	4.56	−.27
Head Start status[b]	−15.14	3.88	−.58**	−14.26	3.83	−.54**
Treatment group[c]	9.21	4.13	.34*			
Number of sessions				0.84	0.33	.37*
R^2		.45			.47	
F		5.26**			5.75**	

Note. HTKS = Head–Toes–Knees–Shoulders task.
[a]Child gender: 0 = female, 1 = male.
[b]Head Start status: 0 = not enrolled in Head Start, 1 = enrolled in Head Start.
[c]Treatment group: 0 = control, 1 = treatment.
*$p < .05$. **$p < .01$.

We conducted an additional post hoc analysis examining whether the number of intervention sessions attended significantly predicted behavioral self-regulation gains in the overall sample of children and for the subgroup of children with low initial HTKS scores. Results of the multiple regression predicting gains in HTKS scores (controlling for Head Start status, child age, gender, and initial HTKS score) for the overall sample ($N=65$) indicated that the model was statistically significant, $F(5, 59) = 6.71$, $p < .01$, $r^2 = .36$, although the number of intervention sessions attended did not significantly predict HTKS gains. We then ran the same analysis (excluding initial HTKS score as a control) for children with low initial HTKS scores ($n = 31$; see Table 3). This model was statistically significant, $F(4, 26) = 5.75$, $p < .01$, $r^2 = .47$, and indicated that the number of playgroup sessions attended significantly predicted HTKS gains for children with low initial HTKS scores, $t(26) = 2.50$, $p < .05$, $\beta = .37$ (accounting for 13% of the explained variance). Specifically, for each additional intervention session attended, children were expected to gain nearly 1 additional point (0.84 points) on the HTKS over the year. If children attended the average number of intervention sessions (11.3 sessions), they were expected to gain an additional 9.5 points on the task. Head Start status was the only significant control variable in the model, $t(26) = -3.73$, $p < .01$, $\beta = -.54$, accounting for 33% of the explained variance. Thus, although overall intervention effects were not detected, post hoc analyses indicated significant effects of the intervention for children beginning the year with low HTKS scores. In addition, the number of intervention sessions attended also significantly predicted behavioral self-regulation gains over the school year for children in the low subgroup.

Research Question 2: Does Intervention Treatment Group Participation Relate to Academic Outcomes Over the Prekindergarten Year?

Prior to testing the second research question, we used multiple regression analyses to determine whether children's behavioral self-regulation in the fall predicted fall letter-word identification, applied problems, and vocabulary outcomes. Fall behavioral self-regulation significantly predicted fall academic achievement when child age, gender, and Head Start status were controlled: letter-word identification, $t(60) = 2.09$, $p < .05$, $\beta = .23$; applied problems, $t(60) = 2.54$, $p < .05$, $\beta = .29$; and vocabulary, $t(60) = 4.67$, $p < .001$, $\beta = .53$. Specifically, for each additional standard deviation children scored on the HTKS, they were predicted to score an additional 1.1 points in letter-word identification, 1.3 points in applied problems, and 1.8 points in picture vocabulary in the fall. Head Start status was also a significant predictor of fall scores on letter-word identification, $t(60) = -4.36$, $p < .001$; and applied problems, $t(60) = -3.05$, $p < .01$; but not vocabulary. Children enrolled in Head Start were predicted to score 3.2 fewer points in applied problems and 4.5 fewer points in letter-word identification than children from more advantaged families.

Multiple regression analyses were then used to determine whether intervention treatment group participation predicted gains in academic outcomes (one each for applied problems, letter-word identification, and picture vocabulary). Gains in all academic outcomes were calculated by subtracting children's scores in the fall from their spring scores on the same measure (see Table 2). Child age (in months), gender, and Head Start status (enrolled in Head Start/not enrolled in Head Start) were control variables in all three analyses.

Letter-word identification. The regression model predicting gains in letter-word identification scores was statistically significant, $F(4, 64) = 2.81$, $p < .05$, $r^2 = .15$ (see Table 4). Intervention group assignment significantly predicted gains in children's letter-word identification scores over the prekindergarten year, $t(60) = 2.32$, $p < .05$, and contributed .07 to the explained variance in letter-word identification gains. Children who participated in the treatment group were predicted to gain 2 more points (a difference of 0.57 SD) on the letter-word identification assessment than children in the control group. Head Start enrollment also significantly predicted change in

TABLE 4
Multiple Regression Results Examining Intervention Group and Number of Intervention Sessions to Predict Change in Letter-Word Identification Scores Over the Prekindergarten Year in the Overall Sample (N = 65)

Variable	Analysis (Intervention Group)		
	B	SE B	β
Child age (months)	0.05	.12	.06
Child gender[a]	−0.76	.90	−.11
Head Start status[b]	−1.72	.85	−.24*
Treatment group[c]	1.97	.85	.28*
Number of sessions			
R^2		.16	
F		2.81*	

[a]Child gender: 0 = female, 1 = male.
[b]Head Start status: 0 = not enrolled in Head Start, 1 = enrolled in Head Start.
[c]Treatment group: 0 = control, 1 = treatment.
*p < .05.

letter-word identification score, $t(60) = -2.02$, $p < .05$, and contributed an equivalent amount (.07) to the explained variance. Specifically, children not enrolled in Head Start were predicted to gain 1.72 more points (a difference of 0.5 SD) in letter-word identification over the year than children enrolled in Head Start.

Neither the regression model for applied problems nor the model for picture vocabulary was statistically significant. Thus, we found no significant relation between intervention assignment and change over the prekindergarten year in scores for applied problems, $t(60) = -0.20$, $p > .05$; or vocabulary, $t(60) = -0.45$, $p > .05$.

DISCUSSION

The present study focused on a set of circle time games aimed at improving behavioral self-regulation skills that predict children's academic achievement (McClelland, Cameron, Connor, et al., 2007; Ponitz et al., 2009). The games resembled popular children's games and required few materials, making them easy for teachers to implement in a classroom circle time setting. Our primary research questions examined intervention efficacy using a direct measure of behavioral self-regulation and tested the effect of treatment group participation on academic outcomes over the prekindergarten year. Although significant intervention effects were not found for the overall sample, post hoc analyses indicated significant gains in behavioral self-regulation for children who entered the study with low behavioral self-regulation and who participated in the treatment group. In addition, the number of intervention sessions attended significantly predicted behavioral self-regulation gains over the school year for children with low initial scores. In the overall sample, intervention participation was also significantly related to gains in children's letter-word identification scores.

Treatment Group Participation and Gains in Behavioral Self-Regulation

Contrary to our expectations, there were no significant differences in behavioral self-regulation gains between the treatment and control groups in the overall sample. The absence of a significant treatment effect in the overall sample may have been because there was little variability in behavioral self-regulation gains for children beginning the year with scores above the 50th percentile. Children beginning the year with high scores on the HTKS likely ended the year with high scores (the task ceilings at 40 points) and thus had little variability in gain scores with which we could detect an effect.

Post hoc analyses indicated that participation in the treatment group significantly predicted gains in behavioral self-regulation for children beginning the year with low levels of these skills (below the 50th percentile in the fall). Children who began the year with low scores had the opportunity for more growth and variability in gain scores, and this may have enabled us to better detect an intervention effect in this subgroup that was not detected in the overall sample. For children in the low group, higher rates of attendance in the playgroup sessions also significantly predicted gains in behavioral self-regulation. Intervention studies including behavioral self-regulation have reported intervention attendance (Pears et al., 2007) without examining the impact of dosage on intervention effectiveness. Other studies of early childhood interventions focusing on behavioral outcomes have shown greater short- and long-term benefits from higher levels of participation (Hill, Brooks-Gunn, & Waldfogel, 2003; Reynolds, Temple, Robertson, & Mann, 2001). The significant treatment and dosage effects found within the low subsample add to the finding in the existing literature that behavioral self-regulation can be improved through intervention for children who have difficulties with these skills (Bierman et al., 2008; Connor et al., 2010; Diamond et al., 2007).

The Importance of Family Income for Behavioral Self-Regulation Gains

In the overall sample and in the subsample of children with low behavioral self-regulation, family income was the strongest predictor of behavioral self-regulation level and gains over the prekindergarten year. Children from low-income families began and ended the year with lower behavioral self-regulation and gained fewer points on a measure of behavioral self-regulation than their peers. These results support previous findings that family income is an important predictor of children's self-regulation (Evans & Rosenbaum, 2008; Howse, Lange, et al., 2003; Sektnan et al., 2010; Wanless, McClelland, Tominey, et al., 2011). In the present study, family income was significantly correlated with maternal education level ($r = .66$), indicating that income may not have been the only factor contributing to low behavioral self-regulation scores for children in the study. Research has shown that children and families who are economically disadvantaged are likely to experience an accumulation of risk factors that affect child outcomes (Dearing et al., 2006). These potential risk factors include fewer family resources (e.g., economic and academic), less parent–child quality time, higher rates of authoritarian parenting and punitive discipline, and higher rates of chronic illness than in more advantaged families (Dearing et al., 2006; Lareau, 2003). Research also suggests that behavioral self-regulation mediates the effect of risk factors on academic outcomes (Dearing, McCartney, & Taylor, 2009; Sektnan et al., 2010), highlighting the importance of targeting children from low-income backgrounds for intervention, as they may be especially at risk for exhibiting poor behavioral self-regulation at school entry (Wanless, McClelland, Acock, et al., in press). In the present study, children who exhibited the greatest self-regulation gains (i.e., children in the treatment group from more advantaged families) may have had the most opportunity to explicitly practice paying attention, remembering instructions, and demonstrating inhibitory control through participating in the intervention and having exposure to resources and family processes that promoted strong self-regulation at home (Dearing et al., 2006; Lareau, 2003).

Behavioral Self-Regulation, Treatment Group Participation, and Academic Outcomes Over the Prekindergarten Year

In the overall sample, prior to the intervention, children's fall behavioral self-regulation predicted fall academic achievement in applied problems, letter-word identification, and picture vocabulary. Specifically, higher levels of behavioral self-regulation predicted higher scores on each of these academic outcomes. These findings add to the growing body of research showing that behavioral self-regulation is an important component of academic success as early as preschool (Matthews et al., 2009; McClelland et al., 2007; Ponitz et al., 2009). In addition, family income significantly predicted fall academic achievement. Children from low-income families began the year with lower applied problems and letter-word identification levels than their more advantaged peers. Previous research has also documented socioeconomic status as an important predictor of early achievement (Sektnan et al., 2010; Wanless et al., in press).

Although treatment group assignment did not predict behavioral self-regulation gains in the overall sample, participation in the intervention treatment group significantly predicted gains in letter-word identification scores. The intent of the intervention games was to help students practice the integration of attention, working memory, and inhibitory control, skills that have been found to predict academic outcomes in preschool and kindergarten, including letter-word identification (McClelland et al., 2007; Ponitz et al., 2009). The significant gains in behavioral self-regulation made by children in the low subgroup provide preliminary evidence that the circle time games did indeed relate to improved behavioral self-regulation skills for some children, and perhaps improvement in these skills (though not detected in the overall sample) led to an increased ability to benefit from letter-word identification activities in the classroom. It is important to note that children in the treatment group did not receive additional direct instruction in letter-word identification, as none of the playgroup games involved letters, words, or emergent literacy activities of any kind.

It is possible that the significant effect of intervention participation on letter-word identification scores and not the other academic measures was due to the explicit focus on emergent literacy instruction (and specifically letter recognition) in the prekindergarten classrooms. Previous research has demonstrated that children are exposed to more literacy-rich instruction prior to kindergarten compared to instruction in other academic subjects (Connor, Morrison, & Slominski, 2006; Miller, Kelly, & Zhou, 2005; National Institute of Child Health and Human Development Early Child Care Research Network, 2002). In support of this, teachers in the present study reported that letter recognition was often the focus of classroom learning activities, whereas vocabulary and applied problems were rarely explicitly taught.

Although vocabulary and emergent literacy are closely related, children in this study experienced very small gains over the year in picture vocabulary scores in comparison to the gains experienced in letter-word identification. Children did make apparent gains in applied problems scores, which raises questions about the lack of a relation between these gains and intervention participation. One possible explanation is that gains in applied problem scores were in large part due to maturation, not classroom instruction, which would explain the gains experienced by children in both the treatment and control groups. Previous research has found evidence supporting this lack of an instructional effect on the development of math skills in preschool (Christian, Bachman, & Morrison, 2001). Another possible explanation is that gains in applied problems, whether due to classroom/home learning experiences or maturation, were not aided by participating in the intervention treatment group. Research (including the present study) has found significant relations between behavioral self-regulation and preschool children's applied problems/math abilities (Matthews et al., 2009; McClelland, Cameron, Connor, et al., 2007; Ponitz et al., 2009); however, additional research is needed to investigate the relation between intervention-related gains and gains in math abilities.

Nature and Implementation of Intervention Games

Our implementation strategy resulted in a number of positive and negative consequences, some of which we anticipated and others we did not. As we had intended, the use of music and movement in the intervention games was highly effective at encouraging engagement. The majority of children actively participated in all of the playgroup games, although a few children chose to watch on occasion. In order to involve all children in the activities, especially those who appeared to be withdrawn/shy or easily distracted, we incorporated opportunities for children to lead each activity. For example, each child had a turn choosing which colors represented stop and go and acting as the stoplight in the game *Red Light, Purple Light*. By leading activities, children could watch the responses of other children to their rules and cues and thus practice behavioral self-regulation skills by modeling the correct behaviors and monitoring other children's behaviors. We made sure that every child had an opportunity to lead the activity in every session, and no child ever declined the opportunity to lead an activity.

The decision to remove children from the classroom to participate in the playgroup sessions had both positive and negative consequences. We were concerned about adding to the workload of classroom teachers, and removing children lessened the burden on teachers. This approach also allowed us to control fidelity of implementation. Removing children from classrooms, however, also led to issues we did not anticipate. For example, playgroup sessions were held at times that were chosen by the classroom teachers. The result was that children in some classrooms missed part of free-play time to participate, whereas others missed outdoor play. Occasionally, children would decline to participate in a playgroup session because they did not want to miss one of these activities. In these instances, the response of the classroom teacher significantly impacted whether the child attended the playgroup session. Classroom teachers who encouraged children to go and reassured them that the activity would be available when they returned facilitated participation, whereas classroom teachers who remained uninvolved in these exchanges did not.

LIMITATIONS AND FUTURE RESEARCH

Although the present study supports the preliminary efficacy of a behavioral self-regulation intervention in preschool for children with low initial behavioral self-regulation scores, there are a number of limitations. The primary limitation is the small sample size. Because the study had a final sample size of 65 children, the power to detect a significant effect was limited, although significant effects were still found. Most notably, children with low levels of self-regulation in the fall (below the 50th percentile) benefited from participation in the intervention. The small sample size, however, also limited the ability to perform statistical analyses on subgroups within the treatment and control groups, such as by family income.

Another limitation of the study was that only one measure was used to assess change in behavioral self-regulation over the prekindergarten year. The circle time games were designed to help children practice the skills measured by the HTKS and were selected for use because of face validity and ease of implementation. Although the findings from this study provide preliminary evidence supporting the construct validity of the games in relation to the HTKS, it is critical that future studies of the games incorporate additional measures of behavioral self-regulation to better establish construct validity. Ideally, a combination of direct measures, teacher reports, and classroom observations would be needed to provide a complete picture of how participating in these playgroup games relates to measures of behavioral self-regulation as well as classroom behavior and academic outcomes. In future studies of these games, it may also be beneficial to videotape playgroup sessions in order to observe and code children's responses to the games and watch for specific behaviors (e.g., length of attention) and change in those behaviors.

Moreover, the scope of this intervention was limited to playgroup sessions that included child involvement. It is clear from the results that family income significantly predicted children's behavioral self-regulation and academic scores across the year. The significant effect of family income on child outcomes highlights the need for interventions that extend beyond the child level to include family characteristics. Numerous family factors and processes (National Institute of Child Health and Human Development Early Child Care Research Network, 2003), including parenting (Calkins, 2004) and the home learning environment (McClelland & Wanless, 2006), have demonstrated significant relations with the development of children's self-regulation. Future interventions should include parent and family involvement to maximize gains in self-regulation for all children.

Future studies should also better establish intervention feasibility by implementing the study games in classrooms, led by classroom teachers.

In the present study, the same researcher (who had previously been a classroom teacher) administered the games in small groups outside of the classroom. Although this helped ensure consistency across sessions, future studies should examine fidelity as a variable because ideally classroom teachers will be leading the sessions, which will likely result in varying levels of fidelity and impact intervention effectiveness. Finally, participants should be followed longitudinally with more time points to examine the potential long-term effects of the intervention on children's behavioral self-regulation and academic achievement.

PRACTICAL IMPLICATIONS AND CONCLUSIONS

The results of the present study support the efficacy of a prekindergarten behavioral self-regulation intervention for children with low behavioral self-regulation skills. The results indicate that a set of circle time games was effective in helping children with low initial behavioral self-regulation improve scores on a direct measure of attention, working memory, and inhibitory control, skills that have been found to predict academic outcomes. In addition, participation in the treatment group significantly predicted gains in letter-word identification scores over the prekindergarten year in the overall sample of children. The games used in the study were implemented in playgroup settings with common classroom materials and could be implemented by teachers in small and large groups of children within classrooms. The intervention presented in this study represents a unique opportunity to improve behavioral self-regulation with limited training and without expensive materials, which increases its potential for use on a larger scale.

The present study has the potential to inform preschool curricula that emphasize behavioral self-regulation as a means of facilitating school readiness. The development of interventions that can be translated to classroom settings and easily implemented by teachers is critical to ensure that all children enter school with the behavioral self-regulation skills they need to be ready to learn.

REFERENCES

Adams, A. M., Bourke, L., & Willis, C. (1999). Working memory and spoken language comprehension in young children. *International Journal of Psychology, 34*, 364–373.

Alexander, K. L., Entwisle, D. R., & Dauber, S. L. (1993). First-grade classroom behavior: Its short- and long-term consequences for school performance. *Child Development, 64*, 801–814.

Barnett, W. S., Jung, K., Yarosz, D. J., Thomas, J., Hornbeck, A., Stechuk, R., & Burns, S. (2008). Educational effects of the Tools of the Mind curriculum: A randomized trial. *Early Childhood Research Quarterly, 23*, 299–313.

Baumeister, R. F., & Vohs, K. D. (Eds.). (2004). *Handbook of self-regulation: Research, theory, and applications*. New York, NY: Guilford Press.

Bierman, K. L., Nix, R. L., Greenberg, M. T., Blair, C., & Domitrovich, C. E. (2008). Executive functions and school readiness intervention: Impact, moderation, and mediation in the Head Start REDI program. *Development and Psychopathology, 20*, 821–843.

Blair, C. (2002). School readiness. *American Psychologist, 57*, 111–127.

Blair, C., & Razza, R. P. (2007). Relating effortful control, executive function, and false belief understanding to emerging math and literacy ability in kindergarten. *Child Development, 78*, 647–663.

Bronson, M. B., Tivnan, T., & Seppanen, P. S. (1995). Relations between teacher and classroom activity variables and the classroom behaviors of prekindergarten children in Chapter 1 funded programs. *Journal of Applied Developmental Psychology, 16*, 253–282.

Calkins, S. D. (2004). Early attachment processes and the development of emotional self-regulation. In R. F. Baumeister & K. D. Vohs (Eds.), *Handbook of self-regulation: Research, theory, and applications* (pp. 324–339). New York, NY: Guilford Press.

Christian, K., Bachman, H. J., & Morrison, F. J. (2001). Schooling and cognitive development. In R. J. Sternberg & R. L. Grigorenko (Eds.), *Environmental effects on cognitive abilities* (pp. 287–335). Mahwah, NJ: Erlbaum.

Connor, C. M., Morrison, F. J., & Slominski, L. (2006). Preschool instruction and children's emergent literacy growth. *Journal of Educational Psychology, 98*, 665–689.

Connor, C. M., Ponitz, C. C., Phillips, B. M., Travis, Q. M., Glasney, S., & Morrison, F. J. (2010). First graders' literacy and self-regulation gains: The effect of individualizing student instruction. *Journal of School Psychology, 48*, 433–455.

Cooper, D. H., & Farran, D. C. (1988). Behavioral risk factors in kindergarten. *Early Childhood Research Quarterly, 3*, 1–19.

Dearing, E., Berry, D., & Zaslow, M. (2006). Poverty during early childhood. In K. McCartney & D. Phillips (Eds.), *Blackwell handbook of early childhood development* (pp. 399–423). Malden, MA: Blackwell.

Dearing, E., McCartney, K., & Taylor, B. A. (2009). Does higher quality early child care promote low-income children's math and reading achievement in middle childhood? *Child Development, 80*, 1329–1349.

Denton Flanagan, K., & McPhee, C. (2009). *The children born in 2001 at kindergarten entry: First findings from the kindergarten data collections of the Early Childhood Longitudinal Study, Birth Cohort (ECLS-B)* (NCES Publication No. 2010-005). Washington, DC: National Center for Education Statistics.

Diamond, A., Barnett, W. S., Thomas, J., & Munro, S. (2007, November 30). Preschool program improves cognitive control. *Science, 318*, 1387–1388.

Domitrovich, C. E., Cortes, R. C., & Greenberg, M. T. (2007). Improving young children's social and emotional competence: A randomized trial of the preschool "PATHS" curriculum. *Journal of Primary Prevention, 28*(2), 67–91.

Dowsett, S. M., & Livesey, D. J. (2000). The development of inhibitory control in preschool children: Effects of "executive skills" training. *Developmental Psychobiology, 36*, 161–174.

Eisenberg, N., Smith, C. L., Sadovsky, A., & Spinrad, T. L. (2004). Effortful control: Relations with emotion regulation, adjustment, and socialization in childhood. In R. F. Baumeister & K. D. Vohs (Eds.), *Handbook of self-regulation: Research, theory, and applications* (pp. 259–282). New York, NY: Guilford Press.

Entwisle, D. R., & Alexander, K. L. (1993). Entry into school: The beginning school transition and educational stratification in the United States. *Annual Review of Sociology, 19*, 401–423.
Evans, G. W., & Rosenbaum, J. (2008). Self-regulation and the income-achievement gap. *Early Childhood Research Quarterly, 23*, 504–514.
Ford, R. M., McDougall, S. J. P., & Evans, D. (2009). Parent-delivered compensatory education for children at risk of educational failure: Improving the academic and self-regulatory skills of a Sure Start preschool sample. *British Journal of Psychology, 100*, 773–797.
Gathercole, S. E., & Pickering, S. J. (2000). Assessment of working memory in six- and seven-year-old children. *Journal of Educational Psychology, 92*, 377–390.
Hill, J. L., Brooks-Gunn, J., & Waldfogel, J. (2003). Sustained effects of high participation in an early intervention for low-birth-weight premature infants. *Developmental Psychology, 39*, 730–744.
Howse, R. B., Calkins, S. D., Anastopoulos, A. D., Keane, S. P., & Shelton, T. L. (2003). Regulatory contributors to children's kindergarten achievement. *Early Education & Development, 14*, 101–119.
Howse, R. B., Lange, G., Farran, D. C., & Boyles, C. D. (2003). Motivation and self-regulation as predictors of achievement in economically disadvantaged young children. *Journal of Experimental Education, 71*(2), 151–174.
Kline, R. B. (2005). *Principles and practice of structural equation modeling.* New York, NY: Guilford Press.
Kopp, C. B. (1991). Young children's progression to self-regulation. In M. Bullock (Ed.), *The development of intentional action: Vol. 22. Cognitive, motivational, and interactive processes,* (pp. 38–54). Basel, Switzerland: Karger.
Ladd, G. W. (2003). Probing the adaptive significance of children's behavior and relationships in the school context: A child by environment perspective. *Advances in Child Development and Behavior, 31*, 43–104.
Landry, S. H., Smith, K. E., Swank, P. R., & Miller-Loncar, C. L. (2000). Early maternal and child influences on children's later independent cognitive and social functioning. *Child Development, 71*, 358–375.
Lareau, A. (2003). *Unequal childhoods: Class, race and family life.* Los Angeles: University of California Press.
Lewis-Beck, M. S., Bryman, A., & Liao, F. T. (2004). *The Sage encyclopedia of social science research methods* (Vol. 1). Thousand Oaks, CA: Sage.
Liew, J., McTigue, E., Barrois, L., & Hughes, J. (2008). Adaptive and effortful control and academic self-efficacy beliefs on achievement: A longitudinal study of 1st through 3rd graders. *Early Childhood Research Quarterly, 23*, 515–526.
Matthews, J. M., Ponitz, C. C., & Morrison, F. J. (2009). Early gender differences in self-regulation and academic achievement. *Journal of Educational Psychology, 101*, 689–704.
McClelland, M. M., Acock, A. C., & Morrison, F. J. (2006). The impact of kindergarten learning-related skills on academic trajectories at the end of elementary school. *Early Childhood Research Quarterly, 21*, 471–490.
McClelland, M. M., Cameron, C. E., Connor, C. M., Farris, C. L., Jewkes, A. M., & Morrison, F. J. (2007). Links between behavioral regulation and preschoolers' literacy, vocabulary, and math skills. *Developmental Psychology, 43*, 947–959.
McClelland, M. M., Cameron, C. E., Wanless, S. B., & Murray, A. (2007). Executive function, behavioral self-regulation, and social-emotional competence: Links to school readiness. In O. N. Saracho & B. Spodek (Eds.), *Contemporary perspectives on social learning in early childhood education* (pp. 83–107). Charlotte, NC: Information Age.

McClelland, M. M., Morrison, F. J., & Holmes, D. L. (2000). Children at risk for early academic problems: The role of learning-related social skills. *Early Childhood Research Quarterly, 15,* 307–329.

McClelland, M. M., Piccinin, A., Acock, A. C., & Stallings, M. C. (2011). *Relations between preschool attention and sociability and later achievement outcomes.* Manuscript in review.

McClelland, M. M., Ponitz, C. C., Messersmith, E., & Tominey, S. (2010). Self-regulation: The integration of cognition and emotion. In W. Overton (Vol. Ed.) & R. Lerner (Series Ed.), *Handbook of life-span human development: Vol. 1. Cognition, biology and methods* (pp. 509–553). Hoboken, NJ: Wiley.

McClelland, M. M., & Wanless, S. B. (2006, July). *Child and parenting influences on early reading and mathematics skills.* Paper presented at the 19th biennial meeting of the International Society for the Study of Behavioural Development, Melbourne, Australia.

Miller, K. F., Kelly, M., & Zhou, X. (2005). Learning mathematics in China and the United States: Cross-cultural insights into the nature and course of preschool mathematical development. In J. I. D. Campbell (Ed.), *Handbook of mathematical cognition* (pp. 163–177). New York, NY: Psychology Press.

Muñoz-Sandoval, A. F., Woodcock, R. W., McGrew, K. S., & Mather, N. (2005). *The Batería III Woodcock-Muñoz: Pruebas de aprovechamiento* [Batería Woodcock-Muñoz: Achievement tests]. Itasca, IL: Riverside.

National Institute of Child Health and Human Development Early Child Care Research Network. (2002). The relation of global first-grade classroom environment to structural classroom features and teacher and student behaviors. *The Elementary School Journal, 102,* 367–387.

National Institute of Child Health and Human Development Early Child Care Research Network. (2003). Do children's attention processes mediate the link between family predictors and school readiness? *Developmental Psychology, 39,* 581–593.

Pears, K. C., Fisher, P. A., & Bronz, K. D. (2007). An intervention to facilitate school readiness in foster children: Preliminary results from the Kids in Transition to School pilot study. *Social Psychology Review, 36,* 665–673.

Phillips, D., McCartney, K., & Sussman, A. (2006). Child care and early development. In K. McCartney & D. Phillips (Eds.), *Blackwell handbook of early childhood development* (pp. 471–489). Malden, MA: Blackwell.

Ponitz, C. C., McClelland, M. M., Jewkes, A. M., Connor, C. M., Farris, C. L., & Morrison, F. J. (2008). Touch your toes! Developing a direct measure of behavioral regulation in early childhood. *Early Childhood Research Quarterly, 23,* 141–158.

Ponitz, C. C., McClelland, M. M., Matthews, J. M., & Morrison, F. J. (2009). A structured observation of behavioral self-regulation and its contribution to kindergarten outcomes. *Developmental Psychology, 45,* 605–619.

Raver, C. C. (2002). Emotions matter: Making the case for the role of young children's emotional development for early school readiness. *Social Policy Report, 16,* 3–18.

Rennie, D. A. C., Bull, R., & Diamond, A. (2004). Executive functioning in preschoolers: Reducing the inhibitory demands of the dimensional change card sort task. *Developmental Neuropsychology, 26,* 423–443.

Reynolds, A. J., Temple, J. A., Robertson, D. L., & Mann, E. A. (2001). Long-term effects of an early childhood intervention on educational achievement and juvenile arrest: A 15-year follow-up of low-income children in public schools. *Journal of the American Medical Association, 285,* 2339–2346.

Rhoads, C. (2009, November). *The implications of "contamination" for experimental design in education.* Paper presented at the Society for Research on Education Effectiveness, Washington, DC.

Rothbart, M. K., & Posner, M. I. (2005). Genes and experience in the development of executive attention and effortful control. *New Directions for Child and Adolescent Development, 109*, 101–108.

Rueda, M. R., Posner, M. I., & Rothbart, M. K. (2004). Attentional control and self-regulation. In R. F. Baumeister & K. D. Vohs (Eds.), *Handbook of self-regulation: Research, theory, and applications* (pp. 283–300). New York, NY: Guilford Press.

Rueda, M. R., Rothbart, M. K., McCandliss, B. D., Saccomanno, L., & Posner, M. I. (2005). Training, maturation, and genetic influences on the development of executive attention. *Proceedings of the National Academy of Sciences, USA, 102*, 14931–14936.

Schrank, F. A., McGrew, K. S., Ruef, M. L., Alvarado, C. G., Muñoz-Sandoval, A. F., & Woodcock, R. W. (2005). *Overview and technical supplement (Bateria III Woodcock-Muñoz Assessment Service Bulletin No. 1)*. Itasca, IL: Riverside.

Sektnan, M., McClelland, M. M., Acock, A., & Morrison, F. J. (2010). Relations between early family risk, children's behavioral regulation, and academic achievement. *Early Childhood Research Quarterly, 25*, 464–479.

St. Clair-Thompson, H., Stevens, R., Hunt, A., & Bolder, E. (2010). Improving children's working memory and classroom performance. *Educational Psychology, 30*(2), 203–219.

Tominey, S., & McClelland, M. M. (2008, April). "And when they woke up... they were monkeys!" Using classroom games to promote preschoolers' self-regulation and school readiness. Poster presented at the Conference on Human Development, Indianapolis, Indiana.

Torgerson, D. J. (2001). Contamination in trials: Is cluster randomisation the answer? *British Medical Journal, 322*, 355–357.

U.S. Department of Education. (2009). *No Child Left Behind*. Retrieved from http://www.ed.gov/nclb/landing.jhtml

Valiente, C., Lemery-Chalfant, K., & Castro, K. S. (2007). Children's effortful control and academic competence. Mediation through school liking. *Merrill-Palmer Quarterly, 53*(1), 1–25.

Vitaro, F., Brendgen, M., Larose, S., & Tremblay, R. E. (2005). Kindergarten disruptive behaviors, protective factors, and educational achievement by early adulthood. *Journal of Educational Psychology, 97*, 617–629.

Wanless, S. B., McClelland, M. M., Acock, A. C., Ponitz, C. C., Son, S.-H., Lan, X., ... Li, S. (in press). Measuring behavioral regulation in four cultures. *Psychological Assessment*.

Wanless, S. B., McClelland, M. M., Tominey, S., & Acock, A. (2011). The influence of demographic risk factors on children's behavioral regulation in prekindergarten and kindergarten. *Early Education and Development, 22*, 462–490.

Wellman, H. M., Somerville, S. C., & Haake, R. J. (1979). Development of search procedures in real-life spatial environments. *Developmental Psychology, 15*, 530–542.

Woodcock, R. W., & Mather, N. (2000). *Woodcock–Johnson Psycho-Educational Battery-III*. Itasca, IL: Riverside.

Parent–Teacher Agreement and Reliability on the Devereux Early Childhood Assessment (DECA) in English and Spanish for Ethnically Diverse Children Living in Poverty

Jennifer Crane

Melissa S. Mincic

Adam Winsler

Research Findings: Social-emotional competence is especially important for children living in poverty, and effective assessment of social-emotional skills is critical. This study examined parent–teacher agreement and reliability of the Devereux Early Childhood Assessment (DECA; P. A. LeBuffe & J. A. Naglieri, 1999) English and Spanish forms in a large ($n = 7,756$) sample of impoverished, ethnically diverse preschoolers. Both forms were reliable. Parents reported greater social-emotional protective factors and behavioral concerns than teachers. Parent–teacher agreement was moderate ($rs = .20–.28$) and consistent with previous research. Parent–teacher agreement was higher when both informants completed the survey in the same language. Agreement was highest for average-functioning children, according to a standardized assessment of cognition, language, and motor skills that was also administered. Parents rated low-functioning children more favorably than did teachers; teachers rated high-functioning children more favorably than did parents. *Practice or Policy:* The English and Spanish DECA forms demonstrate reliability for examining social-emotional skills and behavioral concerns for impoverished, ethnically diverse preschoolers.

Effective social skills and appropriate self-regulation of emotion and behavior are critical for children's school readiness (Denham, 2006; Graziano, Reavis, Keane, & Calkins, 2007; McClelland et al., 2007) and their early academic trajectories in elementary school (Caprara, Barbaranelli, Pastorelli, Bandura, & Zimbardo, 2000; Coolahan, Fantuzzo, Mendez, & McDermott, 2000; Evans & Rosenbaum, 2008). In recognition of this, young children's social, emotional, and behavioral competencies are often the specific targets of early childhood education, prevention, and intervention efforts (Denham & Burton, 2003; Hemmeter, Ostrosky, & Fox, 2006; Raver, 2002). However, the first step in effectively promoting young children's social and emotional skills is being able to assess such skills effectively with a variety of reliable, valid, and practical assessment instruments appropriate for use with an increasingly diverse group of young children. Indeed, the dire need for effective assessments for preschool children's social-emotional and self-regulatory skills as they relate to school readiness was indicated by recent federal interagency calls for the development of early childhood assessment instruments (U.S. Department of Health and Human Services, 2004). This article examines internal consistency reliability and parent–teacher agreement on both the English and Spanish versions of the Devereux Early Childhood Assessment (DECA; LeBuffe & Naglieri, 1999) among ethnically and linguistically diverse children and families living in poverty.

Assessments with school-age children and adults are typically used to document individual cognitive potential, to place individuals into appropriate educational or vocational programs, and to predict later success (Kaplan & Saccuzzo, 2001). Assessment in early childhood has a necessarily different focus—the acquisition of information about a child's development and environment in order to understand that child's strengths and weaknesses and facilitate the creation of curricula and interventions to meet the child's needs (Meisels & Atkins-Burnett, 2000). Standardized early childhood assessment comes with unique challenges, such as children's noncompliance with examiners, young children's short attention spans, children's limited verbal skills for self-reporting, and the difficulty of controlling and standardizing the assessment situation in developmentally appropriate ways for young children (Bagnato & Neisworth, 1991). Given preschool children's limited self-reflection and self-reporting capabilities, parent and teacher reports are often the only sources of information available, especially regarding a child's social-emotional development, for which repeated observations in different contexts and over time are necessary for adequate assessment. For this reason, parents, teachers, and caregivers close to young children are excellent and important sources of information regarding children's behavior and abilities (Bagnato & Neisworth, 1991); however, they do not always agree on children's development and abilities (Achenbach, McConaughy, & Howell, 1987). Questions have arisen regarding the extent of agreement and disagreement between informants; the reasons for, and correlates of, disagreement; and what disagreement might mean for child referral decisions.

PARENT–TEACHER AGREEMENT

A fair amount of research regarding parent–teacher agreement on child behavior and cognitive functioning has been conducted to date (e.g., Achenbach et al., 1987; Ferdinand et al., 2003; Hundert, Morrison, Mahoney, Mundy, & Vernon, 1997; Keogh & Bernheimer, 1998; Keogh, Juvonen, & Bernheimer, 1989; Winsler & Wallace, 2002). Researchers have examined agreement on competence (Keogh et al., 1989; La Paro & Pianta, 2000; Peet, Powell, & O'Donnel, 1997), temperament (Victor, Halverson, & Smith-Wampler, 1988), and psychopathology (Ferdinand et al., 2003; Kumpulainen et al., 1999). In a meta-analysis, Achenbach et al. (1987) reported a mean correlation of .28 between parent and teacher reports of children's behavioral and emotional problems, and there was no significant difference in agreement related to a child's clinical or nonclinical status or to gender. Higher agreement was found for children aged 6–11 than for adolescents. Furthermore, informants were more consistent when rating externalizing than internalizing behavior problems. These researchers concluded that information gained from one informant is unique and cannot be substituted for information gained from another informant. In fact, even the youngest children (6-year-olds) could sometimes give information about their own condition that was different and uniquely useful from the information provided by parents, clinicians, and teachers (Achenbach et al., 1987).

Cross-informant research with preschool-age children, however, is less available. One study that did address cross-informant agreement regarding social-emotional development in preschool-age children was conducted by Winsler and Wallace (2002). These authors examined parent–teacher ratings and independent observer ratings of young children's social skills, internalizing behavior problems, and externalizing behavior problems. They found that parents and teachers more strongly agreed on children's externalizing behavior problems than on their internalizing behavior problems and social skills, and that compared to teachers, parents reported more overall behavior problems in their children. Increased communication between parents and teachers and combined information across different contexts can lead to greater understanding of children's behavior and social-emotional protective factors.

Research on parent–teacher agreement has been conducted with a number of ethnic groups, including Chinese (Deng, Liu, & Roosa, 2004), Japanese (Satake, Yoshida, & Yamashita, 2003), and African American (Cai, Kaiser, & Hancock, 2004) children. However, little research has investigated relations between parent–teacher reports of children's social-emotional protective factors and academic outcomes within low-income, ethnically diverse populations. Children from minority backgrounds, and particularly African American and Hispanic children, are disproportionately more likely to live in poverty (Duncan & Magnuson, 2005) and attend low-quality child care, and they typically have early childhood teachers who are of a different ethnic background (Magnuson & Waldfogel, 2005). Good communication and congruence between home and school is particularly important for such populations, and therefore it is important to understand cross-informant agreement across these two settings in early childhood assessment instruments. Cai et al. (2004) examined parent–teacher agreement on children's behavior problems in a sample of low-income, predominantly African American children. Teachers tended to report problem behaviors affecting academic performance, classroom management, and peer relationships, whereas parent rankings of behavior problems were related to household maintenance (Cai et al., 2004). This is evidence that differences between teacher and parent ratings of behavior problems are at least partly due to differences in the environments in which adults observe children's behavior.

Previous research has also pinpointed differences in parent–teacher agreement depending on children's gender, academic achievement, and both the type and severity of children's behavioral concerns. With a sample of Chinese children ages 6 to 11, Deng et al. (2004) found that parent–teacher agreement was stronger for girls than for boys and stronger for children with higher academic performance. They also reported that parents and teachers most strongly agreed on problems of attention, followed by externalizing behavior problems, then by internalizing behavior problems. It is important to note that Deng et al. also found that agreement between parent and teacher reports decreased with increasing severity of the child's difficulties. Pinpointing levels of disagreement related to the level of child functioning is important because it has clear implications for referrals and for clinical practice. If parent and teacher reports diverge further from one another in a child with lower functioning versus a child with higher-functioning, clinicians may need to use information from each informant very differently or combine the two reports differently for the lower functioning child most in need of services. The present study thus examined whether agreement between parents and teachers on children's social and behavioral skills on the DECA is the same for children who vary in cognitive/language competence. Agreement as a function of child gender and age was also examined for the same reason.

Research on the assessment of bilingual and multilingual preschool-age children is rare (Cofresi & Gorman, 2004). There is no research to date regarding parent–teacher agreement when language differences between parents and teachers are likely. This is an important area for research because of quickly expanding populations of English language learners (National Center for Education Statistics, 2000). Poor communication and a lack of understanding of issues related to learning two languages simultaneously can lead to misdiagnosis, over- or under-referral, and improper enrollment of bilingual children in special education classrooms (Cofresi & Gorman, 2004). Furthermore, assessment instruments are often translated directly from English into another language without going through the proper standardization and/or validation procedures needed in the new language, which is problematic because much can be lost in the translation process because of lack of cross-language equivalence and other differences (Cofresi & Gorman, 2004). In the current study, we examined agreement between parents and teachers who used the same and different language versions (English–Spanish) of the DECA.

THE DECA

The DECA (LeBuffe & Naglieri, 1999) is a 37-item parent- and teacher-report instrument of child social-emotional protective factors and behavioral concerns that is appropriate for use with children between the ages of 2 to 5. It is available in English and Spanish. It was created as a screening device to identify children's individual social and emotional strengths and weaknesses for use in program planning and assessment. One of the features of the DECA that distinguishes it from other available measures of social skills and behavior in early childhood is that it was designed with a focus on children's strengths and resilience, whereas most other measures emphasize child problems and pathology (LeBuffe & Naglieri, 1999). The DECA, for example, yields an overall Total Protective Factors scale that emphasizes the child's strengths in self-control, initiative, and attachment/closeness with adults. Children's strengths in social competence may be conceptualized as potential *protective factors*, which have been defined as "antecedent conditions associated with a decrease in the likelihood of undesirable outcomes or with an increase in the likelihood of positive outcomes" (Kazdin, Kraemer, Kessler, Kupfer, & Offord, 1997, p. 377). Because they reflect positive aspects of children's circumstances, protective factors are important to consider along with potential risk factors that threaten children's early academic and social success. Another unique aspect of the DECA is that the child assessment instrument is embedded within a larger program or curriculum system designed to improve children's social-emotional strengths in early childhood classrooms (Devereux Early Childhood Initiative, 2006). These features have made the DECA a popular tool in many communities throughout the United States (i.e., Miami, Florida; Bristol, Connecticut; Bowling Green, Ohio; Passaic, New Jersey; Pueblo, Colorado) for large-scale early childhood community program evaluation, curriculum development, and assessment/intervention initiatives (Devereux Early Childhood Initiative, 2006).

Only two published studies to date have examined the utility of the DECA and reported psychometric data on the instrument (Jaberg, Dixon, & Weis, 2009; Lien & Carlson, 2009) to compare with the material discussed in the DECA user's manual. Jaberg et al. (2009; see also Mayor's Commission for Children, 2007) examined the utility of the DECA with a sample of 780 children from one community in the American Midwest (88% White, 4% American Indian/Alaska native, 3% African American, 2% Hispanic/Latino, and 2% other). These authors reported parent–teacher correlations (ranging from .20 to .38) and internal consistency reliability coefficients (between .71 and .95) very similar to those reported by the DECA authors (LeBuffe & Naglieri, 1999). The children participating in this study were by and large middle class, as evidenced by the percentage of children who received free or reduced lunch in kindergarten (32%). In addition 79% of these children had parents who were married at the time of the study, and 97% of the parents had a high school diploma or more education (Mayor's Commission for Children, 2007). Although this information is certainly useful, the sample used in the Jaberg et al. study is limited with respect to ethnic and language diversity.

A study by Lien and Carlson (2009) utilized a sample of 1,208 children attending Head Start to examine the psychometric properties of the DECA. These authors reported internal consistency ratings (ranging from .71 to .91) close to those found by Jaberg et al. (2009). These authors also did a factor analysis that revealed some differences in item loadings, but basically the same factor structure was found as that reported in the DECA technical manual. They also found that the children in their Head Start sample scored significantly higher on the Behavioral Concerns scale (i.e., had more behavior problems) and significantly lower on the protective factors scale (i.e., had poorer social skills) than did the sample of children used to standardize the DECA. Unfortunately, demographic information about the children in the Lien and Carlson study were not available. The participating families likely were living in poverty because they were enrolled in Head Start; however, their ethnic backgrounds are not actually known. The authors stated that the study took place in a "diverse area of mid-Michigan" (Lien & Carlson, 2009, p. 389), so perhaps the proportion of African American and Latino children was somewhat larger than that for Michigan as a whole (77% White, 15% African American, 4% Hispanic; U.S. Census Bureau, 2010). However, it does not appear that Hispanic/Latino children were a large part of the sample. Additional evaluation of the DECA for use with ethnically and linguistically diverse children, and specifically for children living in poverty, is clearly needed to inform intervention efforts for at-risk children. The current study thus evaluated reliability and parent–teacher agreement on the DECA with a large sample of ethnically and linguistically diverse children living in poverty in Miami, Florida.

POVERTY AND ETHNIC/LANGUAGE DIVERSITY

Although social-emotional skills and behavior are important aspects of school readiness for all children, they may be especially important for young children living in poverty because such children are at greater risk for numerous developmental problems because of the stressors associated with the impoverished environments in which they live (Brooks-Gunn, Britto, & Brady, 1999; McLoyd, 1998). Children living in poverty have been shown to have particular difficulty with the self-regulation of emotion and behavior (Evans & Rosenbaum, 2008; Miller, Gouley, Seifer, Dickstein, & Shields, 2004), and many early childhood programs target social skills and behavior for intervention (see Webster-Stratton & Reid, 2008, for a review). Therefore, it is important to verify that assessment instruments are effective within specific low-income populations.

Given that ethnic and language minority groups in the United States are more likely to be living in poverty compared to English-speaking Caucasian individuals (Garbarino & Ganzel, 2000), examination of assessment tools for use within low-income families also requires careful attention to issues of language and culture. Instruments need to demonstrate reliability, validity, and measurement equivalence across different populations, languages, and income groups. Standardization samples, although generally large and intended to be nationally representative, typically do not include sufficient numbers of individuals within any one ethnic group to explore such issues adequately, and the DECA is no exception. Several components of social and emotional skills, such as teacher–child attachment relationships (Howes & Smith, 1995) and teacher-reported problems during children's transition to kindergarten (Rimm-Kaufman, Pianta, & Cox, 2000), have been found to vary as a function of either child or teacher ethnicity, typically favoring Caucasian children and teachers. Understanding how ethnically diverse parents and teachers rate ethnically diverse children on social-emotional skills and behavior concerns is important for teasing apart the extent to which differences might be due to the child versus the rater.

Little information is available pertaining to the development, translation, reliability, or validation of the Spanish form of the DECA. The DECA items were first written in English, translated into Spanish, and then back-translated into English. Comparison of the original and back-translated English versions was completed and minor modifications were made (Devereux Early Childhood Initiative, 2001). The Spanish DECA uses the English-normed standardization tables for calculation of the standard scores, a practice justified by the publisher after preliminary analyses revealed that bilingual raters' scores of the same children in English and Spanish did not differ in mean levels (Devereux Early Childhood Initiative, 2001). The present project represents the first external study to our knowledge to examine the utility of the Spanish DECA.

THE PRESENT STUDY

The goal of this study was to examine internal consistency reliability and parent–teacher agreement on the DECA (LeBuffe & Naglieri, 1999). Consistent with calls by scholars to examine phenomena within specific local communities and minority populations (Garcia-Coll & Magnuson, 2000; McLoyd, 1998; Phinney & Landin, 1998), the present study explored the use of both the English and the Spanish versions of the DECA within one large, urban, predominantly Latino and African American sample of children living in poverty in Miami, Florida—an at-risk population that stands to benefit greatly from social-emotional interventions in early childhood. This work emerges from the larger Miami School Readiness Project (Winsler et al., 2008) a large-scale, county-wide, community–university collaborative, program evaluation and assessment/intervention project designed to improve the quality of early childhood programs in the community. Miami is one of the several communities that selected the DECA as their social-emotional and behavioral school readiness assessment tool. Both ensuring the use of reliable instruments and understanding disagreements between parents and teachers on adult reports of children's social skills are critical for effective program evaluation and intervention efforts as well as for accurate and helpful individual child referral decisions. Much of the prior research discussed previously has focused on parent–teacher agreement on mental health problems and among older, monolingual, and often clinical samples. In the current study, we focused on the congruence between linguistically and ethnically diverse parents and teachers in a large ($n = 7,756$) community-based sample of low-income children attending either child care in the community with the assistance of child care subsidies or Title I pre-kindergarten programs in the public schools. Also, whereas prior research has typically examined informant ratings at only one point in time, the present investigation adds to the literature by exploring agreement over time at the beginning and end of the 4-year-old preschool year. To that end, the following research questions were addressed:

1. What is the internal consistency reliability of the English and Spanish versions of the parent and teacher DECA within a relatively high-risk sample of ethnically and linguistically diverse urban children living in poverty?
2. To what extent do parents and teachers agree on the DECA within this population, both at the beginning and at the end of the academic year?
3. To what extent does parent–teacher agreement on the DECA within this population vary as a function of language of the form (English, Spanish), child ethnicity, age, gender, or child cognitive/linguistic competence?

METHOD

Participants

The sample for this study consisted of the child care teachers and parents of 3- and 4-year-old children ($n = 7,756$) attending center-based child care facilities while receiving child care subsidies for low-income families. This overall sample size reflected the total number of children for whom a DECA was completed by any informant at any time (the sample sizes for the various analyses that follow vary depending on the time point and informant[s] included). The sample of children reflected the ethnic diversity of the county in general (57% Latino/Hispanic, 38% African American/Caribbean islander, 5% White/other) and was 49% female. The children were all 3 or 4 years of age at the beginning of the school year; the mean age was 49 months ($SD = 6.9$ months). The mean education level for the parents of children in this sample was 11 years (i.e., less than high school completion). Of a subsample ($n = 3,779$) for which this kind of information was available, only 8%

of the children lived with two currently married parents, 61% of the parents reported being a single parent, and 31% of the parents reported being divorced or separated. Mean family size was 3.35 family members.

These data represent a center-based, child care subsidy–receiving subsample from the larger Miami School Readiness Project, a large-scale university–community collaborative and applied research, program enhancement, intervention, and program evaluation initiative in Miami, Florida (Winsler et al., 2008). The sample here included functionally the entire (consenting) county population of low-income children whose families received child care subsidies to attend non–Head Start community-based child care centers of their choice or who attended Title I public school pre-kindergarten programs. Although center quality in this community varies considerably, with many very fine facilities included, as is true throughout the United States (National Institute of Child Health and Human Development Early Child Care Research Network, 2000), the average quality of the centers is likely mediocre in this community, as indicated by overall Early Childhood Rating Scale–Revised (Harms, Clifford, & Cryer, 1998) scores (for a small, nonrandom, but likely representative sample of 312 classrooms of the participating centers here that was collected for other purposes) averaging 4.88 on a scale of 1 to 7 (scores of 3–5 on this measure indicate average/mediocre quality). Because of the nature of the community-based project, ethnic and other demographic information about teachers was unfortunately not available. However, given the ethnic composition of the area, strong support for Spanish use in the community in general, and the teacher preferences for which language version of the DECA they completed (see below), it is clear that at least half of the teachers were Spanish-speaking Latinas.

All told, 1,454 different teachers were involved in the context of 847 centers/schools. Many teachers had only one participating child in their classroom (25%), and many centers had only one participating child (17%); furthermore, a majority of teachers (60.4%) had four or fewer participating children in their classroom. Analytic procedures such as hierarchical linear modeling that control for the nesting of children in classrooms and/or centers were deemed unnecessary in this study, because (a) in most cases, teachers only completed the DECA on a small number of (subsidy-receiving) children in their classrooms; (b) the very nature of the investigation (teacher–parent agreement) was to examine differences between teacher reports on children (in the context of teachers having multiple children as reference points in the classroom) and parent reports (for which only their own children are present) that are perhaps due to such nesting by design; and (c) we wanted to compare our results to prior reports of agreement that did not involve nested analyses.

Assessments

The DECA (LeBuffe & Naglieri, 1999) is divided into four subscales: Initiative, Self-Control, Attachment, and Behavioral Concerns. The first three scales can be collapsed into a Total Protective Factors score, with larger scores indicating better social-emotional protective factors. The Behavioral Concerns scale is scored such that larger numbers indicate more behavior problems. The DECA has 37 items with responses ranging from 0 (*never*) to 4 (*very frequently*). Identical forms are completed by both parents and teachers. The same standardization table is used for the calculation of Z scores, T scores, and national percentiles for children of all ages (2–5 years) and genders; however, there are separate standardization tables for parents and teachers. The DECA was standardized on a sample of children ($N = 2,000$) representing the U.S. population on demographic characteristics (LeBuffe & Naglieri, 1999). The internal consistencies reported in the DECA technical manual were all greater than .7, and many were greater than .9, indicating high internal consistency. Original correlations between parent and teacher scores were as follows: Initiative ($r = .34$), Self-Control ($r = .23$), Total Protective Factors ($r = .29$), all $ps < .05$; Attachment ($r = .19$), Behavioral Concerns ($r = .23$), nonsignificant (LeBuffe & Naglieri, 1999).

Parents and teachers were asked to complete the DECA (in their choice of English or Spanish) at the beginning of the academic year (September), and parents and teachers of the 4-year-old children (but not the 3-year-olds) completed it again at the end of the school year (May). One survey form went home with the children from the center, and parents were asked to complete it within 2 weeks and return it to the center. The parent or guardian who filled out the DECA questionnaire self-reported his or her relationship to the child on the form. During the September assessment period, 73% of the forms were filled out by the child's mother, 6% by the child's father, and 1% by both parents. Another 18% simply wrote "parent," so it is not known which parent completed the form, and the remaining 2% were filled out by "other relative." The DECA provides separately normed scores for teachers and parents; however, because our goal was to examine teacher–parent agreement in its purest form on the same identically worded items, and because it would be more difficult to interpret the meaning of mean differences across raters using adjusted, within-rater standardized scores, we chose to use raw scores for the analyses. To examine the magnitude and direction of mean differences by rater, we computed mean difference scores between informants (the teacher score minus the parent score). Thus, negative scores indicate that parents scored children higher than did teachers on that dimension, whereas positive scores mean that teachers scored children higher than did parents on that dimension. Scores at or near zero indicate that parents and teachers rated children similarly on that dimension. Finally, for some analyses in which magnitude (and not direction) of disagreement was of interest, the absolute value of the difference score was used.

The children were also assessed at the beginning (September) and end (May) of the school year using the Learning Accomplishment Profile–Diagnostic (LAP-D; Nehring, Nehring, Bruni, & Randolph, 1992) as part of the larger community project. The LAP-D (and DECA) was chosen because it was available in English and Spanish, it fit in well with the state's performance standards (Florida Partnership for School Readiness, 2003), and it had good psychometric properties. The LAP-D is a standardized developmental and curriculum-based instrument that is divided into four domains, with each domain subdivided into two subdomains: cognitive (matching and counting), language (comprehension and naming), fine motor (writing and manipulation), and gross motor (body and object movement). The gross motor scale was not included here. The LAP-D was standardized using a sample of preschoolers ($N = 792$) selected to represent the 1990 U.S. Census. Internal consistency for the LAP-D during standardization was confirmed for each subscale, with alphas ranging from .76 to .92. Internal consistency reliabilities for the LAP-D within the Miami sample ranged from .93 to .95 (Winsler et al., 2008). LAP-D assessments were conducted individually by trained bilingual assessors in a separate room of the child's school. The assessors had master's degrees in social work, education, psychology, or a related field. Standardized national percentile scores were used. The assessment was given in English or Spanish based on whichever language the child's teacher and the assessor believed was the child's strongest language.

RESULTS

Table 1 contains the means and standard deviations for the parent and teacher raw scores at Time 1 and the interscale correlations on DECA scores for parents and teachers for Time 1. Similar means and interscale correlations were run for Time 2 but are not reported here because they were so similar to those at Time 1. As might be expected, the scales belonging to the Total Protective Factors scale were moderately correlated with one another and negatively correlated with Behavioral Concerns. Correlations within the Total Protective Factors scales were similar for both parents and teachers. However, it is evident from Table 1 that the negative associations between the Total Protective Factors and Behavioral Concerns scales were stronger for teachers than for parents, and this was confirmed by Fisher's test for independent correlations ($Z = -16.55$, $p < .05$).

TABLE 1
Means, Standard Deviations, and Interscale Correlations for the Devereux Early Childhood Assessment Scale for Teachers and Parents at Time 1

Variable	Initiative	Self-Control	Attachment	Total Protective Factors	Behavioral Concerns
Initiative	—	.61	.70	.91	−.14
Self-Control	.53	—	.58	.83	−.36
Attachment	.72	.61	—	.86	−.15
Total Protective Factors	.90	.80	.88	—	−.24
Behavioral Concerns	−.33	−.61	−.35	−.49	—
Teacher					
M	26.98	20.85	22.99	70.47	10.39
SD	7.56	5.42	4.74	15.53	5.89
Parent					
M	30.90	21.14	25.95	77.93	11.88
SD	6.63	4.90	4.31	13.81	5.48
Possible range	0–44	0–32	0–32	0–108	0–40
Disagreement (Teacher Minus Parent Scores)					
M	−3.91[a]	−0.28[a]	−2.96[a]	−7.15[a]	−1.48[a]
SD	8.79	6.21	5.73	17.66	6.93

Note. Correlations above the diagonal are from parent forms, and those below the diagonal are from teacher forms. All correlations were significant at the $p < .01$ level.

[a]Significant difference between teacher and parent scores at $p < .01$.

Internal Consistency Reliability

The first research question concerned the internal consistency reliability of the DECA within this low-income, ethnically diverse sample. Cronbach's alphas were computed for the five DECA scales (Initiative, Attachment, Self-Control, Total Protective Factors, and Behavioral Concerns) for both teacher reports and parent reports, in English and Spanish, and these are displayed in Table 2. All alphas were greater than .70 and thus were acceptable; and many were greater than .90, indicating very high internal consistency reliability. Attachment and Behavioral Concerns were the two scales with the lowest (but still acceptable) internal consistency reliability. Generally speaking, teacher-reported scales had higher reliability (by 5 to 10 points for the scales) than parent-reported scales. There were no differences in reliability between the English and Spanish forms. The alpha values reported in the DECA manual for the standardization sample were all very similar to the ones found in this study. Thus, the present investigation showed that the DECA has strong internal consistency reliability in both English and Spanish within a low-income, diverse sample of children. Unless

TABLE 2
Cronbach's Alphas for DECA Scales for Parents and Teachers at Time 1 by Language of the Form and by Child Ethnicity

		DECA Scale				
Variable	Informant	Initiative	Self-Control	Attachment	Total Protective Factors	Behavioral Concerns
Overall	Parent (n=1,893)	.85	.83	.77	.92	.72
	Teacher (n=2,287)	.90	.90	.82	.94	.81
English	Parent (n=1,231)	.85	.85	.78	.92	.72
	Teacher (n=1,203)	.90	.90	.83	.94	.81
Spanish	Parent (n=662)	.85	.79	.75	.91	.72
	Teacher (n=645)	.91	.89	.82	.94	.80
Latino children	Parent (n=1,050)	.85	.82	.77	.91	.71
	Teacher (n=1,246)	.90	.90	.81	.94	.80
African American children	Parent (n=777)	.85	.85	.77	.93	.72
	Teacher (n=961)	.90	.90	.84	.94	.81

Note. DECA = Devereux Early Childhood Assessment.

otherwise stated, analyses that follow were conducted without regard to the language of the DECA form.

The aforementioned analyses examined internal consistency for the entire sample of children. Also of importance, however, was whether the reliability of the DECA is the same for African American and Latino children compared to that reported in the standardization table. We thus selected just those groups of children and reran the analyses to see if there were any differences in reliability as a function of child ethnicity. These alphas by child ethnicity are displayed in Table 2. There were no differences in the reliability of the DECA forms by child ethnicity. The values for African American or Latino children were typically within two hundredths of those for the overall group and quite similar to those reported in the DECA manual, indicating that the DECA has strong internal consistency reliability for ethnically and linguistically diverse children.

Parent–Teacher Agreement

The second research question asked to what extent parents and teachers agree on the DECA. To examine parent–teacher congruence in this population, we conducted two different types of analyses: (a) correlational analyses to examine agreement across informants in terms of children's relative rankings (what is typically done in agreement research) and (b) repeated measures analyses of variance (ANOVAs) examining level, or mean, differences in the raw scores. Differences in raw scores illustrate the overall amount of disagreement between the raters and show the directional pattern of differences across informants (i.e., which adult rates children higher on which scales).

Agreement in terms of relative ranking. Pearson correlations were computed between parent-reported scores and teacher-reported scores at both the beginning and end of the school year (see Table 3). Parent–teacher agreement in this group was fairly similar for all scales, with all correlations ranging from .18 to .30. The highest correlations were found for Self-Control and Behavioral Concerns, and the lowest correlations were found for Attachment. Correlations were all statistically significantly different from zero, and there was very little change in the associations between Time 1 and Time 2. For example, on the Initiative scale, the correlation between parent and teacher scores was .24 at both Time 1 and Time 2. Only the Behavioral Concerns scale included a change of more than .01 in the correlation over time (Time 1, $r = .28$; Time 2, $r = .31$), and even that difference was very small. Fisher's Z tests for significant differences were conducted

TABLE 3
Correlations Between Parent and Teacher Scores on the DECA Scales at T1 and T2

DECA Scale	Overall Group T1 Only[a] (n=5,745)	4-Year-Olds Only		3-Year-Olds Only T1 (n=2,631)
		T1 (n=3,111)	T2 (n=2,553)	
Initiative	.24*	.24*	.24*	.23*
Self-Control	.28*	.28*	.26*	.27*
Attachment	.20*	.19*	.18*	.21*
Total Protective Factors	.27*	.27*	.25*	.27*
Behavioral Concerns	.26*	.28*	.30*	.23*

Note. DECA = Devereux Early Childhood Assessment; T1 = Time 1; T2 = Time 2.
[a]Three-year-old children were only assessed at T1, so for the overall group and for the 3-year-olds only group, only T1 correlations are given.
*$p < .01$.

for each scale and revealed that none of the differences across time were significant, indicating that there was no significant change in parent–teacher agreement over the course of the school year.

Because 3-year-old children were only assessed at Time 1, we felt it important to report the correlations at Time 1 separately for the 3- and 4-year-olds, so the Time 1 and Time 2 correlations just involving the 4-year-olds can be compared directly. This also allowed us to examine whether agreement between parents and teachers differed for 3- and 4-year-olds, which is a reasonable possibility given that social and behavioral developmental expectations change rapidly in the preschool years. As is clear in Table 3, cross-informant agreement for the younger and older children at Time 1 was practically identical.

Directional disagreement. Means and standard deviations for directional difference scores (teacher minus parent) are listed at the bottom of Table 1. A repeated-measures ANOVA was conducted with informant (teacher, parent) as the within-subjects factor to test whether the differences between teacher and parent scores were significantly different for the DECA scales. The results indicated that there were significant differences between raters on all four scales: Initiative, $F(1, 5744) = 1,138.41$; Self-Control, $F(1, 5744) = 11.90$; Attachment, $F(1, 5744) = 1,533.06$; Behavioral Concerns: $F(1, 5744) = 26,404$ (all $ps < .01$). For all scales, parents scored children higher on average than did teachers. Parents reported children as having stronger social-emotional protective factors but also as demonstrating worse behavior problems than did teachers.

Correlates of Disagreement

Child gender and ethnicity. A multivariate ANOVA was conducted using child gender and ethnicity (White/Caucasian, $n = 262$; African American, $n = 2,153$; and Latino, $n = 3,226$) as independent variables and the absolute value disagreement scores on the four DECA scales as dependent variables. There was no multivariate effect of gender, Wilks's $\Lambda = .999$, $F(4, 5632) = 0.89$, $p = .47$; but the multivariate effect of ethnicity was significant, Wilks's $\Lambda = .996$, $F(8, 5632) = 2.70$, $p < .01$. Follow-up univariate tests revealed that the agreement differences related to ethnicity were significant only for the Self-Control scale, $F(2, 5641) = 3.16$, $p < .05$. Post hoc Tukey honestly significant difference contrasts revealed that overall disagreement between parents and teachers on the Self-Control scale of the DECA was slightly higher for parents and teachers of African American children (disagreement $= 5.05$) than for parents and teachers of Hispanic/Latino children (disagreement $= 4.78$, Cohen's $d = .07$); however, the effect size was very small. The multivariate interaction between gender and ethnicity was not significant, $F(2, 5641) = 0.32$, $p = .96$.

Age. ANOVAs were conducted to examine differences in disagreement scores for parents and teachers of younger (3-year-old, $n = 2,534$) and older (4-year-old, $n = 3,111$) preschoolers. Age group at first assessment (3 or 4 years) was entered as the independent variable and disagreement between parent and teacher scores on the four DECA scales was entered as the dependent variable. Differences in disagreement between parents and teachers were significant for the two age groups on only the Initiative scale of the DECA. Disagreement on child initiative between parents and teachers was slightly greater for 3-year-olds (disagreement = 7.7) than for 4-year-olds (disagreement = 7.3, $d = .07$), $F(1, 5744) = 6.23$, $p < .05$, also a small effect.

Language of the form. Children were divided into three groups based on what language their parent and teacher used to complete the DECA. The children were first grouped based on whether the parent and teacher shared a language on the DECA (i.e., both used the Spanish form or both used the English form) or whether the informants used two different languages (i.e., one informant used English and the other Spanish). Then the shared language group was split on the basis of which language was shared across the two informants (English or Spanish). This yielded three groups: child's parent and teacher did not share a language on the DECA ($n = 966$), child's parent and teacher shared English ($n = 2,439$), and child's parent and teacher shared Spanish ($n = 1,194$). Table 4 contains the mean disagreement scores for each of the different language groups. Also included in the last column of the table are parent–teacher agreement correlations done separately for each of the groups. All correlations between parent and teacher scores were significant and moderate and ranged between .15 and .29. The unshared language group showed the lowest correlations for all DECA scales, whereas the shared language groups had very similar correlations for the Self-Control (.28 and .29) and Attachment (both .22) scales. For Behavioral Concerns and Initiative, the both-English group had slightly higher correlations than the both-Spanish group. Fisher's Z tests indicated that the correlations for the both-English and unshared language groups were significantly different for all four scales. The correlations for the both-Spanish and unshared language groups were significantly different for just Self-Control and Attachment. Both-English and both-Spanish correlations were significantly different for just the Initiative and Behavioral Concerns scales.

The effect of language group membership on mean levels of disagreement was significant for all three DECA protective factor scales: Initiative,

TABLE 4
General Disagreement Between Parents and Teachers as a Function of the Language of the Form Used

DECA Scale	Language Group	General Disagreement	Agreement (Parent–Teacher Correlation)[a]
Initiative	Both Spanish	7.9[b]	.21
	Both English	7.3[c]	.27
	Unshared language	7.9[b]	.18
Self-Control	Both Spanish	4.5[c]	.28
	Both English	5.1[b]	.29
	Unshared language	5.1[b]	.22
Attachment	Both Spanish	4.7[c]	.22
	Both English	5.1[b]	.22
	Unshared language	5.4[b]	.15
Behavioral Concerns	Both Spanish	5.4	.24
	Both English	5.5	.28
	Unshared language	5.7	.22

Note. DECA = Devereux Early Childhood Assessment.
[a]All correlations were significant at $p < .01$.
[b,c]Groups with different superscripts were significantly different from one another at $p < .05$.

$F(2, 4596) = 6.21$, $p < .01$; Self-Control, $F(2, 4596) = 8.5$, $p < .01$; and Attachment, $F(2, 4596) = 6.6$, $p < .01$; however, it was not significant for the Behavioral Concerns scale. Post hoc Tukey honestly significant difference contrasts revealed that for the Initiative scale, parents and teachers in the both-English group showed slightly lower disagreement than parents in the both-Spanish group and unshared language group. For the Self-Control and Attachment scales, post hoc contrasts revealed that parents and teachers in the both-Spanish group showed significantly lower disagreement than parents and teachers in the both-English group and unshared language group. Generally speaking, the unshared language group showed the most disagreement.

Child cognitive/linguistic competence. To illustrate relations between disagreement between parents and teachers on the DECA and child preacademic competence, we used correlations and regression analyses. First, Pearson correlations were computed between the child's overall LAP-D score (cognitive, language, and fine motor scales combined) and the disagreement scores. In this case, we found it informative to examine both the absolute value version of the disagreement score (indicating the amount of disagreement in general, forgetting about direction) and the directional disagreement score—thus, both are reported in Table 5. In terms of general (absolute value) disagreement, Table 5 shows that Initiative, Attachment, and Total Protective Factors were significantly negatively associated with children's overall LAP-D scores ($p < .01$). Thus, children who were higher functioning in terms of cognitive, language, and motor skills had parents and teachers who disagreed less (agreed more) about their social-emotional skills (at least attachment and initiative) compared to lower functioning children.

Correlations between the directional disagreement scores and the LAP-D are interesting because they inform about the pattern of parent and teacher ratings depending on child competence. These associations were all modest (ranging from $-.18$ to $.20$) but were significantly different from zero ($p < .01$). Recall that positive directional disagreement scores meant that teachers rated children higher than did parents. So, for example, the positive correlation between the Total Protective Factors directional disagreement score and child LAP-D competence ($r = .16$) indicated that children who were more academically prepared were more likely to have their teachers rate their social-emotional competence higher than parents. The negative correlation between Behavioral Concerns directional disagreement and LAP-D competence ($r = -.18$) indicated that children who were more academically competent were likely to have their parents (rather than their teachers) rate them as having more behavior problems.

Second, regression analyses predicting child competence on the basis of parent–teacher directional disagreement were conducted to help clarify

TABLE 5
Correlations Between LAP-D Overall Scores and Mean Differences Between Parent and Teacher Scores

	Correlation With LAP-D Scores	
DECA Scale	Directional Disagreement (Raw Mean Differences)	General Disagreement (Absolute Value Differences)
Initiative	.20*	−.19*
Attachment	.07*	−.10*
Self-Control	.10*	−.04
Total Protective Factors	.16*	−.15*
Behavioral Concerns	−.18*	.02

Note. LAP-D = Learning Accomplishment Profile–Diagnostic; DECA = Devereux Early Childhood Assessment.
*$p < .01$.

these patterns. This was done for the Total Protective Factors scale and for the Behavioral Concerns scale. For the Total Protective Factors scale, directional disagreement between parent and teacher scores explained a small but significant amount (2%) of the variance in the children's overall LAP-D scores, $F(1,1958) = 48.36$, $p < .001$, $t = 6.95$, $p < .001$, $B = .20$. Children whose parents and teachers agreed the most on the Total Protective Factors scale (i.e., disagreed the least and gave the child the same score) tended to have average LAP-D scores. However, when parents reported much higher scores than teachers on the child's social-emotional competence (as indicated by negative numbers), children tended to have lower than average competence scores; and when teachers reported much higher DECA scores than parents (as indicated by positive directional disagreement numbers), the children tended to have higher than average LAP-D scores. This was a small effect but an important one, indicating that the pattern of parent–teacher agreement on child social skills was related to child functioning in interesting ways. Disagreement between informants was low for average children and higher for children who were more extreme in their academic functioning. For lower-functioning children, social-emotional competence was seen to be higher by parents than teachers, and for higher-functioning children the reverse was true, with teachers (rather than parents) seeing the children as having stronger social skills.

For Behavioral Concerns, differences between parent and teacher scores explained 3% of the variance in the children's LAP-D scores, $F(1, 1958) = 62.43$, $p < .001$, $t = -7.90$, $p < .001$, $B = -.67$. This was another small but important effect. Children with less competence (as measured by lower scores on the LAP-D) tended to have their parents (rather than their teachers) rate them as having more behavioral concerns, and children with higher scores on the LAP-D tended to show greater behavior concerns in the classroom than at home. Again, as with agreement on Total Protective Factors, good parent–teacher agreement on behavior problems was more likely for an average-functioning child.

Finally, simple bivariate correlations were conducted between each informant's ratings on Total Protective Factors and overall LAP-D score, and between Behavioral Concerns and overall LAP-D score. For both parent and teacher scores, the Total Protective Factors score was positively related to overall LAP-D performance (parents: Total Protective Factors with LAP-D, $r = .12$; teachers: $r = .29$). Behavioral concerns were negatively related to overall LAP-D scores (parents: Behavioral Concerns with LAP-D, $r = -.15$; teachers: $r = -.35$). In each case, teacher DECA scores were more highly correlated with overall child cognitive competence than were parent DECA scores (all Fisher's Z's; $p < .05$).

DISCUSSION

The goals of this study were threefold: (a) to examine the internal consistency reliability of the English and Spanish versions of the parent- and teacher-report DECA within a sample of ethnically and linguistically diverse urban children living in poverty; (b) to determine the extent to which parents and teachers agree on the DECA both at the beginning and at the end of the academic year; and (c) to determine how much parent–teacher agreement varies as a function of language of the form, child ethnicity, age, gender, and child competence. Much of the prior research discussed previously has focused on informant agreement on behavior and mental health problems in older, monolingual, and often clinical samples. Also, whereas prior research has typically examined informant ratings at only one point in time, the present investigation adds to the literature by exploring agreement over time at the beginning and end of the 4-year-old preschool year. Because little reliability or validity data are available regarding the Spanish form of the DECA, and because virtually no reliability data are available regarding the use of the DECA within low-income, ethnically diverse samples of children, answers to these questions make a significant contribution to current research and practice.

Regarding the first research question, internal consistency reliability measures indicated that the DECA is a methodologically sound instrument in terms of internal consistency for examining social-emotional protective factors and behavioral concerns in preschool children from low-income and ethnically diverse (Latino and African American) backgrounds. The internal consistency in this sample of children was very similar to that reported in the original standardization sample for the DECA. Social-emotional development is central to children's early academic and social success (Coolahan et al., 2000; Denham, 2006; Raver, 2002), and social-emotional competence and social skills are important for children living in impoverished environments (Brooks-Gunn et al., 1999; Magnuson & Waldfogel, 2005; McLoyd, 1998). Because internal consistency reliability values of the DECA within the current sample, a population that may especially benefit from social-emotional interventions in early childhood because of poverty, were similar to those reported within a nationally normed sample, the DECA may be able to fulfill the need for effective tools for assessing children's social-emotional skills and protective factors during the preschool period, particularly for preschool children living in impoverished environments.

There were no differences in internal consistency reliability between the Spanish and English versions of the DECA. Parents and teachers are excellent consultants for obtaining information regarding children's behavior and abilities (Bagnato & Neisworth, 1991), and according to this study, the language in which they completed the form does not influence the reliability of the instrument. This study is the first to provide internal consistency reliability data for the Spanish form of the DECA. Furthermore, this study is the first to evidence the internal consistency reliability of the Spanish form of the DECA within an ethnically diverse, low-income sample of preschoolers. Thus, these findings add to previous research validating the use of the DECA as a social-emotional assessment tool (LeBuffe & Naglieri, 1999).

This study also shows similar parent–teacher agreement to that found by the developers. As the participants in this study were a very different, larger, and more diverse group, this shows that the DECA is a potentially effective assessment tool for use with both teachers and parents across a wide range of socioeconomic, ethnic, and language backgrounds. The agreement between parents and teachers in this study was also similar to that found in prior research in other domains (Achenbach et al., 1987). It is important to examine instruments such as the DECA in at-risk populations like the one in this study and to confirm that they remain reliable with both parent and teacher reports.

This study did not find major differences in parent–teacher agreement related to the age of the child, the language of the form used, child ethnicity, or child gender. There were, however, differences related to shared or unshared language of the form. For example, this study shows that if parents and teachers do not chose to use the same language for completing the survey, they will disagree more about their child's functioning than if they share the language (English or Spanish) of the form. This is important, as it suggests that perhaps efforts should be made, if possible and appropriate, with truly bilingual participants who do not have a language preference/dominance to have both informants complete the assessment instrument in the same language. In communities like Miami, where large bilingual populations speak English and Spanish regularly, matching the language of the forms completed by parents and teachers may be possible, but this is unlikely in other communities. Fortunately, agreement across informants who completed the DECA in different languages was not reduced much, so comparisons across informants using different versions of the form appear to still be valid. There were small differences between the groups that shared either Spanish or English on the Behavioral Concerns and Initiative scales of the DECA. For both these scales, the parents and teachers who both used the English form had higher agreement in terms of relative ranking. These latter effect sizes were very small, and although they were statistically significant for the large sample here, they are likely not practically significant.

There is very little research relating informant congruence with child functioning, and what does exist has examined parents and teachers of children with developmental disabilities (Hundert et al., 1997). These researchers divided their participants into three groups based on their diagnosis (severe developmental disabilities, mild/moderate developmental disabilities, and no diagnosis) and found that mean differences between parent and teacher scores were related to diagnosis, with the differences being significant only for children with severe developmental disabilities (i.e., teachers tended to score these children higher). It is interesting that our analyses reveal that the direction of informant agreement (whether parent scores were higher than teacher scores or vice versa) was related to children's general competence as measured by a developmental assessment. Children who were less competent in cognitive, language, and motor skills had higher parent ratings compared to teacher ratings on the DECA assessment, whereas children who were more competent had lower parent ratings compared to teacher ratings. Children with average scores in general academic competence were more likely to be rated by both informants at the same numerical level on social-emotional strengths. Disagreements between parents and teachers appeared more often when children were either very high functioning or very low functioning academically. The finding that teachers and parents had higher disagreement when children were either high or low functioning indicates that teachers and parents rate high- and low-functioning children differently than they rate average-functioning children. There are several possibilities for why this is happening: (a) The behavior of high- and low-functioning children may differ depending on the environment more than that of average-functioning children, (b) informants may have a harder time evaluating the social-emotional and behavioral functioning of children who are higher or lower functioning, or (c) informants may be defensive or protective of children who they perceive as being especially bright or as being slow learners compared to other children. This type of protective or defensive behavior by parents and teachers may carry over into home and school environments where high- and low-performing children are treated differently. It will be important for future research to see if the same pattern is true for other instruments that assess social-emotional skills, for assessments of other domains altogether, and with different populations and ages of children.

It is interesting to note that in this sample, parents rated their children systematically higher on both the positive (Total Protective Factors) and the negative (Behavioral Concerns) dimensions. Perhaps teachers are more likely to use the lower half of the choices in rating scales than are parents. As can be seen in Table 1, teachers had larger standard deviations than parents, indicating that there was more variance in teacher scores than in parent scores, so teachers used a larger range of scores than parents. This is an area in which additional research is clearly needed.

There are a number of limitations of the present study because of the nature of the overall larger community project. The fact that this study was conducted in only one community may be seen as a limitation in terms of generalizability; however, it is also a strength given that the particular population examined here, namely linguistically diverse, low-income, Latino and African American children, is a group much in need of study for verifying the utility of the DECA in more diverse populations. Similarly, examining the use of the DECA within a local, large-scale, community-based quality initiative sacrificed experimental control but gained high external or ecological validity by examining the reliability of the DECA in real-world community agencies for large-scale assessment, evaluation, intervention, and policy purposes (rather than simply in the research laboratory). Another clear limitation is that very limited demographic information was available about the teachers and families who participated in the study. Thus, we were not able to examine potentially important variables such as teacher ethnicity, the language environment of the home or school, parent and teacher education, or the English proficiency of the informants. Thus, it is not known whether the differences observed here were in fact due to the language of the DECA form or to other unmeasured cultural or language differences between parent and teacher participants. Another limitation is that our analyses did not account for children being nested within classrooms/centers. Finally, we only examined internal consistency and parent–teacher agreement. To fully establish the utility of an assessment instrument in two languages among diverse populations, one must examine issues of validity, most notably factorial invariance across languages, informants, and populations. This should be the target of future research.

In conclusion, this study shows that the DECA appears to be a reliable and potentially useful instrument for examining social-emotional protective factors and behavioral concerns within a large sample of ethnically and linguistically diverse preschoolers living in an urban, impoverished environment. It is becoming clear that children's social-emotional and behavioral self-regulatory skills must be addressed if children are to thrive in school, and thus empirically validated assessment instruments within this domain are essential.

ACKNOWLEDGMENTS

This project was supported by funding from the Early Learning Coalition of Miami-Dade/Monroe. We would like to thank all of the community partners involved in the Miami School Readiness Project, including Miami-Dade County Public Schools and Miami-Dade County Child Development Services.

REFERENCES

Achenbach, T. M., McConaughy, S. H., & Howell, C. T. (1987). Child/adolescent behavioral and emotional problems: Implications of cross-informant correlations for situational specificity. *Psychological Bulletin, 101,* 213–232.

Bagnato, S. J., & Neisworth, J. T. (1991). *Assessment for early intervention: Best practices for professionals.* New York, NY: Guilford Press.

Brooks-Gunn, J., Britto, P. R., & Brady, C. (1999). Struggling to make ends meet: Poverty and child development. In M. E. Lamb (Ed.), *Parenting and child development in "nontraditional" families* (pp. 279–304). Mahwah, NJ: Erlbaum.

Cai, X., Kaiser, A. P., & Hancock, T. B. (2004). Parent and teacher agreement on child behavior checklist items in a sample of preschoolers from low-income and predominantly African American families. *Journal of Clinical Child and Adolescent Psychology, 33,* 303–312.

Caprara, G. V., Barbaranelli, C., Pastorelli, C., Bandura, A., & Zimbardo, P. G. (2000). Prosocial foundations of children's academic achievement. *Psychological Science, 11,* 302–306.

Cofresi, N. I., & Gorman, A. A. (2004). Testing and assessment issues with Spanish-English bilingual Latinos. *Journal of Counseling and Development, 82,* 99–106.

Coolahan, K., Fantuzzo, J., Mendez, J., & McDermott, P. (2000). Preschool peer interactions and readiness to learn: Relationships between classroom peer play and learning behaviors and conduct. *Journal of Educational Psychology, 92,* 458–465.

Deng, S., Liu, X., & Roosa, M. W. (2004). Agreement between parent and teacher reports on behavioral problems among Chinese children. *Journal of Developmental & Behavioral Pediatrics, 25,* 407–417.

Denham, S. A. (2006). The emotional basis of learning and development in early childhood education. In B. Spodek, & O. N. Saracho (Eds.), *Handbook of research on the education of young children* (2nd ed., pp. 85–103). Mahwah, NJ: Erlbaum.

Denham, S. A., & Burton, R. (2003). *Social and emotional prevention and intervention programming for preschoolers.* New York, NY: Kluwer Academic/Plenum.

Devereux Early Childhood Initiative. (2001). *Research brief: Development of the Spanish language version of the DECA.* Retrieved from http://www.devereux.org/site/DocServer/Bulletin-4.pdf?docID=3566

Devereux Early Childhood Initiative. (2006). *DECI newsletters.* Retrieved from http://www.devereuxearlychildhood.org/newsletters.html

Duncan, G. J., & Magnuson, K. A. (2005). Can family socioeconomic resources account for racial and ethnic test score gaps? *The Future of Children, 15,* 35–54.

Evans, G. W., & Rosenbaum, J. (2008). Self-regulation and the income-achievement gap. *Early Childhood Research Quarterly, 23,* 504–514.

Ferdinand, R. F., Hoogerheide, K., van der Ende, J., Visser, J., Koot, H. M., Kasius, M. C., & Verhulst, F. (2003). The role of the clinician: Three-year predictive value of parents', teachers' and clinicians' judgment of childhood psychopathology. *Journal of Child Psychology and Psychiatry, 44,* 867–876.

Florida Partnership for School Readiness. (2003). *Florida school readiness performance standards for three, four- and five-year-old.* Retrieved from http://www.floridajobs.org/earlylearning/oel_performance.html

Garbarino, J., & Ganzel, B. (2000). The human ecology of early risk. In J. P. Shonkoff, & S. J. Meisels (Eds.), *Handbook of early childhood intervention* (2nd ed., pp. 94–114). New York, NY: Cambridge University Press.

Garcia-Coll, C., & Magnuson, K. (2000). Cultural differences as sources of developmental vulnerabilities and resources. In J. P. Shonkoff, & S. J. Meisels (Eds.), *Handbook of early childhood intervention* (2nd ed., pp. 94–114). New York, NY: Cambridge University Press.

Graziano, P. A., Reavis, R. D., Keane, S. P., & Calkins, S. D. (2007). The role of emotion regulation in children's early academic success. *Journal of School Psychology, 45*, 3–19.

Harms, T., Clifford, R. M., & Cryer, D. (1998). *Early Childhood Rating Scale, revised edition (ECERS).* Williston, VT: Teachers College Press.

Hemmeter, M. L., Ostrosky, M., & Fox, L. (2006). Social and emotional foundations for early learning: A conceptual model for intervention. *School Psychology Review, 35*, 583–601.

Howes, C., & Smith, E. W. (1995). Relations among child care quality, teacher behavior, children's play activities, emotional security, and cognitive activity in child care. *Early Childhood Research Quarterly, 10*, 381–404.

Hundert, J., Morrison, L., Mahoney, W., Mundy, F., & Vernon, M. L. (1997). Parent and teacher assessments of the developmental status of children with severe, mild/moderate, or no developmental disabilities. *Topics in Early Childhood Special Education, 17*, 419–434.

Jaberg, P., Dixon, D., & Weis, G. (2009). Replication evidence in support of the psychometric properties of the Devereux Early Childhood Assessment. *Canadian Journal of School Psychology, 24*, 158–166.

Kaplan, R. M., & Saccuzzo, D. P. (2001). *Psychological testing: Principles, applications, and issues* (5th ed.). Belmont, CA.

Kazdin, A. E., Kraemer, H. C., Kessler, R. C., Kupfer, D. J., & Offord, D. R. (1997). Contributions of risk-factor research to developmental psychopathology. *Clinical Psychology Review, 17*, 375–406.

Keogh, B. K., & Bernheimer, L. (1998). Concordance between mothers' and teachers' perceptions of behavior problems of children with developmental delays. *Journal of Emotional and Behavioral Disorders, 6*, 33–42.

Keogh, B. K., Juvonen, J., & Bernheimer, L. (1989). Assessing children's competence: Mothers' and teachers' ratings of competent behavior. *Psychological Assessment, 1*, 224–229.

Kumpulainen, K., Räsänen, E., Henttonen, I., Moilanen, I., Piha, J., Puura, K., ... Almqvist, F. (1999). Children's behavioural/emotional problems: A comparison of parents' and teachers' reports for elementary school-aged children. *European Child & Adolescent Psychiatry, 8*, 41–47.

La Paro, K. M., & Pianta, R. C. (2000). Predicting children's competence in the early school years: A meta-analytic review. *Review of Educational Research, 70*, 443–484.

LeBuffe, P. A., & Naglieri, J. A. (1999). *Devereux Early Childhood Assessment: User's guide.* Lewisville, NC: Kaplan Press.

Lien, M. T., & Carlson, J. S. (2009). Psychometric properties of the Devereux Early Childhood Assessment in a Head Start sample. *Journal of Psychoeducational Assessment, 27*, 386–396.

Magnuson, K. A., & Waldfogel, J. (2005). Early childhood care and education: Effects on ethnic and racial gaps in school readiness. *The Future of Children, 15*, 169–196.

Mayor's Commission for Children. (2007). *Readiness for kindergarten: A study conducted by the Mayor's Commission for Children*. Retrieved from http://www.ci.springfield.mo.us/children_commission/schoolreadinessfinal.pdf

McClelland, M. M., Cameron, C. E., Connor, C. M., Farris, C. L., Jewkes, A. M., & Morrison, F. J. (2007). Links between behavioral regulation and preschoolers' literacy, vocabulary, and math skills. *Developmental Psychology, 43*, 947–959.

McLoyd, V. C. (1998). Socioeconomic disadvantage and child development. *American Psychologist, 53*, 185–204.

Meisels, S. J., & Atkins-Burnett, S. (2000). The elements of early childhood assessment. In J. P. Shonkoff, & S. J. Meisels (Eds.), *Handbook of early childhood intervention* (pp. 231–257). New York, NY: Cambridge University Press.

Miller, A. L., Gouley, K. K., Seifer, R., Dickstein, S., & Shields, A. (2004). Emotions and behaviors in the Head Start classroom: Associations among observed dysregulation, social competence, and preschool adjustment. *Early Education & Development, 15*, 147–165.

Nehring, A. D., Nehring, E. F., Bruni, J. R., & Randolph, P. L. (1992). *LAP-D: Learning Accomplishment Profile–Diagnostic*. Lewisville, NC: Kaplan Press.

National Center for Education Statistics. (2000). *Schools and Staffing Survey (SASS), 1993–94 and 1999–2000 "Public School Questionnaire" and 1999–2000 "Charter School Questionnaire."* Retrieved from http://nces.ed.gov/quicktables/Detail.asp?Key=1185

National Institute of Child Health amd Human Development Early Child Care Research Network. (2000). Characteristics and quality of child care for toddlers and preschoolers. *Applied Developmental Science, 4*, 116–135.

Peet, S. H., Powell, D. R., & O'Donnel, B. (1997). Mother-teacher congruence in perceptions of the child's competence and school engagement: Links to academic achievement. *Journal of Applied Developmental Psychology, 18*, 373–393.

Phinney, J. S., & Landin, J. (1998). Research paradigms for studying ethnic minority families within and across groups. In V. C. McLoyd, & L. Steinberg (Eds.), *Studying minority adolescents: Conceptual, methodological, and theoretical issues* (pp. 89–109). Mahwah, NJ: Erlbaum.

Raver, C. C. (2002). Emotions matter: Making the case for the role of young children's emotional development for early school readiness. *Social Policy Report, 16*(3), 1–18.

Rimm-Kaufman, S. E., Pianta, R. C., & Cox, M. J. (2000). Teachers' judgments of problems in the transition to kindergarten. *Early Childhood Research Quarterly, 15*, 147–166.

Satake, H., Yoshida, K., & Yamashita, H. (2003). Agreement between parents and teachers on behavioral/emotional problems in Japanese school children using the Child Behavior Checklist. *Child Psychiatry & Human Development, 34*, 111–126.

U.S. Census Bureau. (2010). *State and county quickfacts: Michigan*. Retrieved from http://quickfacts.census.gov/qfd/states/26000.html

U.S. Department of Health and Human Services. (2004). *Developing outcome measures for young children*. Retrieved from http://grants.nih.gov/grants/guide/rfa-files/RFA-HD-04-026.html

Victor, J. B., Halverson, C. F., & Smith-Wampler, K. (1988). Family-school context: Parent and teacher agreement on child temperament. *Journal of Consulting and Clinical Psychology, 56*, 573–577.

Webster-Stratton, C., & Reid, M. J. (2008). Strengthening social and emotional competence in young children who are socioeconomically disadvantaged: Preschool and kindergarten school-based curricula. In W. H. Brown, S. L. Odom, & S. R. McConnell (Eds.), *Social *competence of young children: Risk, disability, and intervention* (pp. 185–203). Baltimore, MD: Brookes.

Winsler, A., & Wallace, G. L. (2002). Behavior problems and social skills in preschool children: Parent-teacher agreement and relations with classroom observations. *Early Education & Development, 13*, 41–58.

Winsler, A., Tran, H., Hartman, S., Madigan, A. L., Manfra, L., & Bleiker, C. (2008). School readiness gains made by ethnically-diverse children in poverty attending center-based childcare and public school pre-kindergarten programs. *Early Childhood Research Quarterly, 23*, 314–329.

Index

Page numbers in **bold** type refer to figures
Page numbers in *italic* type refer to tables

acceptance problems 8
Achenbach, T.: *et al* 168
achievement: and social functioning 61–2; study and effortful control (EC) 57–74, *66*, **69**
aggression 8
Ainsworth, M.: *et al* 9
anger/disappointment 39, 60
Aroian, L.: Meeker, W. and Cornwell, L. 70
assessment: social behavior 18; standardized early childhood 167–8, *see also* DECA
attachment: DECA subscale 176–84
attention/persistence 3, 37, 42–52, 58, 71, 137–42, 161; flexibility 108; focusing 23–5, *see also* classroom games
Attentional Focusing and Inhibitory Control scale 15
attitudes 3; and effortful control (EC) 83–4; indicators 95; and learning approaches 42–52; low income sample study 80–101; and school readiness 42–52, 83–4; teacher-child relationship quality 84–6, 91–2

Baker, B.: Blacher, J. and Eisenhower, A. 11; McIntyre, L. and Blacher, J. 11
Baron, R.: and Kenny, D. 43
Batería III Woodcock-Muñoz 144–5
Bates, J.: and Rothbart, M. 58
Behavioral Concerns scale 171–2; DECA 176–89
behavioral regulation 107–34; definition 108–9; demographic risk factor influences 107–29; descriptive statistics/analysis (gender/education/language) *115*, 119–23; early importance 109; family income contribution 110–11; Head-to-Toes Task (HTT) 109, 116–23, *122–3*; limitations 128–9; low income/ELL contribution 111–13, 122–6; participants 115–16; pre- and kindergarten growth 113–14, 119–23, *121*; study goals and method 114–19; teacher-rated 118, *see also* self-regulatory skills
behaviors: externalizing 61–2, 68, 85
Bennett, E.: Pianta, R. and Nimetz, S. 9
Birch, S.: and Ladd, G. 85
Blacher, J.: Baker, B. and McIntyre, L. 11; Eisenhower, A. and Baker, B. 11
Blair, C. 71; and Diamond, A. 59
bootstrapping 19–20, 24
Box's M statistic test 70
Bracken Basic Concepts Scale (BBCS) 42; Revised School Readiness Composite 42–4
Brock, L.: Nathanson, L. and Rimm-Kaufmann, S. 25
Burgess, K.: and Ladd, G. 8

Cai, X.: *et al* 169
California Head Start Association 112–14
Carlson, J.: and Lien, M. 171–2
Child Behavior Checklist 18, 63, 67
Child Behavior Questionnaire (CBQ) 15, 27, 65–8, 90
child care quality 169, *see also* Head Start
CI mediation method 96
circle time: games study 142–59; trial 135–65

INDEX

classroom games 4; benefits 151–4; circle time trial 135–65; Conducting an Orchestra/Drum Beats 148; descriptive statistics 148–55; Freeze/Color-Matching 147–8; and HTKS Task 140, 144–5, 148–56, *149–50*, 160; and letter-word identification skills 135–55, *149–50*; limitations and implications 160–1; playgroup session format 146–7; Red Light, Purple Light 147, 159; Sleeping 148; study and demographic factor impact 135–61

Classroom Observation System (COS-1) 16–18; negative 16–17; positive/neutral interactions 16; reliability 17–18; unstructured peer 17

classroom relationships 8–9; child perceptions 8–9; conflictual 8; friends and foes 18; observation system (first grade) 16–17; Social Skills Rating System (SSRS) 17–18; student-teacher relationship scale (STRS) 15–16, 91; Teacher Report Forms (TRF) 18, 67, *see also* effortful control

cognitive flexibility 3, 34–56; competence 183–5; and LAP-D 177–85; and school readiness study 34–53

Coleman, C.: Ladd, G. and Kochenderfer, B. 8

communication *see* language/communication

comparative fit index (CFI) 95–6

competence 67; assessment 168; and emotion regulation 167–8, 185, 186–9; language/communication 183–5; motivation 3, 42, 46–8, *47*; social 3, 6–28, 61, 68

Conducting an Orchestra/Drum Beats game 148

conflict: teacher-child relationship 85, 93–5, 100

control: self 176–83, *see also* effortful control (EC); inhibitory control

Cornwell, L.: Aroian, L. and Meeker, W. 70

Crane, J.: Mincic, M. and Winsler, A. 4, 166–93

Curran, P.: West, S. and Finch, J. 68

curriculum: Tools of the Mind 127, 141; variables 89

DECA (Devereux Early Childhood Assessment) 4, 166–93; consistency/reliability study 173–89; English/Spanish versions 4, 166–89; ethnically diverse children living in poverty 166–93; features 170–2; internal consistency 178–9; interscale correlations *178–9*; and LAP-D 177–85, *184*; and parent-teacher agreement 166–89; and parent-teacher disagreement 181–5; participants 174–5; subscales 176–89

demographic factor impact 4, 107–34; and children's behavioral regulation 107–29; and classroom games study 135–61; Parent Questionnaire 143–4, *see also* effortful control

Deng, S.: et al 169

Diamond, A.: and Blair, C. 59

Dinella, L.: and Ladd, G. 100

disability 35; developmental 35, 188; learning 35, 188

disappointment/anger 39, 60

Doumen, S.: et al 100

Duncan, G.: et al 72

Early Childhood Longitudinal Study Kindergarten 111

Early Childhood Rating Scale-Revised 175

effortful control (EC) 6–33, 57–79; and achievement study 57–74, *66*, **69**; analytic plan/results 19–24, *23*; effects, limitations and implications 22–8, 72–4; and maternal sensitivity study 6–28; participants and phases 13; risk factors(income/sex/race) 8, 64, 80–101; and school attitudes 83–4; social competence/relationships 11; student-teacher relationship scale (STRS) 15–16, 91; study overview/data collection 11–18; teacher-child relationship study 6–28, 80–106, *92–7*; variables 19–24, *20–1*

Eisenberg, N.: et al 72; Sadovsky, A. and Spinrad, T. 61

Eisenhower, A.: Baker, B. and Blacher, J. 11

Elliott, S.: and Gresham, F. 17–18

emotion regulation 50, 167; and competence 167–8, 185, 186–9; school engagement 82; and skills assessment 167, 173, *see also* DECA

English language learners (ELL) 107–29, 166–93; Hispanic 107–29, *see also* demographic factor impact

195

INDEX

ethnically diverse children: poverty 166–93
ethnicity as risk factor 64; and Hispanic ELLs 107–29, 166–89
externalizing behaviors 61–2, 68, 85, *see also* effortful control

family 63; income and behavioral regulation 110–11, *see also* low-income families; maternal sensitivity
Finch, J.: Curran, P. and West, S. 68
Fisher's test 177, 182
Florida: Department of Children and Families 87
Freeze/Color-Matching games 147–8
friends and foes 18
frustration tolerance 37; anger and disappointment 39, 60

games: circle time 142–59; classroom *see* classroom games; playgroup 147–8
gift wrap procedure 90–1
gratification delay 58
Gresham, F.: and Elliott, S. 17–18
growth: and behavioral regulation 113–14, 119–23, *121*

Hamm, J.: Vandell, D. and Pierce, K. 67
Hamre, B.: Hatfield, B. and Mintz, T. 3, 6–33; and Pianta, R. 8; Pianta, R. and Jerome, E. 9
Harlan, E.: Kochanska, G. and Murray, K. 7
Harter Teacher Rating Scale 18
Harter's Perceived Competence Scale for Children (1982) 67
Hatfield, B.: Mintz, T. and Hamre, B. 3, 6–33
Head Start pre-school children 34–53, 87, 112–16, 125–7, 171–5; and circle time games study 142–59, *see also* school readiness
Head-to-Toes Task (HTT) 109, 116–23; and classroom games study scores 148–56, *149–50*; construct validity 140–1; Knees-Shoulders version (HTKS) 117–18, 140–1, 144–5, 160; reliability 117
hierarchical linear modeling 175
Hispanic children 107–34; ELL 107–29, 166–93; and income/poverty study 166–89; parenting 112–13
Howes, C.: *et al* 8
hyperactivity 39

impulsivity 39
income risk factor 166–89; and behavioral regulation 110–11; effortful control/school attitudes study 80–101; ELL contribution 111–13, 124–9; ethnically diverse children/DECA study 166–89; importance 156–7, *see also* low-income families
inhibitory control 23–7, 35, 51, 71, 109, 137–42, 161, *see also* classroom games
initiative 37; DECA subscale 176–87
interrater reliability 14–15
Intervention Treatment Group Participation study 141–61; games, nature and implementation 159; participants and measures 142–4; participation benefits 151–4; phases and procedure 145–6; playgroup games 147–8, *see also* classroom games
intraclass correlation coefficients (ICCs) 89, 118

Jaberg, P.: *et al* 171
Jerome, E.: Hamre, B. and Pianta, R. 9

Kenny, D.: and Baron, R. 43; and McCoach, D. 22
Kids in Transition to School program 141
Kochanska, G.: and Knaack, A. 12; Murray, K. and Harlan, E. 7
Kochenderfer, B.: Coleman, C. and Ladd, G. 8
Krull, J.: and MacKinnon, D. 43
kurtosis 68

Ladd, G. 7; and Birch, S. 85; and Burgess, K. 8; and Dinella, L. 100; *et al* 82; Kochenderfer, B. and Coleman, C. 8
language/communication 166–89; competence 183–5; ethnically diverse children study 173–89; of form 182–3, *183*; and LAP-D 177–85
Learning Accomplishment Profile-Diagnostic (LAP-D) 177–85; and DECA study results 177–85, *184*; domains 177; parent-teacher scores *184*
learning approaches 34–56; and attitudes 42–52; components 46–8, *see also* school readiness
learning disability 35, 188

letter-word identification: skills 135–55, *149–50*
Lien, M.: and Carlson, J. 171–2
low-income families 2–4; and circle time games study 142–59; and school readiness impact 80–106

McClelland, M.: *et al* 60; and Tominey, S. 1–5, 135–65
McCoach, D.: and Kenny, D. 22
McElwain, N.: and Volling, B. 9
McIntyre, L.: Blacher, J. and Baker, B. 11
MacKinnon, D.: *et al* 70; and Krull, J. 43
Mashburn, A.: *et al* 110
maternal sensitivity 3; behavior ratings 14–15; and child's social skills 9–10; and effortful control study 6–28
Mayor's Commission for Children 171
measurement model 93–5, *see also* teacher-child relationship EC study
mediation: and social functioning 57–74; teacher-child relationship 86–7
Meeker, W.: Cornwell, L. and Aroian, L. 70
memory: working 35, 51, 71, 108, 137–42, 161, *see also* classroom games
Miami School Readiness Project 173–5
Mincic, M.: Winsler, A. and Crane, J. 4, 166–93
Mintz, T.: Hamre, B. and Hatfield, B. 3, 6–33
motivation 37, 59, 85; competence 3, 42, 46–8, *47*
motor (fine/gross) domain 177; and LAP-D 177–85
Murray, K.: Harlan, E. and Kochanska, G. 7

Nathanson, L.: Rimm-Kaufmann, S. and Brock, L. 25
National Association for the Education of Young Children (NAEYC) 115
National Education Goals Panel (NEGP) 81
National Institute of Child Health and Human Development (NICHD) 3, 6; Early Child Care Research Network (ECCRN) 8, 12–17, 24, 60–2, 71, 160; Early Child Care and Youth Development Study (SECCYD) 3, 9, 12–18, 91

National Task Force on Early Childhood Education for Hispanics 111
Nimetz, S.: Bennett, E. and Pianta, R. 9
No Child Left Behind Act (NCLB 2001) 136

Olson, S.; *et al* 10
ordinary least squares (OLS) regressions 118; exploratory model 119

parent-child relationships 7; and educational involvement/competence 51, 64, 139; temperament measure report 90, 93, *see also* maternal sensitivity
parent-teacher agreement 166–93; and DECA reliability 166–89; and directional disagreement 182–5; relative ranking 180–1
parenting: Hispanic children 112–13
Pearson correlations 183
Peer Competence scale 17–18
persistence 37, 58, *see also* attention/persistence
Pianta, R. 86; and Hamre, B. 8; Jerome, E. and Hamre, B. 9; Nimetz, S. and Bennett, E. 9; and Rimm-Kaufman, S. 62
picture vocabulary 144–5
Pierce, K.: Hamm, J. and Vandell, D. 67
Posner, M.: *et al* 59, 71
poverty 35; and ethnically diverse children 166–89; and school readiness implications 35–6
Pre-School Learning Behavior Scale (PLBS) 34, 40; definition 41–2
Promoting Alternative Thinking Strategies (PATHS) 141
psychopathology: assessment 168

Raver, C. 59–60
Red Light, Purple Light game 147, 159
Rimm-Kaufman, S.: Brock, L. and Nathanson, L. 25; and Pianta, R. 62
risk factors (income/sex/race) 8, 64; accumulation 2; behavioral self-regulation impact 156–7; demographic 107–29; ethnically diverse children in poverty 166–89, *see also* teacher-child relationship EC study
root mean square error of approximation (RMSEA) 22, 95–6

INDEX

Rothbart, M.: and Bates, J. 58; et al 27

Sadovsky, A.: Spinrad, T. and Eisenberg, N. 61
School Liking and Avoidance Questionnaire 91–2
school readiness 3, 110, 139; age/gender analyses 45–7, 51; approaches to learning 37–9; and attitude 42–52, 83–4; cognitive flexibility study 34–56; control theory application 37–53; correlations and results 44–8; descriptive/multilevel mediation analyses 43–8; and Hispanic ELLs 107–29; and low income sample study 80–106; participants and procedures 40–1
self-control: DECA subscale 176–83
self-regulatory skills 35, 58–9; academic outcomes/applied problems 144–5; behavioral 136–61, 167; children at risk 139–40; and classroom games 135–61; definition and importance 136–8; early 84; and family income importance 156–7; and Head-Toes-Knees-Shoulders Task (HTKS) 140–1, 144; intervention research/study 141–8; measurement 140–1; poor 59, 139–40; pre-school years 138–9, see also effortful control
sex and socioeconomic status (SES) 63–5, **69**, 70, 73; family 63; and IQ indices 73
Silva, K.: et al 3, 80–106
skewness 68
skills: assessment and emotion regulation 167, 173; letter-word identification 135–55, *149–50*; self-regulatory 35, 58–9, 84, 135–61; social rating system (SSRS) 17–18
Sleeping game 148
Sobel tests 43, 46–8
Social Behavior Assessment 18
social competence 3; classroom relationships 8–9; and effortful control role 6–28; maternal sensitivity relation 6–28; measures 68; parent-reported 61
social functioning 57–79; and achievement 61–2; effortful control study 57–74; and mediation 57–74
social problems scale 18
Social Skills Rating System (SSRS) 17–18

socioeconomic status see sex and socioeconomic status (SES)
Spinrad, T.: Eisenberg, N. and Sadovsky, A. 61; et al 12
standardized root-mean-square residual (SRMR) 95–6
Steiger, J. 22
structural equation model 95–7, see also teacher-child relationship EC study
Structural Equation Model (SEM) 20–3, 97
student-teacher relationship scale (STRS) 15–16, 91; reliability 16
Sulik, M.: et al 99
switching see cognitive flexibility

Teacher Report Form (TRF) 18, 67
teacher-child relationship 3, 51, 84–6, 91–2, 173; conflict 85, 93–5, 100; effortful control study 6–28, 80–106, *92–7*; implications and limitations 100–1; intervention program 89; mediation 86–7; participants and procedure 87–92; positive 7; quality study 80–106, *92–7*; and school attitudes 84–6, 91–2; variable correlations 94
teacher-parent agreement 166–93
teacher-student relationship scale 15–16, 91
temperament: assessment 90, 93, 168
Tominey, S.: and McClelland, M. 1–5, 135–65
Tools of the Mind curriculum 127, 141
Total Protective Factors scale 170–2; DECA subscale 176–89

Valiente, C.: et al 3, 57–79
Vandell, D.: Pierce, K. and Hamm, J. 67
Vitiello, V.: et al 3, 34–56
Volling, B.: and McElwain, N. 9

Wallace, G.: and Winsler, A. 168
Wanless, S.: et al 107–34
Welsh, M.: et al 61
West, S.: Finch, J. and Curran, P. 68
Winsler, A.: Crane, J. and Mincic, M. 4, 166–93; and Wallace, G. 168
Woodcock-Johnson Psycho-Educational Battery-III Achievement Tests 144–5; Applied Problems subtest 145; Picture Vocabulary subtest 144–5
word: letter- identification 135–55, *149–50*

www.routledge.com/9780415618519

Related titles from Routledge

Language Planning in the Asia Pacific
Hong-Kong, Timor-Leste and Sri Lanka

Edited by Robert B. Kaplan and Richard B. Baldauf

This volume covers the language situation in Hong Kong, Timor-Leste and Sri Lanka explaining the linguistic diversity, the historical and political contexts and the current language situation, including language-in-education planning, the role of the media, the role of religion and the roles of non-indigenous languages. It draws together the literature on each of the polities to present an overview of the research available about each of them, while providing new research-based information.

This book was originally published as special issues of the journal *Current Issues in Language Planning*.

Robert B. Kaplan is Emeritus Professor of Applied Linguistics at the University of Southern California, USA.

Richard B. Baldauf, Jr. is Professor of TESOL in the School of Education at the University of Queensland, Australia.

March 2011: 246 x 174: 264pp
Hb: 978-0-415-61851-9
£80 / $125

For more information and to order a copy visit
www.routledge.com/ISBN 9780415618519

Available from all good bookshops

www.routledge.com/9780415693523

Related titles from Routledge

Education and Religion
Global Pressures, Local Responses
Edited by Keith Watson & William I. Ozanne

In most countries, secular or otherwise, education and religion are closely interlinked; no matter how hard the state tries, it can be difficult to remove the ties between them. This book investigates the links between education, religion and politics.

The dominant feature in creating a common culture between peoples, each of which has its own distinct heritage and practices, is religion. Globalisation is leading to a redefinition of the state, community and local identity. Recent world events have focused attention on the interplay between education, religion and politics like never before. Even more pertinent is the fact that the involvement of politics in decisions about religion and education is often central and impossible to disentangle.

Education and Religion covers all the major religious traditions – Buddhist, Christian, Jewish, Hindu, Muslim, Sikh – and cites global examples throughout the world. It aims to understand the underlying complexities in the struggle to reconcile education, religion and politics in an informative and sensitive way.

This book was originally published as a special issue of *Comparative Education*.

December 2011: 246 x 174: 160pp
Hb: 978-0-415-69352-3
£80 / $125

For more information and to order a copy visit
www.routledge.com/9780415693523

Available from all good bookshops

www.routledge.com/9780789037619

Related titles from Routledge

Family Factors and the Educational Success of Children

Edited by William Jeynes

Family Factors and the Educational Success of Children addresses a wide range of family variables and a diverse array of family situations in order to understand the dynamics of the multifaceted relationship between family realities and educational outcomes of children. It provides research on building effective partnerships between parents and teaches the importance of parental style, parental involvement as a means of improving family life, the influence of family factors on children of color, and the role of religion in influencing family and educational dynamics.

This book was published as a double special issue of *Marriage and Family Review*.

> August 2009: 234 x 156: 420pp
> Hb: 978-0-7890-3761-9
> Pb: 978-0-7890-3762-6
> **Hb: £80 / $130 Pb: £22.99 / $45.95**

For more information and to order a copy visit
www.routledge.com/9780789037619

Available from all good bookshops